CONFRONTATION AT
OCEAN HILL–BROWNSVILLE

Confrontation at Ocean Hill-Brownsville

THE NEW YORK SCHOOL STRIKES OF 1968

EDITED BY

Maurice R. Berube

AND

Marilyn Gittell

FREDERICK A. PRAEGER, *Publishers*

New York · Washington · London

FREDERICK A. PRAEGER, PUBLISHERS
111 Fourth Avenue, New York, N.Y. 10003, U.S.A.
5, Cromwell Place, London S.W.7, England

Published in the United States of America in 1969
by Frederick A. Praeger, Inc., Publishers

© 1969 by Frederick A. Praeger, Inc.

Library of Congress Catalog Card Number: 78–76953

Printed in the United States of America

For Anne, Michael, and Jean (M.R.B.)

———————————————————

For my students (M.G.)

Preface

This collection of documents and analyses of the Ocean Hill–Brownsville controversy attempts to provide an accurate record of the circumstances of that confrontation. It is our view that this dispute, much larger than a local labor conflict, has bearing on public schools in our cities and on the future relations between the races in this nation. Although the editors strongly hold to one interpretation of these events, we intend no polemic; rather, an understanding of the forces determining the events requires that all the powerful opinions evoked be presented as impartially as possible.

We have avoided no aspect of the controversy, not even one that might cast our own opinions in doubt. We have included as many pertinent documents and significant interpretations as space would allow, so that the major protagonists and the varying opinions are represented. Documents have been edited where the excluded material was extraneous to the general context of the controversy. Opinion pieces, however, have been reprinted virtually intact; although these accounts tend to cover some of the same ground, we refrained from editing them in order to preserve each author's handling of fact, crucial to the conclusion drawn.

The documents and analyses are arranged to suit the issues and events as they developed. A brief chronology supplies a running account of the major events in the dispute, and editorial summaries at the beginning of each chapter focus on the thread of the debate. The errors of fact in the various pieces would fill a volume were they corrected; since they are, for the most part, minor, we have preferred to rely on corrections made by other authors in other selections.

By no means does this volume constitute a comprehensive reader in decentralization and community control; many perceptive articles have been excluded because they did not deal directly with the events and issues at Ocean Hill. Perhaps most regrettably, we have had to omit many excellent articles directly pertaining to the Ocean Hill controversy because of space limitations. The decision to omit a piece was, in most instances, very hard to make; to those readers who find their own favorite article missing, we can say only that we tried to choose fairly and to achieve balance and interest.

We are grateful to the periodicals and contributors for permission to reprint their materials. Mrs. Marian Wood, our editor, constantly furnished gracious help and perceptive guidance. We should also like to thank Mrs. Ione Harris, Mrs. Lucille Hubert, and Mrs. Phyllis Treitler for aid in preparing the manuscript. A special debt of gratitude belongs to Mr. Arnold Dolin, editor-in-chief at Praeger, for his willingness to embark on yet another venture that might clarify what is happening in city schools.

MAURICE R. BERUBE
MARILYN GITTELL

Contents

Prologue

The Struggle for Community Control

Few events in the history of American education have been as portentous as the strikes that closed New York City schools in the fall of 1968. The dispute underlying those strikes was no parochial issue. The battle for control of city schools, waged between school professionals and the black community of Ocean Hill–Brownsville, had political, educational, and social implications for the whole nation. The outcome would affect not only public education in the nation's cities but also the political and social fabric of a democratic society, for on trial were some of our most cherished concepts: politically, the public's right to determine the policy and course of education; educationally, the moral imperative to provide quality education for all in publicly supported schools; and socially, the egalitarian ideal of a just, interracial society.

The failure of city schools to educate a predominantly black population is a national disgrace. The public has only recently become aware of this failure. Most of America's schools function behind a curtain of ignorance. Scant information is available on the achievements of pupils, and educators bitterly resist a national assessment, although, under pressure from civil rights groups, educators in some cities have begun to disclose the results of standardized tests. In New York City, one out of three pupils is a year or more behind the norm in reading; in Washington, D.C., pupils in four out of five schools perform below national norms. In the black ghetto, the figures are even more stark: nearly 85 per cent of Harlem school children are more than two years behind the norm in reading and, in one recent year, only thirteen Harlem

3

youngsters in the only high school in Harlem received an academic diploma. The racial gap increases the longer the black student remains in school. By the last year of high school—assuming he goes that far (which is unlikely)—the black child is, on the average, educationally three and a half years behind his white counterpart.

City school systems have been unable to stem this failure. Each year, as the number of black poor increases in the school population, school bureaucracies face greater educational challenge. Members of the urban black poor have begun to hold the schools responsible for their children's educational failure and have been demanding the right to participate in the operation of the public schools. This demand far transcends the right to elect school boards that fashion school policy; it reaches into the democratic ethic, projecting a communal involvement through the public school and making the school the agent for transforming the ghetto into a community.

In most American cities, the public has little say about how their schools are run; urban school systems, dominated by professionals, remain isolated and unaccountable to their public. This condition, uncommon to American suburbs and rural areas, results from the white middle-class urban reform movement that at the turn of the century sought to protect the public school from big-city political machines. Over the last fifty years, however, educational needs and school conditions have changed immeasurably. Isolated city school bureaucracies, having shown themselves incapable of adapting to shifting educational needs and lacking the regenerative power to reform from within, are being challenged by outside groups.

All public functions are by nature political, and any group using public funds for public purposes automatically becomes political. Since the largest share of local expenditures is spent on education, to deny the political nature of decision-making in this area is foolishness. Unfortunately, educators disparaging politics strengthen the wall of separation between the school and the public.

Over the past decade, the leadership of the school reform movement has changed. No longer does a mostly white middle class supply the power to improve the schools; the impetus now derives from the poor. This political development can only be welcomed. If educational institutions are to function effectively, the poor must be involved in their improvement. Presently, the poor and the middle-class school professionals are competing for power.

The struggle will continue until the poor achieve a guarantee of their participatory role.

In New York City, the United Federation of Teachers and the Council of Supervisory Associations are the heirs of middle-class reformism. Such reform has preserved the civil service system from easy access by minority groups. Those who benefit from the system oppose any revision of school civil service qualifications; yet, the *stasis* of urban government, overcentralized and unresponsive, can be largely attributed to the protective maze surrounding civil servants and to the routinization of procedures. If city government is to become viable once again, some measure of accountability must be introduced into the civil service system. So far, decentralization and community control of public schools present a plausible *modus operandi*. Cohesive, strong local units could revitalize the inflated city government structures, and the stature of the American mayor, shrunken by proliferating bureaucracies, could be enhanced—community control might even re-establish the political primacy of urban mayors.

In the Ocean Hill–Brownsville confrontation, the limits of the old reformism are illustrated by the issue of due process. The UFT translated the transfer of nineteen teachers and principals into a threat to job security and a violation of due process. Due process in the transferring of teachers tends to entrench an already unresponsive bureaucracy, but teachers should be entitled to hearings in cases of involuntary transfer. Nevertheless, at Ocean Hill the emphasis was in the wrong direction. The already overly protected civil service was protected without thought for the rights of clients, and the public was left without recourse to legal channels to assert its own rights. Whereas the protection of workers was a major social priority in the 1930's, the right to hold public groups—even labor unions—accountable to an urban alienated poor emerges as the prime social priority of the 1960's. The unions, however, are still operating on a 1930's program. In short, the battle for social justice is no longer being waged by American labor.

The black poor demand equality of educational opportunity. For black parents in the ghetto, this means holding teachers and principals accountable for the quality of education children receive. Too many teachers and principals long ago decided that the ghetto child frequently is ineducable. At best, they show their attitudes in low expectancy of academic achievement. At worst, they are racist.

In the Ocean Hill controversy, there was little public discussion of holding teachers and principals accountable. How may ghetto parents insure that teachers will not adversely influence their children? We don't know. We can only speculate that the sweep of the community control movement will ultimately change the prevailing atmosphere in ghetto schools. The teachers who are most deleterious to black children may seek to leave the system; the surge of parental interest may renew the interest of the most dedicated teachers and help recruit additional sensitive people. Yet, there are no guarantees that this will come about. Educators must direct their attention to creating formal roles for parents so they can hold teachers and principals accountable without violating their rights.

Essentially, the question is one of making democratic theory work, for what distinguishes a democratic system is its participatory character, and inherent in the democratic concept is the individual's right to take part in the formulation of policy if he chooses. Therefore, the political system must provide for the opportunity to formulate policy. In urban education, increased participation can be achieved only through decentralization. If school professionals succeed in halting the political drive of the black communities, we can anticipate the end of public education. Most probably, the energies of the black and white underclass would be redirected toward establishing alternative forms of school systems that are more attuned to their needs.

The struggle for community control bears grave educational consequences for city school systems. At present, most observers of this struggle stress political motivations, either neglecting or dismissing the educational merit of the plan. If the historical political disenfranchisement of American blacks is considered, this stress is understandable. Nevertheless, community control originated as an educational movement, when integration no longer seemed a reasonable probability. Since the Supreme Court's desegregation decision of 1954, more black segregated schools have come into existence than ever before; within a generation, demographers predict, black majorities will dominate major American cities. The educator's traditional answer to the educational needs of the poor—the same educational fare, but more of it—has not met those needs; compensatory education programs have had no notable effects. Predictably, most educators have claimed that socio-economic background determines achievement: failure is not so much the fault of the school as of the society, which neglects to provide for its poor. In effect, this line of reasoning blames the child. Although a great deal of the educational and sociological research of recent years has emphasized social and economic factors, there is sufficient evidence to challenge this view, and ghetto parents certainly no longer accept this easy explanation. They argue that the school system's responsibility is to educate—regardless of the background of the child. They know through experience that this can be done. However, if it is to be done in public schools, the atmosphere currently stifling public education must be changed. Before any compensatory program can hope to succeed, the system of public schooling itself must be reformed.

No evidence exists to show that participation will raise academic achievement: no urban school system has been decentralized and placed under the control of the community. However, there are encouraging signs as well as a growing body of educational research. One community control experiment in Washington, D.C., the Adams-Morgan school, reports noteworthy academic results during its short existence. One can infer from the success of Headstart programs that parental involvement plays a crucial role.

Some major research studies indicate that community control may offer the most positive educational formula. These studies show teacher and pupil attitudes to be critical to learning. The largest educational study conducted in the United States—the U.S. Office of Education's "Equality of Educational Opportunity," commonly referred to as the Coleman Report—concludes that a student's feeling of control over his future is a factor influencing achievement, a factor of more weight than all other factors combined. Furthermore, Greeley and Rossi, in their 1966 investigations of the Catholic school system (*The Education of Catholic Americans*) link achievement with student feelings of security as offered by the religious communal atmosphere. Rosenthal and Jacobson's 1968 study of teacher attitudes (*Pygmalion in the Classroom*) confirms the generally held notion that teacher expectation bears on the performance of pupils. If community control produces affirmative attitudes in teachers and students, it may well be of paramount value. Surely, it is a move in the right direction.

The demonstration districts in New York already give the impression that ghetto parents and children are revamping their attitudes toward the public school. The school, school officials, and the learning process are no longer seen as oppressive and alien.

What was a fortress school, separated from the community, now appears to be the first communal institution. Visitors to Ocean Hill during the crisis could not help but note the involvement and enthusiasm of parents and students, in marked contrast to the *anomie* of schools in other ghettos. In the broadest sense, *participation* is an educational experience.

Educators, however, have long been ambivalent to lay participation in the schools. Although rhetorically committed to parents' taking greater interest in schooling, they actually are apprehensive about lay control and involvement. Most educators are accustomed to reform from within (with negligible results) and do not welcome outside reform. With measured regularity over the past thirty years, educators have recommended that urban school systems be decentralized in order to increase both professional and lay initiative. With the same regularity, colleagues have ignored the recommendations.

Socially, the Ocean Hill–Brownsville confrontation questions the very substance of American life. Can this nation avoid bifurcation into a black society and a white society? In this instance, the school controversy may well be a paradigm of America's racial problem. What is most distressing is the failure of many American liberals to perceive the nature of the struggle. Instead of recognizing the community control movement as part of the same fight for respect, dignity, and democratic rights as the civil rights struggle in the South was in the early 1960's, many northern liberals condemn school activists as extremists. That traces of white paternalism should be found among many liberals should not surprise anyone, but it certainly gives one pause when considering the racial prospect of this country.

The Ocean Hill–Brownsville confrontation was a unique social phenomenon. A large Jewish community, fearful of undercurrents of black anti-Semitism, was hesitant to ally itself with the black cause; for many Jews already weary of the black struggle, a convenient escape hatch was placed before them. Some white liberals, comfortable with the rhetoric and distant reality of integration, inveighed against community control as separatist—an easy position, as integration affected few and little was at stake. Community control, on the other hand, entails a more potent and divisive element—the redistribution of power, much of it from white liberals to the black poor.

Many liberal spokesmen, of course, defended local control. But a significantly large and articulate segment vociferously decried its impact. In this sense, the Ocean Hill confrontation revealed an entanglement of strange alliances. For the most part, conservatives and the more radical left empathized with the black poor. The beneficiaries of the New Deal liberal social revolution were juxtaposed against them. These new political and social alignments caused by the school crisis indicate a confusion widespread in the nation. People most reluctant to change, those nostalgically yearning for the Roosevelt era, are reactionary liberals. Theirs is basically a quantitative social philosophy conceiving the root cause of poverty to be merely a lack of money. They naturally resist structural and qualitative change.

The struggle for community control of public schools is only the beginning of a larger movement. In education, it continues to spread throughout the country. The number of community schools is increasing, and four states—Massachusetts, California, Michigan, and New York—have considered bills to decentralize city schools.

This struggle is at the core of the new black militancy. While espousing the traditional ethnic political cohesion, Stokely Carmichael and Charles Hamilton add one unique ingredient to the concept of black power. "The goal of black self-determination," they write, "and black self-identity—Black Power—is full participation in the decision-making process affecting the lives of black people, and recognition of the virtues in themselves as black people."* Community control and the concept of "participatory democracy" posited by the most socially concerned and radical of this student generation are closely related; so, too, is the mandate of the poverty program to allow the poor to participate in decision-making. Community control applies not only to the black poor. It offers members of the white community an opportunity to renew their involvement in the life of our institutions. The black Harlem mother and the white Queens mother share the burden of inadequate public schooling, although the former is more aggrieved.

The idea of public control of urban public institutions has also taken root in other, noneducational, areas such as welfare, health, and housing. For too long, an outmoded welfare state has bred

* Stokely Carmichael and Charles V. Hamilton, *Black Power* (New York: Random House, 1967), p. 47.

pathological qualities of subservience in its client poor. The struggle for community control attempts to restructure public institutions so that they will accomplish the ends they were designed to achieve. More than token public involvement is required. Power must be transferred, for, as one critic has remarked, "participation without power is a ritual." At present, the struggle for community control seems to be the best way of improving the quality of life in America.

PART ONE

Prelude

1. The Lines Are Drawn

On the opening day of the 1966 fall term, angry Harlem parents boycotted one school: Intermediate School 201. They demanded that the school be integrated or, failing this, that control be turned over to them. "Future historians," Martin Mayer wrote, "will have no difficulty dating precisely the moment of decision that the New York schools could not be significantly integrated." The boycott marked the end of the school integration movement.

Parent boycotts spread rapidly throughout the city, and the concept of community control spread with them. Officials cloistered in the sanctums of the city, state, and federal government bureaucracy and in the unions and the foundations watched the unrest in the schools with mounting concern. During the winter of 1966–67, the school superintendent met with community leaders, union representatives, and Ford Foundation personnel to devise a blueprint for giving parents some role in school policy-making.

Of the dissatisfied parents, those from the depressed Brooklyn communities of Ocean Hill and Brownsville had gone further than most. Their grievances were all too familiar: segregated schools, an unsatisfactory principal, and dismal academic results. Banding together, these parents formed a group, which then declared itself the rump local school board in District 17. The group sought support from the United Federation of Teachers, and the UFT welcomed them, perceiving an opportunity to advance teacher goals—in particular, the More Effective Schools program, which is the union's compensatory education plan. On recommendation of the union, the Ocean Hill–Brownsville group was included as one of three experimental districts to be governed by local boards in the plan that was developed by the New York City Board of Education. The other districts were the IS 201 Complex in Harlem and the Two Bridges Model District in the Lower East Side.

Despite the temporary accord, the union and the black communities may well have been far advanced on their collision course. The union was on the verge of becoming a major educational influence. In its September, 1967, strike, the UFT wrote school policy into its contract. One clause provided for the study and recommendation of an educational program, with $10 million set aside to implement the program suggested. In terms of power, the union had come of age. The contract represented a historic first for both labor and education. On the other side, parents were now seeking the power to run their own schools, a power long enjoyed by most American suburban and rural school districts. Teacher power and parent power were destined to clash.

More threatening to educators than the three experimental districts was the prospect of city-wide school decentralization into community-controlled school districts. Shortly after the experiments were created, Mayor John Lindsay received a mandate from the state legislature to submit a school decentralization plan. On the promise of an additional $54 million in state aid, the mayor was to produce a plan for the 1968 legislative session that would "foster greater community initiative and participation."

The Mayor's Advisory Panel on Decentralization issued its report—commonly referred to as the Bundy Plan, after Chairman McGeorge Bundy, Ford Foundation president—recommending sweeping change. From thirty to sixty autonomous local boards would be elected by parents, with a minority membership appointed by the mayor. These local boards would have final authority over the key areas of school policy: budget, curriculum, and personnel. The Board of Examiners, an agency regulating city civil service qualifications, would be abolished for school staffing; state standards for school personnel were to suffice.

The Bundy Plan was widely attacked by school professionals. The UFT, the Council of Supervisory Associations (CSA), and the Board of Education all successfully lobbied against its passage in the spring legislative session.

Against this background, the Ocean Hill experiment was framed. To many, Ocean Hill was a paradigm of proposed school decentralization as conceived by the Bundy panel. The success or failure of Ocean Hill and the two other experiments would determine whether urban parents could and should control their schools. Consequently, wary observers watched the demonstration school districts closely. To the critics, the experiments constituted living examples of the pitfalls of city-wide school decentralization as conceived and proposed by the Bundy panel. In early November, Eugenia Kemble, a UFT staff writer, began a series on the experiments, in which she voiced teacher discontent. To those supporting the experiment, various forces—teachers, unions, the central headquarters staff—harassed and undermined the project. Such supporters point to a number of instances: eighteen assistant principals and five principals requested transfers out of Ocean Hill at the start of the project; the CSA filed suit challenging the creation of a position of demonstration school principal based on state (not city) civil service qualifications; union teachers seceded from the project. Frustrations extended to constant haggling with headquarters staff over approval of staff positions and budget allocations; yet, negotiations to obtain a clearer delineation of powers proved fruitless.

In May, 1968, the Ocean Hill board transferred involuntarily thirteen teachers, five assistant principals, and one principal to central headquarters for reassignment. Some of those transferred were felt by the Ocean Hill board to be sabotaging the project. The union quickly branded the transfers "firings." It demanded that the nineteen be given due process hearings, and it struck the Ocean Hill schools for the remainder of the school year. Thus, a confrontation between a predominantly white union and a black community had occurred.

The documents in this section describe the events and the difficulties of that first year. The Board of Education's original guidelines creating the three demonstration districts are exceedingly vague. The proposal submitted and accepted by the central board empowers the local board only to seek election and to select supervisory personnel. As a result of this clouded grant of power, the central board and the Ocean Hill board were to haggle over responsibilities throughout the first year. The demonstration districts negotiated with the central board for more control, the guideline memorandum of March 26 being part of their attempt to clarify and expand their powers. In turn, the central board's Advisory and Evaluation Committee on Decentralization (the Niemeyer Committee) proposed its own guidelines, and stalemate ensued.

The Niemeyer Committee, chaired by the president of the Bank Street School of Education, was set up in July, 1967; it observed and studied the three districts from their inception, and, on July 30, 1968, it submitted its report to the central board. The excerpt that is included here details the early history of Ocean Hill, presenting the image of a district struggling to function. The most critical question throughout was that of control over personnel. Perhaps the severest blow the Ocean Hill board suffered was the New York State Supreme Court decision in favor of the CSA, dismissing the board's establishment of a new supervisory position for the demonstration school district. This job category, bypassing city civil service regulations, had enabled the Ocean Hill board to seek school supervisors from a wider background, substituting state qualifications for city license. The decision was ultimately reversed in the Court of Appeals, nearly a year later. In the intervening months, the question of teaching personnel and, particularly, of the local board's right to hire, fire, and transfer, exploded; the Ocean Hill board's letter transferring nineteen teachers and supervisory personnel completes the documents of this early period.

The articles also depict the formation of the lines of confrontation. Eugenia Kemble charts the feelings of key union teachers in Ocean Hill, from mild support to hostility. UFT disenchantment with the local board set in early, leading the union to begin talks with the central board in order to increase the right of teachers to transfer from the district. On the other side, Unit Administrator Rhody McCoy relates the painful struggles, small and large, that were his lot. Convinced the experiment represents the most far-reaching attempt to better the educational fortunes of the children in the community, McCoy argues that community control will blaze a path for urban schools nationally.

In the final article Richard Karp charges that the Board of Education had no intention of allowing the project to succeed. Accordingly, central headquarters deliberately refrained from offering real help and found a willing ally, Karp adds, in the UFT, which saw itself defending the existing system from extremists.

DOCUMENTS

Board of Education Policy Statement on Decentralization

All members of our board are committed to the principle of decentralization of operations. In a city as large and varied as New York, we believe it is essential to have as much flexibility and authority at the local level as is consistent with our need for centralized standards. Two years ago, the Board of Education and the superintendent of schools took the first steps in a decentralization program based on the principle of strengthening and enlarging the responsibilities of the various districts: their boundaries were adjusted to equalize their burdens, and their number was increased to thirty.

The board at that time considered and rejected the idea of decentralizing by boroughs, which has been tried in the past and has failed. Concentrating therefore on the districts, the board and the superintendent decided to place the high schools, as well as junior high and elementary schools, under the jurisdiction of the district superintendents in their respective districts and to phase out the high school, junior high school, and elementary school divisions at headquarters.

Now the board proposes to further facilitate decentralization in the districts, in two major directions.

The first . . . confers increased responsibilities, especially in administrative matters, on the district superintendents and principals and the local school boards. The second embodies the superintendent's recommendations, requested and approved by the board, regarding various demonstration projects that would permit experimentation to determine more effective methods for achieving greater community involvement within different types and sizes of districts. Proposals for implementing these recommendations

ADOPTED BY the New York City Board of Education in public session, April 19, 1967.

are under study and will be presented for public discussion in the near future.

.   .   .

On October 20, 1966, and again on February 17, 1967, the board announced its desire to experiment with varying forms of decentralization and community involvement in several experimental districts of varying sizes. Its purpose is to find means of strengthening decentralization by deepening and broadening the relationship of the communities to the schools.

Pursuant to the board's request, the superintendent of schools has recommended that demonstration projects be organized in several ways so as to evaluate different approaches. Possibilities included: (1) the division of a current school district into two smaller districts, each with its own local school board and district superintendent; (2) the setting up, within a school board area, of a small grouping of schools, possibly including a high school and feeder intermediate and primary schools. The experiments could include services by a contract with a university. (3) a demonstration district of a small size to involve representatives of the community, parents, and staff more effectively in the conduct of school programs as well as in new approaches to teacher training and in curriculum development; (4) several demonstrations in single schools probing parental and community involvement in a school's program, such as the strengthening of early childhood education or the improvement of instruction in the fundamentals.

Since the date of the board's announcement, we have received many imaginative proposals from interested groups and universities regarding the nature of the demonstration projects that might be organized. All are now being studied.

The board has requested the superintendent to formulate and present to it, as soon as possible, specific proposals for the implementation of the above recommendations. Appropriate discussions with both local school boards and parent and community groups will take place before any plans are finally adopted.

Through one or more of these demonstration projects, we hope that new techniques and new approaches will be developed for teacher training and instruction and for increasing parental and community involvement and [will] thus strengthen our educational program.

Draft Guidelines for a Demonstration Project

Preamble: In order to demonstrate the manner in which community control of the school system can improve the schools as basic and essential institutions of our society, the Board of Education and the governing board of the _____ Demonstration Project hereby declare these to be the guidelines for the operation of the _____ Demonstration Project.

Article I: Demonstration Project

Section 1: Creation of Demonstration Project

a. There is hereby created a Demonstration Project for _____, hereinafter designated as the Demonstration Project.

Section 2: Area of Operation

a. The following are the geographic boundaries of and the schools within the Demonstration Project:

Section 3: Administration of the Demonstration Project

a. The Demonstration Project shall be administered by a governing board as established under Article II of these guidelines.

Article II: The Governing Board

Section 1: Selection and Composition

a. The parents, residents, and, if so designated by the bylaws, the professional staff of the Demonstration Project shall select the members of the governing board. Elections of members of the governing board shall be conducted in accordance with a published set of election rules and procedures established by bylaws to ensure a fair and honest election.

b. The Board of Education recognizes the existing governing board of the Demonstration Project as having been elected in accordance with subsection (a) of this section.

SUBMITTED BY the Ocean Hill–Brownsville governing board to the superintendent of schools, March 26, 1968, as part of the negotiations for a clear grant of power to the local board.

c. Governing board members shall serve for a term to be fixed in the bylaws of the governing board. Terms of office of the members shall be staggered.

Section 2: General Functions of the Governing Board

a. The Board of Education hereby recognizes the governing board as the agency responsible for the conduct within the Demonstration Project of the education of the children of the community in the public schools under the jurisdiction of the governing board. In the exercise of those functions, including functions described in sections 3–6 of this Article, the governing board shall be accountable to the parents and residents of the community.

b. The governing board shall adopt such bylaws for the performance of its functions as it deems appropriate.

Section 3: Instructional Functions

a. The governing board shall establish the curriculum and program to be taught in each school within its jurisdiction.

b. The governing board shall select and purchase directly the textbooks to be used in the schools within its jurisdiction.

c. The governing board shall determine the methods of instruction and shall exercise control over other educational policies in the schools within its jurisdiction.

d. In the exercise of functions vested in the governing board under this Article, the governing board shall consult with the unit administrator created by section 4 of this Article.

Section 4: Personnel

a. The governing board shall appoint a unit administrator who shall be the chief professional supervisory officer of the Demonstration Project. His powers and responsibilities shall be as provided by Article III of these guidelines.

b. All power of appointment of other instructional and supervisory personnel presently exercised by the Board of Education and the superintendent of schools is vested in the governing board acting upon the advice of the unit administrator.

c. The governing board may appoint consultants to assist it in the performance of its functions, which positions shall be exempt from regular civil service and Board of Education regulations with respect to appointment.

d. The governing board, upon the advice of the unit administrator, may remove or deny tenure or suspend any teacher or supervisor who fails to meet standards of performance established by the governing board. Removal, suspension, or denial of tenure of a teacher or supervisor under the jurisdiction of the governing board may be effected only upon a recommendation of suspension, removal, or denial of tenure by the governing board.

e. The governing board shall have the power to transfer teachers and supervisory personnel among the schools within the Demonstration Project.

f. The Board of Education shall establish schools within the Demonstration Project as training schools for teachers; the governing board shall have the same power over the operation and staffing of those schools as would the Board of Education.

g. In the process of collective bargaining with representatives of teachers and supervisors, representatives of the governing board shall participate in all matters pertaining to the governing board; in addition, the governing board may enter into supplemental agreements with representatives of teachers and supervisors.

h. The governing board shall function as the "district level" in the processing of grievance proceedings under the existing collective-bargaining agreement between the United Federation of Teachers and the Board of Education.

Section 5: Budgetary Powers

a. The Board of Education shall, for each fiscal year, allocate a sum of money to the governing board for the performance of its functions. That allocation shall be based on a per capita grant per registered student in the schools under the jurisdiction of the governing board and may not be less than the average planned per capita expenditure, including salaries to instructional and supervisory personnel, by the Board of Education on all pupils in the New York City School System.

b. Funds allocated to the governing board shall be obligated and expended by the governing board as it determines appropriate for the accomplishment of its educational responsibilities. The by-laws of the governing board shall specify at least two persons who must sign an obligation of funds or an order for the expenditure of funds.

c. The governing board may apply directly for government and private funds to supplement the allocation by the Board of Education of budgetary funds.

d. The governing board shall undertake construction or major renovation of schools to serve the Demonstration Project. The funds for such construction or renovation shall be allocated to the governing board.

Section 6: Contractual Powers

a. The governing board shall have the same power to contract for goods and services, including textbooks, supplies, maintenance, and construction as has been delegated by state law to the Board of Education.

Article III: The Unit Administrator

Section 1: Powers and Responsibilities

a. The unit administrator shall have such powers as are delegated to him by the governing board.

b. The unit administrator shall be responsible to the policy directives of the governing board.

Article IV: Legislative Change

Section 1: Additional Powers

a. Such additional powers as may be granted to the Board of Education by new legislation for the benefit of the Demonstration Project shall be vested in the Demonstration Project by the Board of Education. The Board of Education agrees to join with the governing board in seeking enactment of the proposed legislation attached hereto.

Section 2: Decentralization of the New York City School System

a. The Board of Education agrees to join with the governing board to bring about necessary changes in any legislation designed to decentralize the New York City School System to ensure that the governing board and the Demonstration Project may be continued as provided in these guidelines.

Article V: Evaluation

Section 1: In General

a. The governing board shall maintain a continuing evaluation of the Demonstration Project, which evaluation shall be reflected in annual reports to the community.

Section 2: *Standards of Evaluation*

a. The Board of Education and the governing board shall formulate immediately criteria of evaluation on the basis of which all evaluations will take place. The Board of Education shall then employ an independent agency mutually agreed upon by the governing board and the Board of Education to make an initial evaluation, according to such criteria, of the present state of schools in the Demonstration Project. This evaluation shall serve as the base year evaluation for later comparison.

Section 3: *1971 Evaluation*

a. During the months of February and March of 1971, the governing board, through such means as it deems appropriate, supported by funds allocated for this purpose by the Board of Education, shall conduct a thorough self-evaluation.

Section 4: *1973 Evaluation*

a. During the months of February and March of 1973, the Board of Education shall employ an independent agency mutually agreed upon by the governing board and the Board of Education to evaluate the Demonstration Project.

Article VI: Effective Date and Continuation

Section 1: *Effective Date*

a. These guidelines shall become effective when signed by the president of the Board of Education on behalf of the Board of Education and by the chairman of the governing board on behalf of the governing board. Such signature shall constitute official recognition of the governing board and of the Demonstration Project by the Board of Education.

Section 2: *Fifth Year Review*

a. The continuation of the Demonstration Project shall be reviewed in the Spring of 1973.

Article VII: Resolution of Disputes

Section 1: *Arbitration*

a. If the Board of Education and the governing board cannot agree on the interpretation of any provisions of these guidelines, the matter shall be referred by either party, after prior notice to the other party, to [the state commissioner of education for resolution of the dispute] [an arbitration board consisting of one appointee of each party and a third to be agreed upon by the two appointees].

Excerpts from the Niemeyer Report

In February, 1967, partly in response to the controversy surrounding IS 201 in Manhattan and partly as the result of a parent movement to gain representation on the local school board, members of the Ocean Hill–Brownsville community began to plan for some means to participate more directly in school affairs. From that time until they received their Ford planning grant in July, 1967, a number of key participants, including poverty workers, parents, neighborhood association leaders, and religious leaders, met to discuss how they would assume control of the schools in the area. They were in contact with the mayor's office and held exploratory discussions with members of the Board of Education's administrative staff.

Once they received the Ford grant of $44,000, they set out to complete the planning phase according to a deliberate, twenty-six-day timetable. Parents, community leaders, and teachers became involved. A number of parents were paid on a weekly basis to participate. They met regularly, both day and evening, to discuss the various specific means for achieving community control of the schools.

Most teacher representatives were appointed by their respective faculties at staff meetings held before the close of the school year. For the most part, these were teachers who indicated that they would be in New York during the summer and were willing to participate in the planning phase. At this time, the teachers were participants in the demonstration project, which they characterized as [meeting] the following conditions: (1) full participation by par-

EXCERPTED FROM the final report submitted to the New York City Board of Education by its Advisory and Evaluation Committee on Decentralization (Niemeyer Committee) on July 30, 1968; chap. II, pp. 72–77, 82–85, 91–94.

ents, teachers, and community in the planning and implementation; (2) confidence of each group in the others; (3) an absence of attitudes detrimental to the plan; (4) open, honest, and unbiased discussion of all issues; (5) consensus on all items involved in a plan; (6) impartial procedures for selecting the best-qualified personnel to become involved in the plan; (7) maintenance of the highest professional standards; (8) the primary objective of improving education through the use of every resource and concentrating on educational programs; (9) accountability to all interested parties throughout the planning.

Later, toward the end of September, the teacher representatives were to complain bitterly that they had been bypassed in the planning phase and that, in fact, they were seldom listened to. They described the general atmosphere of the planning meetings as "extremely hostile and negative. There was a constant stream of remarks to teachers which stated that teachers were bigoted, incompetent, disinterested, obstructive, and were attempting to sabotage the plan," and "The atmosphere became so hostile that teachers hesitated even to ask a question or express an opinion. Any attempt at teacher comment was met with insults and charges of obstruction."[1]

On July 29, at the end of the twenty-six days, the Planning Council produced a written document, which they submitted in August to the Board of Education. This differed from the original proposal used to secure the Ford Foundation grant in that it changed the method of selecting the project administrator and principals when vacancies should occur. It also abandoned the request that the project schools be given the More Effective School (MES) status and other supplementary educational services. The teachers later opposed the changes.

The specifically proposed powers, responsibilities, and functions of the project board, as stated in their document, were as follows:

1. The board will be responsible and answerable to the New York City superintendent of schools and the state commissioner of education in all matters pertaining to the schools of this district.

2. The board will be responsible for selecting and recommending for appointment a project administrator.

[1] Statement by the teachers of the Ocean Hill–Brownsville experimental district, September 27, 1967.

3. The board will approve the project administrator's recommendations of principals for existing vacancies at PS 178, PS 87, PS 155, PS 144, and IS 55.

4. The board will select and recommend for appointment a business manager.

5. The board will select nominees for community-relations liaison and community-school worker positions from among community residents.

6. The board will determine policy for the guidance of the project administrator in areas of curriculum, program, and professional personnel.

7. The board will determine budgetary needs and allocate funds for same. In line with this, the nature of such an experimental school unit makes it imperative that needs be met as they arise. The projects, therefore, shall be permitted to apply directly for federal, state, and private funds to supplement the school board's allotment.

8. The board shall make provisions for periodic evaluations of the total program. Such evaluations will include the project administrator, principals, teachers, community workers, etc. This is not to be construed as meaning the board will do the evaluating. Existing Board of Education procedures for evaluating teachers will remain intact.

9. The board will make periodic visits to schools in the experimental unit as provided by state regulations.[2]

During the summer the Planning Council held a number of meetings with Superintendent Bernard Donovan and his staff in order to clarify their intentions and differences. During this planning period the Council conferred with a variety of consultants, especially persons connected with Brooklyn College. In addition, they retained as their Project Administrator Rhody McCoy, an assistant principal with eighteen years of service in the New York City School System.

. . .

A vigorous campaign was waged in Ocean Hill–Brownsville for election to the project board. A brief training program for parents was instituted during the planning period. All the procedures and supervision of this election were established by the Planning Coun-

2 "A Plan for an Experimental School District: Ocean Hill–Brownsville," July 29, 1967 [unpublished].

cil without consultation with or advice from the Board of Education. It was an unorthodox election, but observers considered it one in which an honest effort was made to obtain the votes of all parents of children in the schools. It extended over a period of three days. The first day was normal; people came to the individual schools to vote. The Planning Council secured police cadets and students from Brooklyn College to conduct and/or supervise the election. Although the cardboard boxes and desk drawers that were pressed into service as ballot boxes could easily have been opened and tampered with, no charges were made or misdeeds observed. For the next two days, those parents who had not voted were canvassed at their homes and thus given an opportunity to vote. There was no evidence of coercion during the nominating process or during the election period itself.

Once the parents and teachers who were members of the project board were selected, they in turn designated the community representatives.

. . .

Once the election was over in Ocean Hill–Brownsville, the project administrator began to pull his staff together and proceed with a training program for the new board members. He encountered a number of problems in securing the necessary agreements to assemble a staff for the demonstration project that would be able to move into the regular school system at the end of the experiment. He tried to secure tenure and other benefits for the employees who would join him in this experiment. At the same time, he tried to create either new positions or new classifications of positions in the project administrator's staff. He succeeded in gaining a relative degree of flexibility when he was given a lump sum budget for his central staff. A formula was developed to give him his proportionate share of financing for a normal district superintendent's office having comparable problems. Nevertheless, McCoy complained that it was insufficient. He appealed unsuccessfully for aid from the Ford Foundation and now remains within the amount allocated him by the Board of Education. However, as in the other demonstration projects, he receives technical assistance from the Ford Foundation-sponsored Institute for Community Studies of Queens College.

The project board immediately was faced with a number of vacancies at the supervisory level. For example, four principalships

were open at the beginning of school. The remaining four positions either became open during the semester or will be filled at
the beginning of the 1968–69 school year. The vacancies occurred
as incumbents requested reassignment or as the newly built IS 55
created a new principalship. There were also some rearrangements
as one junior high school became an elementary school. Thus, the
project board in concert with the Board of Education and the state
Commission of Education evolved a new concept called the demonstration principalship as a means of recruiting a supervisory staff
that would be more sensitive and responsive to the special needs
of the local community (in this case the disadvantaged minority—
Puerto Rican and Negro—areas). This concept has been successfully challenged in the courts by the Council of Supervisory Associations and the UFT.

In setting up new criteria for the demonstration principalships,
Superintendent Donovan appointed a committee consisting of the
Board of Education's administrative staff, a representative from the
state Commission of Education, and the project administrators
from the three demonstration projects. The committee and the
Board of Examiners formulated the following criteria for examining candidates for principalship positions in these demonstration
projects:

Preparation: (*a*) A permanent New York State certificate valid for
service as principal of an elementary school or a New York City
license as principal of elementary school; or (*b*) A baccalaureate
degree and, in addition, 30 semester hours in approved graduate
courses; said preparation shall include 32 semester hours in appropriate professional courses, 8 of which shall be in supervision and
administration or organization. (*c*) Preparation under (*a*) or (*b*)
above shall include or be supplemented by 6 semester hours, in
either graduate or undergraduate courses, in one or more of the
following fields: community organization, urban education, urban
planning, community planning, urban social problems, or social psychology.

Experience: (*a*) Three years of teaching in day schools, one of
which shall be under regular license and appointment including
either two years of teaching in a disadvantaged area (as defined in
Title I of the Elementary and Secondary Education Act or as defined by the Board of Education for the purposes of said Act) or two
years of teaching in a special service school or one year of super-

visory experience under regular license and appointment in such a disadvantaged area or in a special service school; and (b) Two years of full time supervisory experience in youth or community activities or two years of supervisory experience under appointment in a school in a disadvantaged area as described above or in a special service school, said experience to be in addition to experience offered under (a) above and not concurrent therewith; and (c) Candidates must render 100 hours of noncompensated service in school or youth or community activities in an authorized demonstration project area or in a disadvantaged area as defined above. Said noncompensated service must cover a period of not less than three or more than ten weeks.

Time extension: For the first examination only, the 8 semester hours in supervision and administration or organization required under *Preparation* (b) and the 6 semester hours required under *Preparation* (c) may be completed within three years from the date for meeting the academic and professional qualifications as prescribed in Section 238. Upon the failure of a candidate to complete said requirements by such date, the license shall terminate.[3]

The final recommendations are now before the Board of Education, as of July, 1968. No action has been taken on the proposals.

It should be noted that the Ocean Hill–Brownsville demonstration project now has a virtually new set of top administrators, including the project administrator and seven of the eight principals of the schools in the cluster. As the 1967–68 school year opened, most (seventeen of twenty-one) assistants to principals offered their resignations. These supervisors are in the process of being transferred out gradually. The gradual procedure is due, on the one hand, to the desire to ensure stability for the demonstration project, and on the other, to find vacancies for the supervisors in other parts of the system. All new assistants to principals for the demonstration project must come from the competitive list. The project board asked to apply the concept of demonstration principal to this position as well. This request was denied by both the superintendent of schools and the state commissioner of education.

As school opened in the fall of 1967, a twelve-day teacher walk-

[3] "Eligibility Requirements for Principal of Demonstration Elementary School," memorandum from Bernard E. Donovan to the Board of Education, March 19, 1968.

out created considerable community tension. The project board tried to man the classes. At the same time, the teachers lodged serious complaints against the project board and its administrative staff, charging lack of community support for their walkout as well as the fact that the Planning Council did not listen to or consult with the teacher representatives. At first, the teachers refused to assume their roles or places on the project board, which has four teacher representatives from the eight schools. These teachers were elected in "rump" session at the opening of school, but they are not recognized by the UFT. A meeting in November, 1967, of the project board and the top leadership of the UFT failed to resolve the problems between the project board and the professional staff, but it did formulate the principle that the professional staff would treat this situation like any labor-management relationship and urged a wait-and-see attitude on the part of the teachers. If at some point the conditions become unworkable, the professional staff may decide to strike. These conditions prevailed in May, 1968, when the project board attempted to transfer and/or dismiss nineteen members of the professional staff.

. . .

During the summer of 1967, the members of the Ocean Hill–Brownsville Planning Council formulated their own proposal. They held many discussions with representatives of the Board of Education and met directly with Superintendent Donovan and the Board of Education. Throughout this period, many key issues were clarified. There appeared to be general understanding and agreement of the specific allocations of authority that were proposed to be granted the project board. In fact, the local community interpreted the appointment of the project administrator as formal recognition of the demonstration project. However, the Board of Education did not explicitly grant full recognition, because they, in turn, sought explicit acceptance of their own guidelines by the project board. Both parties are still awaiting the specific delineation of powers and authority to be granted.

The project board has been meeting since September, 1967, to resolve operational problems in concert with the project administrator. They have spent considerable time formulating specific bylaws to guide their own conduct and decision-making procedures. In January, 1968, they were given a copy of the suggested guidelines on the structure, function, procedures, and grants of authority, as prepared by the Advisory Committee and approved by the Board of Education. They discussed these guidelines with representatives of the Board of Education and among themselves at their own meetings. These discussions developed the following points, which they have held from the very beginning. First, the project board want their project administrator to be responsible *solely* to them. Second, they are dissatisfied with the arrangement for evaluation. They insist that the academic year 1967–68 not be considered as one when they had control of the schools; they want the process of evaluation to be considered as beginning in the academic year 1968–69.

The Board of Education, on the other hand, disagreed with the project board's proposal on four points and made the following four recommendations: (1) provision for a fixed term in office for project board members; (2) recognition of the responsibility of the project board to [the] central Board of Education; (3) application for federal and state funds—this must be done within the framework of existing laws; (4) a statement indicating the project board's acceptance of the requirements of the Board of Education's guidelines.[4]

The project board met with the Board of Education and stated at the outset their dissatisfaction with the suggested guidelines. They want a more specific delineation of their authority and power; for example, they have expressed the need to control their own budget (on a number of occasions they have proposed that they have their own bank account). They want the right to hire and fire the staff and to engage in contracts and subcontracts, using local citizens, of course. They have candidly discussed all three issues with the Board of Education.

A meeting also took place between the project board's lawyer and representatives of the Board of Education. On this occasion, the project board representatives reiterated and expanded on four requests: (1) to apply directly to the federal government for funds (they do not agree that all federal and state funds must be channeled through the city, which recognizes only the Board of Education as the legal educational entity); (2) to bypass city requirements entirely, establishing curriculum subject only to state standards; (3) to establish at least one school in the demonstration project as

---

[4] Letter to Rev. C. Herbert Oliver from Norman Brombacker, special assistant to the superintendent of schools, February 19, 1968.

a training school, with the result that selection of personnel need not follow normal procedures (this section, although still part of state educational law, has not been invoked for several decades); and (4) to intermingle funds—for example, to apply part of the money allocated for textbooks and supplies against maintenance needs.[5]

The issue of obtaining outside funds also came up at this meeting. The representative of the Board of Education stated emphatically the board's commitment to experimenting with the ways and means of increasing parental participation. Thus, if the demonstration project gains substantial sums from other sources, then the possibility of showing the effectiveness of local control will be uncertain. The board contends that experimental variables must be limited in order to pinpoint the cause-and-effect relationship so that the experience can be replicated in other areas. To increase significantly the amounts of monies spent in the demonstration project would not prove the value of community involvement. The board prefers to test whether community involvement will affect student achievement levels. However, former board president Alfred Giardino stated that the board would welcome any new funds, although such monies must be channeled through and approved by the central agency.

Both the Board of Education and the project board had hoped that this phase of securing formal approval might be concluded in time for formal approval and full authority to be granted by the end of March [1968]. The project boards did not share in the normal budget-making process, which began in April. The Board of Education has not yet granted *formal* approval to the project boards because they were constrained by the state Education Law and by union contracts to accede to the demands of the project board. This impasse has given rise to a series of problems concerning the operation of the three demonstration projects and raised the question of who has authority to operate the schools. At this point, the controversy over operational powers with respect to assignment of personnel is focused on the Ocean Hill–Brownsville demonstration project.

[5] The representative of the Board of Education responded that permission would have to come from the city budgetary officer.

Letter of Transfer

May 8, 1968

Dear _____:

The governing board of the Ocean Hill–Brownsville demonstration school district has voted to end your employment in the schools of this district. This action was taken on the recommendation of the Personnel Committee. This termination of employment is to take effect immediately.

In the event you wish to question this action, the governing board will receive you, Friday, May 10, 1968, at 6 P.M. at Intermediate School 55, 2021 Bergen Street, Brooklyn.

You will report Friday morning to Personnel, 110 Livingston Street, Brooklyn, for reassignment.

Reverend C. Herbert Oliver,
Chairman, Ocean Hill–Brownsville
Governing Board

Rhody McCoy
Unit Administrator

cc   Bernard Donovan, Superintendent of Schools
Theodore Lang, Deputy Superintendent for Personnel

VIEWPOINTS

Ocean Hill–Brownsville / EUGENIA KEMBLE

The painfully obvious results of a failing school system—low reading scores, joblessness among school graduates as well as among dropouts, mounting parent concern over the failures of schools,

REPRINTED WITH permission from the *United Teacher*, official publication of the United Federation of Teachers, Local 2, AFL-CIO, December 20, 1967.

hostility and animosity both against those responsible for the educational inadequacy of the schools as well as against the teachers who work in them—all of these ever more obvious symptoms of a dying school system had much the same effect in Ocean Hill– Brownsville as they had in other poverty areas of the city.

Last winter, parents and teachers worked cooperatively in voicing their dissatisfactions with the schools in that area. The two groups demonstrated together on behalf of increased personnel for these schools and other forms of school improvement. In Ocean Hill, functioning parent-teacher councils were in operation.

Residents of Ocean Hill–Brownsville had another cause for complaint. They were not represented on the local school board for District 17. They solved this problem by forming their own independent board, which in turn became concerned with the opening of a new school in the area, IS 55. It was the emphasis and concentration placed on the future of this new school that led to the eventual drawing up of a community-wide proposal for an experimental district. What had originally amounted to a plan for community participation in the management of one new school soon expanded, under the direction of a Catholic priest, Rev. John Powis, to encompass seven existing schools and an eighth school yet to be built, IS 55.

While the IS 201 negotiating committee was working with two professors from Yeshiva University, Harry Gottesfeld and Sol Gordon, in drawing up a decentralization plan for their district, the Ocean Hill–Brownsville group made contact with the same pair in hopes of obtaining their assistance for a similar purpose. United Federation of Teachers representatives, who were in contact with both groups at the time, worked to assure that both plans would contain the same safeguards for teachers. Of special importance, for example, was a provision in the original plan that stated that any conflict between groups on the governing board provided for in the plan would be talked over until a "consensus" could be reached. If an impasse developed, any question would be referred to a mediating body composed of a teacher, a community representative, and an impartial party acceptable to both the others. Teachers were also instrumental in assuring that educational programs to supplement the new administrative format be included in the plan. "Learning centers" and MES elementary schools were two kinds of supplementary programs added to the plan.

When the Ford Foundation, after having made contact with

Father Powis, announced its grant of $44,000 to the Ocean Hill–Brownsville project, teachers were quite surprised. By this time, July 6, 1967, teachers had been seriously involved at only one school, JHS 178.

When the Ford Foundation announced financial support for the three demonstration projects, it stated in its press release that "The new school units will devote the next few months to preparing new program plans . . ." which would in turn be presented to the Board of Education for "review."

The grant made to the Ocean Hill–Brownsville district was to be administered through Our Lady of Presentation Church, the church of Rev. John Powis. It was "to cover preparation for elections, efforts to involve parents and other residents more in school affairs, training institutes for governing board members and community school workers, educational consultants, and budgetary specialists."

Ford said that the preliminary plans used as basis for the project "call for establishment of a local governing board composed of eight parents, five community representatives, eight teachers, and two supervisors for a unit comprising JHS 271 and its feeder schools PS 73, 155, 87, and 137 and IS 55, and its feeder schools, PS 144 and 178."

The functions of the future governing board, as they were enumerated at this point, were that it be

> responsible for hiring an administrator of the program; selecting principals in consultation with the administration as positions become vacant; setting educational goals and standards within the schools; recruiting and selecting staff; adapting curriculum; arranging contracts with an independent evaluative agency; developing policy toward other public and private agencies; and maintaining fiscal control of the central Board of Education's budget allocation. The local board will also be responsible for preparing community-school workers, for in-service training of inexperienced or new teachers and members of the student government.
>
> The experimental unit is expected to include special reading programs, parent teacher liaison at each grade level to discuss curriculum standards and goals, and adult education in each school.

An early version of the plan itself contained a number of provisions for special programs including the increase of specialists in the schools, special reading programs, committees of parents and teachers at each grade level to discuss standards and goals of curriculum regularly, school-wide parent-teacher councils, adult education programs, and the reorganizing of each elementary school into an MES school. A special note attached to this plan stated that "Dr. Donovan has indicated he could not promise to provide *all* the special services listed below. He has said that there will be no expansion of the MES program at all, but that instead there would be a 'beefing-up' in the early childhood grades; for example, each first grade will have two teachers to every class of thirty."

It was precisely this deleted part of the plan that teachers felt was particularly valuable, and it was with these features in mind that the UFT had urged teachers to cooperate in the initial phases of the planning. They felt that administrative change without additional substantive programs would not erase the inadequate features of the schools.

Attached to this first plan was a total budget of $37,000. Of this, $10,000 was earmarked for publicity and preparation for elections. Ten community people were to be hired for door-to-door canvassing on a full-time basis for eight weeks at $100 per week. Another $5,000 was earmarked for "innovative allowance, governing board," and another $5,000 as "contingency funds"; $5,260 was allotted for a "governing board institute" and a "community-school worker institute." The money was to be paid to those who participated in these training sessions at the rate of $15 per session. Some also was intended to pay speakers. The remainder would cover typists, bookkeepers, accountants, and other personnel.

Harriet Goldstein, chapter chairman at PS 144 and representative to the planning board, said that this budget was removed in copies of the plan sent to teachers.

Isadore Tuchinsky, a teacher at JHS 178 who was elected during the last days in June to serve as a teacher representative to the planning board, outlined some of the problems he and other teachers elected to the planning board encountered during the summer. Originally, the steering committee that initiated the project was formed to develop a plan for only JHS 178. This group included representatives of parents and teachers at JHS 178. But, at the last minute (about June 15), the project plan was revised to include other schools in the district, he said. Whereas the group had, up to this point, been considering Rhody McCoy for the position of principal of JHS 178, he soon became their prospective candidate for "acting unit administrator" of the whole project. Tuchinsky was uncertain as to how McCoy was actually appointed to this position, but added that he believed neither the union nor the teachers knew about or participated in the selection.

(Rhody McCoy, a former acting principal of both PS 148 Manhattan and PS 614 Queens and now unit administrator for the Ocean Hill–Brownsville project, says he was called in to be interviewed for the position of principal by the original steering committee at JHS 178. When the nature of the project expanded he was considered as a prospective "acting unit administrator." He said that the steering committee interviewed a number of candidates for the position. But Lee Olshan, chapter chairman at JHS 178 and a member of the original steering committee, said he did not know how Rhody McCoy was appointed.)

Tuchinsky noted that no standard organizational procedure was set up by the other members of the planning board for communicating with the teachers elected to it. For some time, he didn't know who the teacher representatives from other schools to the planning board were. A number of teachers who were active on the planning board during the summer said they had been promised by Father Powis that each school would be able to vote at the end of the summer as to whether or not it would continue to participate in the project. This promise was never fulfilled.

Natalie Belkin, representative to the planning board from PS 155 and eventually elected vice chairman of the governing board, also remarked on the nature of communications the board had with teachers. She said that one teacher from PS 137 attended a number of meetings of the board as a representative from that school, though she had never been elected to do so. The person who had been elected, Burt Landsman, was not informed of the meetings.

Teacher criticism has also been directed at the way in which the original plan was revised. In a statement made public in mid-September, these criticisms were delineated in a paper signed by the chapter chairmen from all seven of the participating schools and a number of teacher representatives to the Planning Board. The statement said:

Attempts to clarify ambiguous sections in the plan were taken as an attempt on our part to destroy the original intent. This was not our intention. . . . The community group had begun expanding on the plan without our presence. We were given the suggestions in written form and we objected to many parts. Our suggestions were ignored, or, when we objected enough the topic under discussion was dropped rather than revised. We were told by Mr. McCoy that the governing board itself, when it took power, would make its own rules and expand on the plan. Without our knowledge or presence, part of the plan was rewritten and submitted to Dr. Donovan. One change was made to guarantee only one possible selection of a unit administrator. The original proposal had provided for the submission of 3–5 candidates to Dr. Donovan, who would then make the selection. . . .

Another important change was made with regard to the selection of principals. Instead of teacher-parent-community participation in the selection through the governing board, principals were now to be selected by the unit administrator, with the governing board's approval but not participation in the original choices. Furthermore, the names were submitted to the Board of Education for approval before teachers were informed of them.

At a meeting with teachers on Thursday, December 7, 1967, Rhody McCoy remarked on the change in the provision for 3–5 candidates. He said it had been decided that general nominations for candidates would be accepted by the governing board and the "one who emerged" would be approved by the superintendent of schools. At an interview a day later he said that three such candidates had been nominated: himself, Dr. Melvin Moore, and Dr. Jack Bloomfield.

McCoy responded both days to the question of why teacher suggestions for changes in the original plan had been ignored. Generally, he believed that the bylaws for the governing board could not be set up before that body was officially constituted. Instead, he said, a committee of the governing board, which is now at work, would announce the powers of that body soon. The reason teacher proposals could not be included before, he added, was because the board was not yet in existence.

"Nobody in their right mind would set bylaws for a body that is not in existence. . . . Our intent is to establish a community group, and then to set up the bylaws," he said.

Teachers objected to this view since it would give the governing board free reign to determine its own powers.

Teachers acknowledged that one of their suggestions, though

modified, had been incorporated after three revisions into the later plan. Their concern was that an independent agency be contracted to evaluate the project and participate in it. In the original plan, the governing board and the principal could judge teachers "unfit" or "incompetent." In the later plan, a provision was included stating that, "The board shall make provisions for periodic evaluations of the total program. Such evaluations will include the unit administrator, principals, teachers, community workers, etc. This is not to be construed as meaning the board will do the evaluating. Existing Board of Education procedures for evaluating teachers will remain intact." Teachers emphasized that this provision was the only one of their many suggested revisions that was included in the later plan.

Another bone of contention teachers raised with regard to the plan was that they did not know who had been responsible for rewriting it. Isadore Tuchinsky said that he didn't believe parents knew who rewrote the plan. He said that when he had asked McCoy himself who had done the job the first answer given was, "I don't know." He was later told that a professional writer rewrote the plan. McCoy had said then that teachers on the original steering committee had been involved in the revision process. McCoy said at a recent interview that those who had drawn up the first plan had also drawn up the second. However, Lee Olshan, a teacher on the original steering committee, said he had been instrumental in drawing up the first plan but did not know who had done the second.

Dan Goldberg, representative to the planning board from JHS 271, complained that no term of office had ever been set for the unit administrator. He said that this had been a concern of teachers at the beginning of the summer but that it had never been resolved. No term of office has yet been set. He also pointed out that the original provision that members of the governing board must come to a "consensus" before decisions are made had been abandoned.

Goldberg and Fred Nauman, chapter chairmen for JHS 271, raised questions over the way elections for the governing board had been conducted as well as over the confused role of teachers in the process of appointing the unit administrator and the new principals. They objected first to the fact that many of those who were elected to the governing board had been the same people who had been doing the electioneering.

The matter of the governing board election was looked upon in askance by some and with approval by others. Rhody McCoy says that at last count more than 1,050 parents voted for their representatives to the board, but he didn't know how many teachers had voted for those who now claim to represent teachers on the board. He said that an "amalgamation" of college people kept track of the voting, none of whom he knew by name. He did not mention which universities or colleges they were from.

Apparently, according to an article published in an August 28 issue of "The Center Forum," a publication of the Center for Urban Education, nonvoting parents in the community were to be canvassed after the election to give them an opportunity to vote. Isadore Tuchinsky . . . pointed out that there is no way of knowing exactly how many parents voted, since all records kept were those of the board itself, and no outside agency such as the Honest Ballot Association, was called in to observe the election. He and other teachers believed that canvassers went into the homes of community people after the election to try and seek out more votes.

Mario Fantini, program officer for the Ford Foundation, said that one factor surrounding the election was the pressure "to do everything possible with the time and resources." He said it could have been done better and that, were it to be done again, the Honest Ballot Association would be brought in. He believed that the present leadership was legitimate and remarked that, "the fact is, the people who spearhead a movement are those most likely to be elected." He also said that the participation in the governing board election was broader than that for most public elections in the area.

Dan Goldberg added that one key to many of the problems that arose during the summer was that "the group running the thing was in a great rush." He said that teachers were first told that the money from the Ford Foundation had been given so a plan could be set up and a governing board trained. But, during the course of the summer they were told that a governing board would be elected by summer's end.

Goldberg and Nauman both said that the staff of JHS 271 had voted in favor of the concept of decentralization, but teachers had hoped that the plan devised would contain educational programs and would outline the powers of the governing board.

A statement written by a committee of "interested teachers" in their school, composed of fifteen signatories said:

We feel that the concepts behind the plan and the general courses of action offered are completely sound and deserving of our full support. The development of an experimental school district, the involvement of parents, teachers, and community at the highest level of planning is daring and imaginative. These three groups, who are in, or intimately associated with, the school, who have the most to gain if the school functions at its highest level, would, out of a natural self interest, create a climate of educational excellence.

The statement, which went on for two pages concluded with:

We therefore make the following motion:
   a. The faculty of JHS 271 heartily endorses the *concept* of an experimental school district in District 17.
   b. The faculty of JHS 271 declines at this point to vote for or against the *plan* for an experimental school district as proposed.
   c. We elect a planning representative to meet with the group which we trust will create a workable plan this summer and submit it for our approval in the fall.

These teachers saw the whole operation as a chance for teachers and parents to work together and hoped it would help erase any antagonisms that existed between the two groups.

Though Goldberg met with an open committee of teachers from JHS 271, and took their suggestions to the governing board, he felt that the final plan produced was "skimpy," contained no educational plans and no bylaws defining how the governing board would function. He added that, despite the fact he had been asked for a summer address list of teachers so that copies of the new plan could be sent to them, none received it until they returned to school.

Ronnie McFadden, a black teacher from the same school, who generally supports the present governing board, served as an alternate to Dan Goldberg over the summer and went to two meetings of the planning board. He said that teachers were under a false impression in June if they felt they would be able to do planning rather than elect representatives to a governing board. There was a necessity to draw out parents and other community representatives to go ahead with an election—to go ahead and choose representatives without delaying over a plan . . . to my understanding teachers would have preferred to delay and work on the plan—I think the planning board people were right in what they did. There are times when the cart comes before the horse.

McFadden explained that he had been elected to serve on the present governing board by approximately 35 teachers in his school. Of a staff of 140 teachers, 41 had voted. He also said that of the seven parents who now serve on the governing board, all but two are PTA presidents. The parent representative for JHS 271, he added, makes regular reports on the activities of the governing board to the parents of that school.

He went on to discuss what he felt to be the rationale behind the Ocean Hill–Brownsville demonstration project. "We have to realize that the community people will now have a greater voice . . . there is a need to have more black people in the schools . . . the community people feel greater allegiance to a black administrator."

As far as the elections for administrators were concerned, mixed views were in evidence as to the logic of the role teachers played. Isadore Tuchinsky noted that the teachers who had served as representatives to the planning board were called to a meeting of the new governing board to vote on the selection of unit administrator. Since they felt they were not legally elected representatives to the new governing board, they were hesitant in voting. When they realized they could be accused of obstructing the operation of the project, they went ahead and voted. Natalie Belkin, UFT chapter chairman of PS 155, was elected to be vice chairman for the board at a second meeting in a closely contested vote.

Confusion erupted when, at a third meeting of the governing board, principals were to be selected. Teachers knew through the press that Herman Ferguson was to be presented as a candidate for the principalship of IS 55. (It has been alleged that he was connected with the Revolutionary Action Movement, a group that intended to assassinate a number of moderate civil rights leaders. Though he is under indictment, trial has not been held and therefore these allegations have never been proved or disproved.) Since they were not governing board members, they were in doubt as to what action they should take with regard to the appointments. They were worried that the appointment of such a controversial figure as Ferguson might cast doubt on the nature of the project. Teachers abstained in the voting, saying that they had no right to vote, but at the same time allowing a vote to be registered so they would not be accused of blocking the project.

As a result, these teachers were accused, instead, of fence straddling to suit their own ends. Parents, community people, and even some teachers accused them of claiming the right to vote when it was in their own interest to do so and refusing it at other times. Ronnie McFadden said parents were angry since they "were under the assumption that the teacher planning board members, since they had gone along all the time, would vote in the election." Natalie Belkin also felt that it was wrong of teachers to operate on the basis of these two different policies. In the end, the Board of Education vetoed Ferguson's immediate appointment, though three other of the principals nominated have been appointed.

Some teachers were bothered by the fact that they had not been invited to participate in press conferences called by the planning board. Harriet Goldstein, representative to the board from PS 144; Sandra Adler, chapter chairman from PS 73; and Natalie Belkin, chapter chairman from PS 15, reported one incident which they resented. At one press conference for a story which came out in the September 2, 1967, issue of the *Amsterdam News*, teachers were invited only to have their picture taken with the governing board, but not to make any statement to the press. Isadore Tuchinsky said that teachers never were given the opportunity at any conferences called by the board to make a statement.

Rhody McCoy, unit administrator, responded to a question on this subject at a recent interview. He said that there had been "no deliberate attempt to keep teachers out of press conferences. . . . They weren't invited because of the nature of the conferences. Each one was held at the time of an election when the press wanted to interview either the parents elected or the new unit administrator. People were invited depending on whom the press wanted to talk to."

With the advent of the teacher walk-out [September, 1967], new problems arose. The governing board members expressed a "negative attitude" toward the walkout according to the statement of criticism drawn up by teachers. Despite this, many felt that the community at large did not express open opposition. Isadore Tuchinsky said that though parents were asked to scab, only one person, Mrs. Hattie Bishop who is the JHS 178 parents represen-

tative to the governing board, came into his school. He felt that
the community was not aware of the opposition of the governing
board people to the walkout, nor had community people directed
the parent representatives on the board to try and keep schools
open.

Ronnie McFadden, made a more general remark on the whole
parent-teacher relationship. "Parents do not feel they have the
good wishes of the teachers in what they are doing," he said.

What friction did arise immediately before and after the opening of school resulted in reports that teachers were being threatened
and that great numbers of them wanted to leave the district. Frank
Lanza, a former chapter chairman at PS 144, who is presently
awaiting his transfer assignment from the Board of Education,
reported a number of "threats" that he believed were made by
people who had some connection with members of the governing
board. One day after picketing during the walk-out, his car was
stopped by another car about half a block from the school. One
of four young men in the car got out and said to him, "Don't
come back here or else. . . ."

On another occasion, Lanza, upon request, went to speak before the Parents' Association of his school. Two of the same group
who had stopped his car began shouting at him, "whitey . . . he
lies . . . don't listen to him. . . ." Apparently many of the parents
were embarrassed at the outbreak and managed to stop the shouting. Ten or twelve of them walked out. Lanza said that after the
meeting, one of the same young men came up to him and told
him he was threatening Lanza's life. The apparent connection,
in both these instances, was that one of those in the group was
the son of a member of the governing board.

Dan Goldberg, representative to the planning board from JHS
271, said that as far as he was concerned there is "no connection
to my knowledge of any threats to me as an individual with anyone on the governing board." He added that as far as he knew,
teachers in other schools had been "threatened."

Harriet Goldstein, representative to the planning board from
PS 144, said that one assistant principal reported that he had been
"threatened," and that all assistant principals had requested transfers from the district. Though all the requests have been granted,
some are still awaiting appointment.

Sandra Adler, chapter chairman at PS 73, said that her principal
had been shouted down during a PTA meeting and that loud

coughing had been used as a technique to prevent him from speaking and being heard. She also said that her principal's car was discovered to be missing and was not found until a few days later when it was seen parked around the block.

Harriet Goldstein made clear that she didn't "believe there was anti-Semitism, but I do think there was anti-teacher and anti-white feeling."

Rhody McCoy, unit administrator, believed the talk about threats had been exaggerated. He said that the extent of the kind of remarks he had heard were such comments as "You ruined my life—you're not going to ruin my children's too," and he didn't believe that such a comment constituted a serious "threat."

During the Board of Education meeting held September 27, at which Rhody McCoy and the three new principals for the district were appointed, an atmosphere of hostility pervaded, which heightened the tempo of the ever-mounting controversy over the project. Shouting, pushing, name-calling, and the shuffling of chairs were all charges made against some of those who attended the meeting.

Both Rhody McCoy and Mario Fantini, program officer for the Ford Foundation, attribute much of the atmosphere at the meeting to a series of rumors that began circulating shortly before it. There were rumors that the Board of Education was not going to approve the appointments. There were rumors that teachers were going to fill all the seats so that community people couldn't get in. There were rumors that community people were going to fill all the seats so that teachers couldn't get in. There were rumors that the meeting would be canceled; there were rumors that a group from the Bronx was planning to come to question Al Shanker, UFT president, on the "strike."

McCoy said that many remarks were made and that, though many such remarks were attributed to Ocean Hill–Brownsville people, they did not make them. For whatever reason, the meeting was chaotic and the appointments made in an unfriendly, suspicious, and hostile atmosphere.

At a recent meeting of teachers at JHS 178, Rhody McCoy was asked a number of specific questions by teachers. When queried as to the number of teachers who had requested transfers from the district, he replied that each school had been asked to submit to him a list of all those who want transfers. Though he has received lists, many of those who originally requested to leave the district have now decided to stay. He told this reporter the next day that of the thirty-eight who had requested transfers, ten had withdrawn their names from the lists.

At the meeting, the teachers presented McCoy with a petition asking that their present principal, William Harris, who was appointed at the September Board of Education meeting, be allowed to move with them to their new school, IS 55, and become its principal rather than Herman Ferguson whose appointment is still pending. McCoy replied that Ferguson would remain as "principal of record" for the new school until the governing board changes its mind or definite legal action is taken on his case.

Teachers also raised the question of services the governing board was intending to bring to the schools. This concern for program and educational services has been raised often by teachers ever since the beginning of the project. The final plan for the experimental project has no provision in it whatever for educational programs or services. When McCoy was asked what new facilities or services IS 55 will have when it opens, he said that he had requested a number of services for the school but did not expect many of those requests to be filled by the Board of Education. Instead, outside agencies would help out in this area, he anticipated.

In a later interview, he said that the Board [of Education] was planning to initiate three programs with funds distributed under Title I of the Elementary and Secondary Educational Act. One of these would include a "material-centered library" with extended hours, larger space, and greater opportunity for individual research work.

A number of reading projects are also in the offing. One of them is based on a "skills center" program, which, according to a plan drawn up by Dr. S. Alan Cohen of Yeshiva University, would involve "a high intensity, individualized, diagnostic, self-directed program for improving reading and for influencing psychosocial behaviors."

A second reading project suggested by Dr. Cohen would introduce "the use of entirely new materials and approaches to affect reading achievement. Examples of the new materials include "Imperial Productions Phonics," "Fries Linguistic Readers," and "Wollensak Tape Records," among others. A third proposal would involve "Bonus Book Home Libraries." Under this plan, "over 300 first-graders across five elementary schools will be given

one children's book to start a home library. . . . For every five
books read, a child receives a bonus book to add to his home
library which he keeps permanently. Once a week children try to
'sell' their private books to other children to exchange for new
books." A fourth Cohen suggestion would utilize paraprofessionals, project assistants, and skills center training teams to work on
materials for the other projects. One additional plan McCoy and
the governing board hope to initiate is an "in-service training program for library assistants."

How realistic these grand plans are becomes a pointed question
when one looks at the present financial situation of the demonstration project. Having run out of the Ford Foundation grant, McCoy
says they are relying on "faith, hope, and charity" to pull the
project through until February when grants are expected from
other sources. He says the project has been "enticed, seduced, and
compromised to the tune of $55 million." The state has promised
$4.6 million for special programs, and $11 million for buildings.
Ford Foundation has promised an additional $5 million; $6.6
million should be in the works from Education Commissioner
Harold Howe and the Office of Education. The Welfare Department has promised $12 million in services. February 1 is the magic
date when the realities of these promises should be known.

Among the other questions directed at McCoy during the JHS
78 meeting was one that asked him if he attributed educational
problems to teacher inefficiency. He criticized teachers for not
being strong enough in their opposition to a system marked by
"atrocious conditions." They are not responding as professionals,
he said, and "then when parents protest you look down on them."
As for the UFT, he said, "At one time the union could have
helped, but now I don't know . . . Until such time as it changes
its direction, and that may depend on when it reaches an apex in
salaries—I don't know." He also felt that teachers' colleges were
partly to blame since they didn't prepare teachers adequately.

As to the question of whether the staffs in the demonstration
project schools should be all black, McCoy didn't understand how
anyone could suggest that since "It's not possible." He added that
he felt images were important to children "particularly when the
image of the black male has been relegated to a third-class position." Yet, "if I were beginning to look at the color of faces before
I look at the job being done, I wouldn't be here—and I feel the
same way about teachers." He also said that he felt teachers

should serve on governing boards since "I feel they have much to contribute." He said nothing about the UFT policy opposing teacher participation on governing boards. On this last point, Ronnie McFadden of JHS 271 had also made a comment. He said that "teachers on the board create friction since teachers are blamed for the kids failures."

The avowed aim of the experimental project, to involve parents in the affairs of the schools, has, according to McCoy, been met. "Nowhere else in this city are parents involved to the extent they are here," he said. They are working on problems outside the schools too—on problems of housing and welfare, as well as on questions of curriculum. He says there are larger turnouts at governing board and after school meetings than formerly.

Natalie Belkin, chapter chairman at PS 155, had a different dimension to add to this observation. She observed that there were fewer parents in for open school this year than in the five previous years. Nor did they come to the private conferences, she said.

Two of the new black principals appointed to the Ocean Hill–Brownsville demonstration schools seem more concerned with the internal workings of their respective schools than with the in's and out's of governing board activity. William Harris, formerly a principal at PS 4 in Queens, is already such a hit with his staff that they want him to stay with them when they move from JHS 178 to the new IS 55. Harris, who says he will follow the recommendation of the governing board no matter what it is, said that naturally he would prefer to follow his staff to the new school. "I have developed a rapport with the people I work with here," he says, "and feel it would be advantageous for me to go ahead to IS 55."

Harris remarked on the effects of teacher attitudes toward the project on their ability to work in his school. "We have a job to do—I don't want opinions to interfere with the job to be done. They have attempted to do the job—the whole faculty has been very cooperative. They have not let their diverse feelings about the project interfere with the job to be done here in this school."

As to the question of whether a school composed of black teachers and black administrators would be more effective, Harris said that he felt that it was important that teachers help children with their image problems. "But," he added, "it is also important that teachers do a job. The real thing people want here is that their children come out of these schools so they can take their place in society along with others."

Harris felt that plans for decentralization would not have a marked affect in the Ocean Hill–Brownsville area as far as integration was concerned. There would be a majority of Negroes here regardless, he said. Maybe in fringe neighborhoods it would make a difference, but not in this core area.

Some of the programs Harris is planning to implement in his school include those now being considered by the governing board. He added that he hoped to raise the level of attendance in his school by using young people in the schools as tutors. Some teachers have already developed a special group activity that involves taking children to plays, museums, and other places of special cultural interest. In-service training for teachers, special training for parents—including Spanish-speaking parents—so that they can help in the schools, and a special math program are a few of his other ideas for the school's future. Harris added that no teachers in his school had requested transfers as a result of the demonstration project.

The new principal for PS 144, Ralph Rogers, comes from PS 58 in Manhattan, a 600 school. Though never an administrator, he says he has taught in the school system for twelve years. He believes that many of his teachers are making constructive suggestions for programs in the school involving audio-visual instruction, new books, and teacher orientation programs. He said he has had two meetings with the governing board, but so far nothing new has been added to the curriculum as a result of them. "I imagine they are working on plans," he says, "but I have no way of knowing."

As for the racial composition of his staff, Rogers says:

I'm taking teachers and people who are going to do a job—I don't care if you're black, white, gold, or polka dot—if you teach you can come here. I see no color at all; all I see is education and it has no color. Education is education and that is all it ever has been. Teachers are doing a good job though they could be doing better. We are starting programs to help the new ones. I don't think these teachers look at education in terms of black or white.

Rogers says that the new programs in his school will come through the governing board [and include] a new math program and the eventual departmentalization of math teaching. He also said he hoped to be able to start language instruction in the third, fourth, or fifth grade.

Attitudes, as Rogers sees them, are generally good. "We just had a parents' meeting today which they tell me had the biggest turnout ever." About 30 to 35 were present, he said. Teacher attitudes are getting better too, since they now feel they can do more new and creative things, he added.

Despite the many seeming irregularities and the misunderstandings that arose as a result of them, many of those skeptical teachers who had originally taken part in the planning believe now that there is a turn for the better taking place as far as the attitudes of teachers are concerned. Harriet Goldstein from PS 144 says that the new principals in the schools are working to establish good relationships with the teachers and that there is a definite effort under way to lessen the influence of hotheads and *provocateurs*. She believes that both sides are moving toward each other as a result of necessity and practicality.

Natalie Belkin of PS 155 said she had made suggestions to her principal and he had accepted and used them. She believes that now that teachers realize decentralization is here they are not opposed to community participation. She says that teachers just want to be sure that participation stays within constructive limits. One reason the views of teachers hardened so was because they kept reading and hearing over and over again about the problems and hostile atmosphere characterizing the project.

The UFT has been negotiating with the Board of Education for a transfer plan that will enable teachers to leave, although the union has encouraged them not to leave their schools. Sandra Feldman, UFT field representative, says that the history of the project was a frustrating one for teachers. The efforts the UFT made last year to cement ties between parents and teachers raised hopes, which were seriously undermined by the events of the summer. The transfer plan being settled upon would give teachers the option of transferring at two points during each school year for as long as the experiment continues. With such opportunities made available to them and with the decline in the harassment of teachers in the project recently, a better atmosphere has been created in the project, Mrs. Feldman says.

Rhody McCoy believed that one cause of problems was that the UFT walkout came at a most "inopportune time" which in turn contributed to a breakdown in communications. He was critical of some of the demands being made by the union and said, for example, "To my knowledge the community was never consulted on the question of the disruptive child." As far as MES goes, he said the community felt that "additional services should be made to coincide with the felt needs of the community. A given district may have been able to utilize the funds and services of MES in ways different from the prototype."

The future of his project is in doubt, he admitted, now that the Bundy Report had been released. Since there is already an elected board in Ocean Hill–Brownsville, to change it might leave the community disillusioned. He added that he had been assured by the Ford Foundation that the substance of the Bundy Report was still subject to modification.

Isadore Tuchinsky of IS 178 had the following analysis of what kinds of teacher attitudes now exist in his school. First there is a group whose ideological agreement with those running the project and frustration over the school system compliment one another. There are those who sympathize emotionally with what is intended but don't agree with the way it is being done. Some, says Tuchinsky, completely disagree but will not say anything for fear of being called Uncle Tom's. The last group he sees are those who for opportunistic reasons cooperate with all the activities of the project.

Lee Olshan, chapter chairman for the same school, has a different view. He says that teachers in his school do not have decided opinions on the project. They did have fears, he said, but these were the result of rumors. Now the rumors have subsided, and this school has a new principal whom teachers like, and their attitude has improved. They are still apprehensive of the idea that Herman Ferguson might become the principal of IS 55, he added.

What turns the degree of cooperation between parents, teachers, and community people in Ocean Hill–Brownsville will take remains to be seen. It does appear that the peak of resistance and hostility has been reached and passed. Whether constructive steps have actually been taken and educational improvement will follow is as yet an open-ended question.

The Year of the Dragon / RHODY McCOY

In Ocean Hill–Brownsville, there are people groping in the dark; they are people who for a long time have felt themselves outside the mainstream of public concern. The city takes no notice of them. These people are obscure, unnoticed—as though they do not exist. They are not censured or reproached; they simply are not seen. They are the invisible residents of a demoralized, poverty-ridden inner city. To be ignored or overlooked is a denial of one's rights to dignity, respect, and membership in the human race. These residents have been frustrated at every turn in their attempt to reverse the process.

The local school board (District 17) is a typical example of the obscurity Ocean Hill–Brownsville residents have experienced. For well over two years, district residents have not been represented on the board nor have their contributions or attempts to contribute been accepted or considered meaningful. They have been ignored.

With increasingly poor academic performance from pupils attending our schools—with all district schools having student reading levels at least two years below city grade norms—there exists the continuous production of imageless children who take no special interest or pride in school achievement. This manifests itself in the increasing dropout rate even at the junior high school level. The physical plants are, for the most part, unfit to house students, let alone to permit teachers to perform in an effective manner. Many have been condemned only to be subsequently reactivated. The alarming turnover in staff, coupled with high pupil mobility and substandard physical conditions, results in minimal learning.

The parents of Ocean Hill–Brownsville are determined to have a permanent voice in matters pertaining to their schools and to have it now. They are dedicated to the goal of joining forces to bring about better educational results for their children. The community, generally acknowledged by the various social and political forces as, in every respect, the most disadvantaged in the city, has

---

THIS IS an edited version of an unpublished address delivered in January, 1968, at a Harvard education conference.

finally risen to demand a change—to make history. And it is demanding not only change but also a share in bringing about that change.

A new concept of a partnership in education, one that incorporates community investment, is beginning to emerge in the educational circles of our country. In keeping with this new trend, on April 19, 1967, the Board of Education of the city of New York declared for decentralization and for greater community participation in the school system. A group of parents, who had banded together originally to obtain a voice in the selection of the principal and teaching staff in the newly built intermediate school (IS 55), quickly moved to have the board's new policy implemented in the Ocean Hill–Brownsville school district.

It is generally assumed that people are political creatures and that even an abuse of spirit can be worked out in the political realm. Such an assumption is a denial of the fact that men are capable of ending the intolerable without recourse to politics. As history has so frequently recorded, the end of oppression has often become a reality only after people have resorted to violent means. Ocean Hill–Brownsville was at such a point of desperation when the Board of Education issued its April (1967) policy statement indicating a readiness to experiment with various forms of decentralization and community involvement. The voices of reason prevailed and urged the community to challenge the sincerity of the board. The community responded. A planning or steering committee was formed; it was made up of people determined to accept the challenge of such an edict, ready to assume the responsibilities for the education of the children—*their* children—and anxious to effect a change that would benefit all children in minority groups. The plan this committee drafted is acknowledged to be the last demonstration of the community's faith in the school system's purposes and abilities.

Opportunities can arise as a result of negative circumstances. Awareness of the need to make change in this chaos remained always on the tip of the tongue and brain, primed for the right occasion. Teachers asked for help in "ridding" one school of a principal—the beginning of overt unity. Repeated denial of a voice at the district superintendent's level led to severe problems—concerned citizens banded together. Those who persisted emerged as leaders; this leadership grew in stature, responsibility, and responsiveness as more was demanded of it; people with causes presented their problems to the various emerging leaders who, with shared talents and contacts, moved toward their solution. The seriousness of the problems promoted immediate action as the following grew. An unauthorized committee sanctioned by needs moved toward action. The tempo of the times mandated that change occur in the schools. Those who demanded it were suddenly a pressure group, but the history of education clearly indicates that all educational change has been born of one pressure group or another. First, a chant for representation at the local board level, then, a demand for change in the architectural design of a building, and, finally, a request for consultation in the selection of principals: a once nebulous group attained structure, purpose, authenticity, support, and recognition. What resources were available to these change agents? Nothing but their experience, their recognition of needs, and their desire to survive.

What of the educator in this process of change? Change is really a new role for the educator, since he belongs to the very system on which he must turn. Individual teachers, sensitive to the needs of the people and aware of the ineffective efforts of their colleagues, joined the ranks of the followers. Their voices lent another dimension to the militant group—sophistication. Teachers did not produce change, but they did lend stability. They brought another resource, too: the teachers' union. This resource, though reluctant, joined because a representative body of its membership demanded it and because community involvement and support was strong. History will one day clearly show that the actions of this community were instrumental in bringing together a sufficient number of change agents to force the Board of Education and the UFT as well as politicians and foundations to declare publicly their support for change.

Regardless of splits, enclaves, and factions, the community had no alternative but to support the effort, for the education of its children was at stake. Outside institutions recognized and felt the appeal of the change, but were not fully responsive; their followers, other than in the community, were aware of their own "danger." Could they sell the product to their followers? How much time did they have? Could they renege on their commitment? Could they serve two masters? What were the interactions? Who were their allies? Enemies? All these questions led to a variety of strategies.

The steering committee involved the union in developing the

proposal for the community to become architects of the educational fate of its children. The community placed its faith in the ability of the professional organization to interpret and translate its needs into the professional jargon. The union, in turn, involved the college. This move should have made the college an ingredient for change, but it retained its ivory tower status. It waited for the community to come on its knees for help. It was obviously insensitive to the pride and new status and responsibility the community had developed.

The union, parents, and a college professor prepared a plan to be presented to the Board of Education. Before the submission of the report, the Ford Foundation entered the picture to give support to the venture. Repeated conferences and dialogues between these representatives reached the point where all parties accepted the concept. Each of the elements now had a commitment to the concept, and each had its role: the parents had to inform the community; the union was called on to inform all teachers in the affected schools; the Board of Education was asked to sanction the concept; and the Ford Foundation, to finance the planning phase. From this point on, the action of some of the groups becomes vague and disputable.

The specifics of the final proposal called for an election of one governing board member from among the parents for each specific school. The campaign began on July 5. An information sheet was distributed, and a cadre of parents and community people went from door to door and held innumerable meetings to inform the community. Signatures attesting that the program had been explained to them were required of parents. They were requested to indicate their approval or disapproval of the concept. Coincidental with this was a petition inviting parents to nominate candidates to the governing board. A community population of approximately 3,100 families yielded 2,200 signatures. The election process was then launched with posters, newspaper ads, flyers, radio announcements, television broadcasts, mass meetings, and church announcements. August 4 was election day. The community had exercised its responsibilities.

The professional staff was to be notified of the pending program by a union representative. Regardless of the extent of the union's completion of this phase of its responsibility, each school sent to the project a representative chosen by its staff to work with the parents during the summer. There were meetings with the teachers, run by the "summer coordinator," who was selected by the steering committee. Joint meetings were held with the teachers, the steering committee, and residents of the community. Many differences were brought to the fore and some solutions were developed. There were many unresolved issues with the teachers during the summer. Some of these remain problems: (1) teacher representation on the board; (2) teacher responsibility to the board; (3) supervision, tenure, and evaluation; (4) voting; (5) the legality of the decentralization operation.

August, 1967. The parent elections were held with 1,100 parents voting. The initial proposal was modified in about three areas. The two elected factions, together with the teachers, elected a unit administrator and a college representative. The name of only one candidate for appointment by the superintendent of schools was submitted rather than the requested three names recommended in the original proposal. The community representatives were selected by the elected parent representatives rather than by the entire governing board, and the item referring to teachers—the famed item six—was modified at the request of the teachers, though not to their satisfaction.

The community representatives comprised two clergymen, one assemblyman, a community center director, and a Spanish-speaking lady from a poverty agency. The selection of these representatives was a point of contention with the teachers, who felt they should have had the right to vote on the candidates. The issue emanated from the determination of teachers to see that no militants or black-power advocates were selected. This, to us, was an attempt to exclude a vital segment of the community and to deny the exercise of free choice.

Teacher voting became a "charged" issue, which still persists. The issue of the selection of principals to fill four existing vacancies clearly evidenced the split between the teachers and the community. On this issue, teachers claimed they were not given the right to vote. A number of candidates for principalships spent a couple of weeks being interviewed by parents and teachers in the community before their names were presented to the governing board. The only segment of the governing board unrepresented was the supervisors.

The proposal, the results of the election, and the names of candidates were presented to the superintendent of schools and to the

Board of Education. At that time, the UFT and the Board of Education were involved in contract negotiations, and the threat of a strike was imminent. One issue the community—and black teachers in it—was opposed to in the negotiations was the problem of disruptive children. The black teacher organizations and the various civil rights groups were publicly opposed to the UFT proposal. When the strike occurred, the first decision of the new governing board was to keep its schools open—this coincided with the Board of Education's determination to keep schools open and to use parents and community people to run the schools—but, the governing board took this decision in August, before the union made the strike a reality.

The teachers returned from vacation on September 8. The governing board members gave them a luncheon and had a panel of governing board members visit each school and recapitulate the events of the summer. Then all hell broke loose. It is not my intent to state the cause, but consensus indicates it was sparked by the UFT"s summer representatives. Objections included open resentment to parental control, charges of black-power takeover, and the use of undemocratic processes. The summer teacher representatives appeared at the governing board meeting and asked for support of the strike in exchange for teachers' support of the community control concept. The community refused the compromise. Then came the strike and the city-wide split between black and white teachers over the disruptive child issue.* In this demonstration unit, the split was poignant and traumatic. Black teachers in our schools supported the community effort to man the schools. Black teachers who would not go into their schools in other areas of the city came to the schools in our area to assist. Then we were hit with two issues: black versus white teachers, and white teachers versus the community. The governing board survived these issues with determination, commitment, and drive. Those days were pure hell!

The formal acceptance of the governing board's proposal by the Board of Education was placed on the calendar for public approval. The union, its strike over, flexed its muscles and zeroed in—in a most unprofessional and vindictive manner. This was the second time the charged atmosphere caused the initial acceptance

---

* A key union demand in the 1967 strike was to give teachers the right to remove "disruptive" pupils from the classroom. Civil rights groups criticized this demand as being subtly racist.—Eds.

of the proposal by the Board of Education to be postponed. The events of that day are too numerous to reconstruct here, but every effort was made to eliminate the program by various groups. Racism was rampant. Nonetheless, the unit administrator and principals were accepted by the Board of Education.

It is relevant now to examine briefly the other demonstration districts: Harlem's IS 201 and lower Manhattan's Two Bridges. IS 201 was still a planning operation. Two Bridges, also in the planning stage but slightly more advanced than IS 201, was comprised mostly of teachers and was not attacked by the UFT. It was also the only demonstration project not in a black community. The famous day of acceptance by the Board of Education of the governing board of Ocean Hill–Brownsville also saw the acceptance of the unit administrator for Two Bridges, which for all intents and purposes was illegal because no board had been elected. It is also odd that, during the heat of the battle of the UFT versus the demonstration projects, no reference was made to the legality of Two Bridges. This type of behavior strongly suggested racism. Yet, during the period when racism and other threatening, traumatic, and emotional charges were made *against this community*, it was unable to defend itself: it did not have the resources of the mass media. For the same reason, many positive developments went unheralded.

The parents of the demonstration district had made plans to open and man the schools in the event of a strike by the teachers. The confidence of these parents was at its highest peak, and all efforts to convince them that they should open only three or four of the seven schools were to no avail. Even the suggestion that the schools be open only a half day was vetoed. They were determined to give evidence to all that they had accepted the challenge and would assume full responsibility. They had had many training sessions—some conducted by our own teachers, some conducted by members of the African-American Teachers Association and several conducted by Mr. Herman Ferguson, one of the newly selected principals. In none of these schools was there any friction or problem during this period. The sensitivity and past experience of the community provided ample preparation for difficulties in certain schools; additional parents and selected personnel were mobilized for these schools. The strike served to solidify all segments of the community, for they had an opportunity to work with their children; even more important, they observed at first hand the educational deprivation of the children and the sub-standard conditions under which the learning process was supposed to take place. What the parents found, they shared, and this sharing intensified their commitment.

The events during this period that highlight, crystalize, and delineate our problem were represented by PS 144. Resentment of the concept on the part of supervisory personnel was manifested in lapses of memory, the need for clarification of standard practices, inability to respond to directives, interruptions of schedules, and many other omissions. Finally, accusations of assault were made at this level. This spread like wild fire and became the basis of the charges of racism. Each event mushroomed and was grossly distorted. During this period, there were several changes in the leadership, but the school remained orderly, and the parents were proud of their accomplishments. In order not to cloud issues, I will assume that all incidents during the strike, regardless of their nature and severity, may be attributed directly to strike conditions. These conditions did have a positive effect on us: they prepared us for the eventual UFT and CSA onslaught, and they made the city acutely conscious of our situation.

There are many implications for the educators. Desire and raw determination and commitment cannot replace the need for sophisticated preparation for dealing with change. The unit administrator and the key people of the community were perceptive enough to anticipate and prepare for many of the opposition moves, and we were able to structure some diversionary tactics of our own to soften the impact. Yet, we were not sophisticated enough to develop a publicity committee or to set up a process whereby only selected people would discuss our project. The opposition capitalized on this; yet this, too, became an asset—the public received honest and sincere responses. During this period, the governing board members, key community people, and the unit administrator worked long, arduous hours to inform the teachers in an attempt to win them over at least to a point of "wait and see."

During this period, the governing board was meeting twice a week. In addition to these meetings, intensive workshops were being conducted; also, communication centers were established in the community. Many meetings were strategy sessions designed to deal with supervisory staff problems, with the Board of Education and the superintendent of schools, and with the teachers. Board members held open community meetings, attended PTA meetings, and spoke on invitation to a variety of audiences. They discussed educational policy, staffing, construction, and a variety of topics with the unit administrator. A curriculum committee and a by-laws committee were formed. Confidence was bolstered with the selection of additional principals. Ways were sought to assure the teachers of their acceptance. Attention was directed to the opening of the new IS 55. Board members were involved in answering UFT charges. They met with college representatives to discuss program and affiliations. They met with student teachers and their supervisors. They spent innumerable hours interpreting the program to the community and attempting to maintain solidarity and support. They practiced self-restraint and reason throughout. They worked diligently with the principals to ascertain school needs. They enlisted parent volunteers and worked to establish paraprofessional training programs. They instituted public relations and information centers for the community. They attended Board of Education meetings on budget, organization, and governing board elections. They worked closely with the unit administrator, supporting, informing, and learning. Each of these involvements sharpened the operational structure of the board and contributed to its increased effectiveness.

The unit administrator was involved in establishing, strengthening, and maintaining rapport with the professional staff, particularly with the teachers who were in the schools prior to the new organization. This effort consisted of many meetings with segments of the staff as well as with the total staff. The unit administrator made numerous attempts to ascertain the basis for the many requests for transfer made by assistants to principals and to cope with the situation. From the standpoint of progress, support from teachers increased in direct proportion to the opportunities they had to ask questions and to eliminate misinformation. An appeal to professionalism, a commitment to it, and a dedication to provide the ingredients for it sustained the interests of some while placing the unit administrator and the governing board in a position of having to deliver what they may not be capable of doing.

The unit administrator battled with the superintendent and with bureau personnel over the appointment of new assistant principals. Specifically, the unit was forced to take assistant principals from the existing civil service list according to their numerical rating without consideration of subject competence. This method was and is detrimental. Every attempt was made to select people at this level who could complement each other and be a meaningful resource for the staffs they were to serve. They would, likewise, be a resource to the total complex. The process and source of selection of principals outside of the civil service list placed us in litigation with the New York City Council of Supervisory Associations. It is noteworthy that this body of educators, representing years of experience and leadership, has not as an association developed a single program to improve education in the city; rather, as an effective political lobby, it has reacted negatively to most programs. It enjoys a reputation of being against minority group education.

Another responsibility placed upon the unit administrator was that of assisting in the development of criteria for the selection of principals in accordance with the ruling of the commissioner of education. This meant justifying the difference between a demonstration principal and a regular principal. The unit administrator was daily involved in the recruitment, selection, and assignment of teachers, assistant principals, and potential principals.

The unit administrator, with limited time, had the problem of developing his own staff. He had to fight daily to establish positions in his office in order to be effective in the execution of his functions. The superintendent of schools reluctantly allowed the unit administrator to create a unit administrative staff that was effective because of the rank of those selected and their competence to perform, for which they were recruited. Ours has been a radical departure from existing district superintendent's staffs. It is interesting that the Assistant Principals Association, in its recently published version of the Bundy Report, recommends a similar organization: they suggest putting people of authority—decision-makers—at the district superintendent level. Every effort was made to select skilled and experienced people at this level. This necessitated going outside of the system more often than not because existing Board of Education policies as they related to promotion and tenure have tended to screen out competent people. Such people require a great deal of orientation, and arrangements must be made for their housing and for other affairs; hence, this has not been as effective as was hoped. However, the quality of the people and their determination and commitment have enabled them to grow rapidly.

The unit administrator has had countless meetings with the superintendent of schools, the Board of Education, and several deputies of the superintendent. These meetings have covered a variety of subjects and disciplines—for example, the legality of the elections, the background of the governing board members, the accusations made by those who oppose the program, the selection and appointment of administrative and supervisory personnel, budget limitations and restrictions, procedures and policies as they conflict with existing Board of Education policies, and payroll problems. Licensing procedures for union staff members are still unsettled and hotly contested. The governing board still has not been officially recognized and authorized. Housing and budget for the unit administrator's office have not been officially established. In effect, the office of the unit administrator does not officially exist.

In addition to these meetings, there have been those jointly attended by the representatives of the state. They were called ostensibly to discuss the qualifications of principals, but their real purpose was to ascertain candidates' affiliations or degree of militancy. Lately, these meetings have centered around the definition of eligibility criteria for principals of demonstration schools for the purpose of preparing a new examination within the scope of the civil service law. The state representatives' contribution is usually twofold: one is as a trouble shooter, and the other is as the interpreter of state law.

Many other factors or responsibilities exist, and the unit administrator must address himself to all. Priorities change from day to day, demanding immediate and time-consuming attention. The unit administrator must of necessity be flexible as well as perceptive enough to decentralize his responsibilities and yet stay abreast if progress is to ensue. Some of his responsibilities are: (1) seeking financial aid; (2) developing programs and inviting proposals; (3) entering into dialogue with the poverty agencies; (4) communicating with city and state agencies; (5) promoting college affiliations, especially student teachers; (6) suspending pupils; (7) interpreting governing board objectives and procedures to the professions; (8) establishing public relations to and for the community; (9) re-educating experienced professionals who have memory lapses or who request interpretation of policies and procedures of the governing board; (10) maintaining relationships with the Niemeyer Committee—an evaluating team authorized by the New York City Board of Education to evaluate the demonstration projects; (11) attending community meetings, professional meetings and professional kangaroo courts; (12) preparing the opening of a new school and the selecting of principals.

As unit administrator, I admit that to give concise and up-to-date information would take another thirty pages, and even at this writing more problems and possibilities are developing. I can only hope that this paper will create a desire for more information in the hearts and minds of the readers and thus invite those interested parties to come and see. I am convinced that what is happening in Brooklyn will play a large part in inner-city education across our country. We at Ocean Hill–Brownsville realize the gravity and implications of the program we are committed to, especially in light of the Bundy Report. We feel strongly that many of our key people will disappear—become consultants and leaders—as we will be more than a prototype for the Bundy Report. We will become faceless, unheralded, and unrepresented in a new milieu of educational change, but we will know in our hearts that our action, determination, and commitment, born of our rights to be human beings and citizens in this great society, will not have been in vain. We will have effected some degree of change and, perhaps, better education for all our children.

School Decentralization in New York /
RICHARD KARP

Ocean Hill is a tiny piece of urban blight resting on a gently sloping section of glacial moraine in Brooklyn. From one side of this ancient hill spreads the vast wretchedness of Bedford-Stuyvesant, from the other, the equally vast wretchedness of Brownsville. The two great Negro ghettos of Brooklyn merge at Ocean Hill, but Ocean Hill has never quite belonged to either slum. It is a no-man's-land between two no-man's-lands. Its inhabitants are the overflow of hopelessness and poverty from two of the most desolate communities in the land, perhaps the most unlikely of slum-dwellers to band together for community action.

But in September, 1966, an issue arose around which they could

REPRINTED FROM *Interplay Magazine* © August–September, 1968.

rally. That month, parents in a Harlem school district demanded from the New York Board of Education the right to veto the selection of a principal for the newly completed IS 201. They had, in effect, asked for the first time to have some real say in the administration of a local school. The cry for "community control" that went up in Harlem was heard far out in the forgotten ghetto of Ocean Hill.

The schooling of children in the Ocean Hill community had long been a failure, and all efforts at reform a failure as well. The Board of Education's plan for "quality integrated education" through busing Negro children to white schools was a farce. Ocean Hill sent 4,000 black children into white communities. They were put onto buses, dropped off at the white schools, and welcomed with little more than suspicion and bigotry. Some principals in the white schools herded the Negro children into separate classes because their reading level was lower than that of the white students. Many Negro children could not keep up with the work and failed. White parents vehemently protested the arrival of black children in their neighborhoods. Segregated by their school administrators and frozen out by the anger and hatred of the white communities, many Negro children begged to be sent back to their local schools, wretched as those schools were.

As if this weren't enough, there was another cause for desperation by the fall of 1966. Until 1965, the Ocean Hill area had been part of the Bedford-Stuyvesant school district, represented by one member on the district school board. In the spring of 1965, the Board of Education created District 17, a long strip of Brooklyn with white middle-class East Flatbush at one end, the black ghetto of Brownsville in the center, and Ocean Hill at the other end. The school board of this "racially balanced" district was weighted heavily in favor of the white areas: Ocean Hill found itself worse off than it had been as part of the Bedford-Stuyvesant district. On the new board, it had no representative at all. The people of Ocean Hill saw acted out before their eyes what they had, perhaps, always believed in their hearts: that the whites would cajole and control them, but never integrate with them.

With talk of "community control" spreading in the Negro ghettos of New York in that fall of 1966, the Ocean Hill community took what must have been to them a drastic step. In November, all the groups with which the Board of Education normally deals, including the parents' associations in the schools, cut off all relations with the District 17 school board and the central Board of Education. Local chapters of the United Federation of Teachers, the official union of New York City teachers, joined and supported them, seeing in the movement for community control a chance to form an alliance with parents against their traditional enemies, the members of the Board of Education. As we shall see, their support was short-lived.

At any rate, in November the loose assembly of parents and sympathetic teachers, now joined by an ever growing number of agitators, got together and issued a plan for unilateral action. They stated three aims: one, to form a small, totally independent school district of Ocean Hill; two, to create an independent governing school board of teachers and parents; and three, to hold public meetings in the community to discuss school problems and future action. Not constituted into any cohesive body, and without any authority whatsoever, this aggregate of community groups met regularly during that fall and winter. They discussed the chronic problems of the ghetto school: lack of discipline, on the one hand, and, on the other, the suspension of students—the latter a sore point to the parents of Ocean Hill, who had seen large numbers of their young ejected into the streets without diplomas.

The Board of Education, a deeply entrenched and virtually autonomous arm of the city bureaucracy for seventy years, remained disdainful of the pretenses of the Ocean Hill groups. As the central command post of a centralized system, the board had complete power, and though its attempts at reform were failures, its authority went unchallenged. But this time a spasm of fear ran through it. Something unprecedented was happening. In December, an angry mob of black parents marched on the board's headquarters on Livingston Street in Brooklyn and for three days occupied its executive offices under the name of the "People's Board of Education."

For the first time, the board realized it was up against real pressure. If its members did not yield, they would, at least, have to listen—or pretend to listen. The people of Ocean Hill did not miss their opportunity and, for the rest of the winter they pressured the board for change. They demanded that it dismiss a principal of one of the Ocean Hill elementary schools who was considered incompetent and was widely disliked by the parents. The board acquiesced, and the principal was soon out of the school. Emboldened by this novel success, the insurgents were ready to lay claim to a more fundamental power.

Due to be completed the following fall was IS 55, and its principal had not yet been named. The Ocean Hill militants began agitating for the right, which no local community in New York possesses, to choose a principal for the new school; they continued agitating until April, 1967, when a far broader prospect appeared on the horizon. That April, Mario Fantini of the Ford Foundation appeared on the scene. The Ford Foundation had been working with the parents' groups of IS 201 in Harlem since their September confrontation with the board, with the idea, according to Fantini, of "seeking out alternatives to the way the schools were being run. We were disturbed at the way the Board of Education was running the school system." Community control in some form was the chief alternative the Ford Foundation had in mind. The foundation, like other critics of the school system, had lost faith in the system's power to reform itself.

Why the Ford Foundation entered the fray between Ocean Hill and the Board of Education is a matter of dispute. Fantini asserts that the board asked the foundation to fund such educational programs as the Ocean Hill groups might propose. Ocean Hill community leaders, on the contrary, say that the board had no intention of asking the Ford Foundation or anyone else to help the community. The Ford Foundation, they believe, saw in the events of that winter a chance to experiment with its own educational theories. "Ford went to the Board of Education and, with its power and prestige, pushed the Board into accepting them as advisers and letting them use Ocean Hill as a laboratory," says Father John Powis, a white Catholic priest who has been active in the Ocean Hill movement from the beginning. "The 'liaison' business is a lot of nonsense."

Whatever its motives, the Ford Foundation, in April arranged a meeting between the Ocean Hill parents' groups and Dr. Bernard Donovan, the superintendent of schools and the chief executor of board policies. Although the meeting was ostensibly held to discuss the problem of a principal for IS 55, it brought to light the basic conflict that was to set the pattern for all future dialogue between the Board of Education and the groups seeking reform in New York City schools. The Ocean Hill parents brought up their plan to create a local governing school board. In their proposal, the board would consist of eight parents—one from each school in the district—elected by the parents of children in the schools, and eight teachers—one from each school—elected by the teachers in each school. There would also be five representatives from the community at large, elected by the eight parent representatives from among Ocean Hill residents on whose behalf petitions had been circulated that contained at least 200 signatures. In addition, there would be two supervisors (principals) on the board, elected by all the supervisors in the district. The board thus constituted would elect one professional educator from a university faculty.

In essence, the proposal meant direct community control of local schools and the virtual end to the Board of Education's long-held power to control, down to minute details, the 900 schools and 1 million students comprising New York's stagnating school system. This the board dreaded and secretly opposed. Under the eyes of the decentralization-minded Ford Foundation, however, and remembering the seizure of their headquarters by angry parents, the board agreed to the proposal "in principle." "In principle" meant that the Board of Education would now deal with the Ocean Hill groups simply as upstarts rather than as outlaws.

The reckoning came swiftly. By the end of the month, the Board of Education issued its "policy on decentralization." The last article of the document was directly related to Ocean Hill: it proposed to set up "demonstration projects" in certain districts "for increasing parental and community involvement" in order to "strengthen our educational program." Ocean Hill would be the site of a "demonstration project"; two others would be in Harlem and in Manhattan's Lower East Side.

The board statement of "policy" meant little: for community *control* the board substituted the term *involvement*, which meant that at its own pleasure it would hear complaints from, and grant privileges to, the districts in the "demonstration." It would not, however, yield a jot of power. By holding out the promise of local involvement rather than control, the board had perpetuated its authority; by putting some unruly communities in the "demonstration" category, it hoped to make them docile "creatures of the Board of Education." This last remark was actually made a year later, by Norman Brumbacker, the superintendent of schools' liaison man with the "demonstration projects."

In April, 1967, however, the Board of Education's resolve to obstruct decentralization was not as evident as it is now, and the people of Ocean Hill hopefully began planning for the election of a local governing school board according to its original proposal. Thanks to the Board of Education's acquiescence to a "demonstration," moreover, the Ford Foundation felt sanctioned to give direct aid to the "demonstration projects," and, in July, it announced that it would fund the planning and establishment of governing boards in Ocean Hill and the two other districts. Ocean Hill received $44,000 to plan and hold elections that summer.

Trouble began when the community groups began planning to elect their parent representatives. To register the parents eligible to vote, they needed the names and addresses of the students— and these were in the Board of Education's files. They appealed to the board for help. The board told them the community groups could get the necessary names and addresses only by hiring two Board of Education secretaries to go into the files. When the community leaders agreed to do this, they were informed that the two secretaries had gone on vacation and that no one else was available. The Ocean Hill leaders were dismayed, but they got sympathetic teachers to canvass students for their addresses. Then, by going from door to door, they finally got 2,000 parents registered by August.

On August 3, Ocean Hill parents voted for their representatives. For many of them, it was the first experience of voting in any election. At the polls were observers from the UFT and the Niemeyer Committee the latter a group of professional educators set up by the Board of Education ostensibly to give assistance to the community. Both groups grumbled about the election: the UFT questioned its legality and the Niemeyer group suggested an irregularity because the Fair Balloting Association did not officiate at the polls. Neither group took a very strong stand, however, and it is fair to assume that neither unearthed any significant mischief.

The Board of Education accepted the election of the governing board and agreed to grant it two important powers: first, to elect a district superintendent, to be known as the "unit administrator," and second, to elect principals to the eight schools in the district. At its first meeting, at the end of August, the governing board held an election for unit administrator. There were two candidates: Rhody McCoy, a Negro, who had been in the school system for many years and had been, until that summer, the acting principal of a school in Manhattan; and Jack Bloomfield, the principal of JHS 271 in Ocean Hill, who was essentially the Board of Education's candidate. Rhody McCoy won the election; the Board of Education recognized him as the unit administrator of Ocean Hill and agreed to pay him a salary as such.

But if the Board of Education had sought to obstruct the election of the governing board by denying help to the community in registering voters in July, it was now bent on pushing the locally administered school district into chaos. To avoid conflict between himself and the new unit administrator, Bloomfield asked the board to transfer him out of the district. It was obvious to him, as it would have been to any experienced administrator, that the divided authority and conflicting loyalties would sow discord and confusion in one of the key schools of the district. The Board of Education refused the transfer, and pressured Bloomfield to remain in Ocean Hill for another six months. It was an act that would provoke animosity, and it did. When Bloomfield finally left, in January, 1968, the enemies of decentralization could truly say that he had been pushed out by "extremist elements."

The Board of Education was not alone in its determination to disrupt and discredit community control. It had powerful allies of the kind that shows how politics makes strange bedfellows. Among them was the giant UFT, the board's traditional foe, with its loyal legions of white middle-class teachers. The UFT had seen, in the events of the previous year, that the Board of Education was beginning to lose its grip on the school system. It could no longer be depended upon to preserve the *status quo*. The union itself would have to fill the gap and become the first line of defense against reform.

The UFT was ready to move, and, on September 2, Ocean Hill received its first volley of shot from the teachers' union. On that day the Ocean Hill governing board held its third meeting and elected five principals for the schools. The five vacancies had been created by the voluntary departure of five incumbent principals after the demonstration project had been established. The teacher representatives on the governing board refused to vote and bolted the meeting. What irked them, and what frightened a large number of union members, was the fact that the principals chosen by the community were not on the approved civil service list. No one denied the merit of the elected principals, but the sight of educators chosen with no regard to bureaucratic procedures seemed to strike symbolically at every teacher's job security, their most pre-

cious (and, in some cases, virtually their only) professional posses-
sion.

This was a preliminary probe; the fury of the full offensive was
unleashed the following week. The UFT called a city-wide teachers'
strike that effectively closed down the entire school system. According to the teachers, the strike was aimed at getting a pay increase and smaller classes; in fact, it was a massive show of strength
designed to show that no one had better dare make trouble for the
teachers. In effect, it threw up a mighty roadblock to the movement toward community control.

Nevertheless, the posture that a "liberal" union cared about
reform had to be maintained, so the striking teachers went to the
Ocean Hill governing board and asked them to support the strike.
When the governing board refused, as the teachers knew they
would, the teacher representatives resigned and joined in the
chorus of those who were busily fanning public fears that "extremism" and "black power" would prevail in the communities. To
prove that black racists had taken over at Ocean Hill, they never
returned to the board.

The strike not only brought about a catastrophic suspension of
public education in New York, it exposed the deep animosity
existing between the white middle-class educational establishment
and the Negro community. After the strike, the teachers who returned to Ocean Hill did so with bitterness and were met by the
community with equal bitterness. JHS 271 was figuratively torn apart
by antagonism between the white teachers who had struck in
September and the black teachers and parents who saw the strike
as a betrayal of community control. When Principal Jack Bloomfield left in February, 1968, he was followed by all the assistant
principals, thirty teachers and five of the six secretaries.

JHS 271 is still the scene of antagonism between white and
black. In the teachers' cafeteria, the black teachers sit on one side
of the room, the white teachers on the other. The wall of fear and
hatred between the two groups makes for communication that is
at best polite, more often curt, and most of the time nonexistent.
To the black teachers, their white counterparts are part of the
conspiracy to obstruct progress toward local control. "The white
teachers are working for the UFT and not the children," the black
teachers assert. "They are letting the students run wild to discredit
the program. The white community says that Negroes have no

pride or ambition, and then, when we show some pride and ambition, they do everything they can to suppress us."

Any one of the Negro teachers could tell of a dozen instances of white teachers "disrupting the program." On Friday, February 23, the day after Washington's birthday, one Negro teacher asserted, twenty-eight teachers were out "sick" from one school alone. "Absenteeism" on the part of white teachers is one of the more common complaints of the black teachers. One "incident," which became a *cause célèbre*, involved a white teacher who was allegedly found pouring paint on a classroom floor to "blame it on a black student as proof of riot and insurrection in the community."

How true these stories are is hard to determine. They might be exaggerations, but, if so, they rise out of the frustrations of trying to deal with men who, because they are still using the rhetoric of another age, cannot and will not understand. The white teachers in Ocean Hill, like the white teachers in the rest of the city, believe in two political principles: labor unionism and the idea that society's problems should be solved by centralized boards of experts and professionals. For these two principles they may well do some improbable things.

Confronted with the Negroes' allegations, the white teachers in Ocean Hill sanctimoniously proclaimed that they were not against, but actually in favor of, community control; only, they had reservations. "We believe that the people of this community are not educated and socially elevated enough to run the schools. They must become middle-class before they can participate." These timid and totally uninspired job-holders put themselves forward as paragons, unaware of how fatuous they sound, or, for that matter, of the unfairness of their assertions, considering that, thanks to them, community control has never been given a chance to prove itself.

"We believe in community control," the white teachers say, "but we could only accept a governing school board if it were made up of representatives of the church, the business world, and influential organizations like the NAACP or the Urban League" The teachers ignored the fact that nationwide "influence organizations" have little or no relation to the exercise of power on the purely local scene.

The sentiments quoted were not only repugnant to a poor community seeking some influence over the education of its own children; they defied America's enduring faith in the common man. The tenacity with which they were maintained by the white educational establishment in New York made inertia and obstructionism more and more blatant in Ocean Hill as the months passed. Since the July agreement to accept the election of a governing board, the Board of Education has not, in fact, made a single gesture toward recognizing the governing board's authority.

The Board of Education allowed the poor people of Ocean Hill to form an administrative unit with the understanding that it would relinquish some of its authority to it. The board clearly hoped the experiment would fail and fall into chaos. When the Ocean Hill people demonstrated that they could elect competent administrators, that they could develop, at least on paper, programs to improve education, that, in fact, the "worst damn schools in the city," according to Rhody McCoy, could be improved under community control, the board merely waited for the Ocean Hill governing board to wither away in bitter impotence.

That it hasn't withered away is a miracle. The planning money granted by the Ford Foundation ran out in the fall of 1967, and an additional $15,000 of Ford money ran out soon after that. After promising $250,000 to fund the Ocean Hill board's programs, the foundation announced that it could make no more grants until the Board of Education or the state legislature recognized the local board as the official governing authority. Fantini declared, understandably, that "we cannot take the place of the Board of Education." This denial of funds meant that the governing board was reduced to a debating society, without the means to implement any programs in its schools.

Ford's decision was a great blow to Ocean Hill; to the people involved, it was betrayal, pure and simple. The Ford Foundation was, they believe, bending to pressure from the Board of Education, from obstructionist groups like the UFT, and from less organized, public pressure generated by racism and an uncomprehending press. Mario Fantini said, "We are waiting to see what happens next." So far, nothing has happened.

The latest and perhaps most effective drive to quash the "rebellion" in Ocean Hill was led by the Council of Supervisory Associations, a quasi-labor union of principals and assistant principals. This group took the Board of Education to court, charging that the principals it had hired in the fall on the recommendation of the Ocean Hill governing board were hired illegally because they were not chosen from the civil service list of candidates. In March, the judge ruled in favor of the CSA, and until an appellate court rules to the contrary—if it does—all the principals elected by the Ocean Hill board are holding their positions illegally.

Without funds to carry out educational reforms and the power to hire and dismiss personnel, the school board of Ocean Hill is wholly unable to administer its schools. As the people of Ocean Hill have painfully learned, the ideal of local control of New York schools is, within the framework of existing laws and confronted with a Board of Education that will not relinquish an iota of its authority, an empty dream.

The so-called decentralization proposals issued by the Ford Foundation, Mayor Lindsay, and, most recently, the state Board of Regents represent an effort to present to the state legislature programs that would break up the Board of Education's power to obstruct reform. The leaders of Ocean Hill are not entirely happy with the various proposals, since they do not, it is asserted, grant enough local power. Experience has made these people skeptical and wary. But if the state legislature could shake itself free of inertia and enact laws that would give real power to the communities, it would relieve a very grave situation.

In Ocean Hill, the situation became critical. Shown to be powerless against a deceitful established bureaucracy, the governing board all but lost the respect and allegiance of the community. Angry and frustrated parents' groups demanded action. Because the governing board could not act, it was ready to turn the schools over to the parents. At a public meeting on March 19, the governing board announced to an auditorium full of parents that, if the Board of Education did not accept community control within ten days, the governing board would "resign"—that is, end all relations with the Board of Education.

Three weeks later, on April 10, parents staged a boycott that closed down all the eight schools in Ocean Hill. The same day, Superintendent of Schools Donovan publicly declared, "it is unfortunate that the children should be denied education over a matter that should be discussed around the table by adults."

What is really unfortunate is that the Board of Education never looked upon the people of Ocean Hill with anything but contempt. The truth is, the Board of Education never treated the governing board of Ocean Hill as adults.

Since last April, events in Ocean Hill have finally demonstrated to the public at large the enormous proportions of the crisis in New York City public education. In the wake of the April 10 student boycott in Ocean Hill, the groups supporting decentralization renewed their efforts to persuade the New York State Legislature to pass a strong decentralization bill. The state Board of Regents, which had announced in March a far-reaching plan for decentralizing New York's schools, now decided to intervene directly in the fray. At the end of April, the Regents went to the legislature and asked it to pass their March proposal into law. At the same time, both Mayor Lindsay and Governor Rockefeller announced their support of the Regents Plan, and urged the legislature to take swift action. But the adjournment-minded legislature remained unmoved. It seemed prepared only to enact a weak bill, proposed by a state senator from New York City, John J. Marchi, which would have sent the decentralization issue back to the Board of Education (whose antipathy to decentralization was by now public knowledge). There it would be "discussed" and then reintroduced to the legislature in 1969. In effect, all action on decentralization would be postponed for at least a year.

While the weak Marchi bill was drifting toward enactment in Albany early in May, the governing board in Ocean Hill, probably with the tacit approval of the mayor and other sympathetic members of the "establishment," took drastic action. On May 10, the governing board formally dismissed nineteen teachers and supervisors in Ocean Hill, charging them with having attempted to "sabotage" the demonstration project. The result of this action was complete dislocation. Superintendent of Schools Donovan ordered the nineteen to ignore the governing board's dismissal order and return to their schools. The Ocean Hill parents vowed to prevent the ousted nineteen from returning and, on Monday, May 13, blockaded the entrance of JHS 271 and told the teachers they could not enter the building. Police surrounding the school that day threatened to escort the ousted teachers through the parent blockade but made no actual move to do so.

The parent blockade of JHS 271 lasted until Wednesday, May 15, when policemen appeared in large numbers, surrounded the school, and proceeded to admit all "authorized personnel." Since the end of the blockade, chaos has reigned in Ocean Hill. Parent boycotts have been answered by teacher counter-boycotts. Black parents have hurled charges of racism and police brutality at the city, and they, in turn, have been accused by the UFT of "vigilantism" and black racism. UFT President Albert Shanker hinted at a city-wide teachers strike, and a prominent civil rights leader who closed the schools in 1964 to protest *de facto* segregation threatened to do the same thing again if Ocean Hill did not get its way.

With the situation in Ocean Hill threatening to explode into racial violence by mid-May, Governor Rockefeller and the Board of Regents began again to pressure the legislature to pass a strong decentralization bill and drop the meaningless substitute proposed by Senator Marchi. On May 14, legislative leaders agreed to work on a strong decentralization bill based on the Regents Plan, and, on the following day, a group of pro-decentralization legislators threatened to "sit-in" outside the govenor's office if the plan were not adopted swiftly. On May 18, the Board of Regents announced in Governor Rockefeller's office a new, strong decentralization bill that would replace the Board of Education with a three-member commission that would have one year to decentralize New York's school system and create nearly autonomous local school boards.

On May 21, Governor Rockefeller predicted that a strong bill would be passed in Albany. The day before, Albert Shanker and 500 New York City school teachers arrived in that city to lobby against the impending legislation. Two days later, on May 22, the accord reached on a strong decentralization bill collapsed in the legislature. Shanker and his supporters had poured into the corridors of the state capitol, passing out leaflets stating that local school districts would operate "on the basis of local prejudices based on color, race, or religion." They flooded New York's newspapers and radio stations with anti-decentralization advertisements and threatened the state legislators with massive political retaliation. The legislators, a few days later, enacted a slightly amended Marchi bill, to the consternation of *The New York Times*, among many others.

By almost single-handedly preventing radical school decentralization, the teachers' union, by a single stroke, cleared the air surrounding the school reform controversy in New York City. They revealed that the 50,000 teachers were the real power behind the *status quo* in New York schools. This was a revelation indeed, since the teachers' union had always before depended on the Board of Education to block reforms, while blandly garbing itself in a cloak of liberal idealism. It now stood plainly exposed as an employee's protective association and little more. The legislative victory was thus a Pyrrhic one; its vast body of automatic liberal support would soon be looking on it with new eyes.

To the people of Ocean Hill, who were never very satisfied with even the strongest decentralization plans, the teachers' unsheathing of their raw power was a welcome change. The struggle for community control, as they see it, can now be waged in the open field, against an uncamouflaged enemy. Unfortunately for New York, the battle may be fought in the streets.

PART TWO

Confrontation

2. Due Process

During the summer, the lines hardened. With official board sanction, Rhody McCoy and the Ocean Hill board recruited new teachers to replace those still striking the district. In July, Mayor Lindsay appointed five members to the Board of Education: four of the appointments were made under the new Marchi law, which had expanded the central board's membership; the fifth was a replacement for Alfred Giardino, who had resigned in June. The resulting "new" board, sympathetic to decentralization, adopted an interim decentralization plan for all thirty school districts and the three demonstration projects. The interim plan was to be in effect until the state legislature enacted a final version in the spring of 1969. In August, special trial examiner Francis E. Rivers, who had been appointed the previous June by the "old" board to hear the case against the Ocean Hill teachers, ruled to reinstate them in their schools. When, in September, the Ocean Hill board refused to accept the teachers, the union struck all city schools.

After two days of negotiation, the union and the Board of Education agreed to the return of the transferred teachers, and the Ocean Hill board promised not to "prevent" that return. When, however, the disputed teachers were permitted entry but refused classroom assignments, the UFT claimed a violation of the agreement and struck again. This strike ended several weeks later when the board guaranteed that returning teachers would have classroom assignments. Ocean Hill refused to accept the UFT-board agreement, and, a few days later, the UFT, charging that its teachers were being harassed by teachers "loyal" to the governing board, called its third strike. UFT demands during this strike were broadened to include the closing of JHS 271, where the harassment had

79

allegedly occured; the reassignment of Unit Administrator McCoy and all those of his principals who were "guilty of intimidation"; and a declaration that the Ocean Hill experiment had failed and the district was to be returned to the regular system. Meanwhile, Ocean Hill had reversed its position and offered to assign the disputed teachers to classrooms.

The strike was to drag on through mid-November. In October, the Board of Education suspended McCoy and the local board. Earlier in September, State Education Commissioner Allen had offered the first of several compromise proposals. The Allen compromise that was ultimately to settle the strike called for placing the Ocean Hill district under a state trusteeship, to operate during the remainder of the 1968–69 school year. The union, the district, and the board agreed to the proposal; McCoy and the Ocean Hill board were reinstated, charges of harassment against "loyal" teachers were dismissed for lack of evidence, and the transferred teachers returned to their classrooms.

Throughout the strikes, the key issue was the question of administrative transfer. From the first, the union maintained that the teachers had been discharged, without benefit of formal charges or hearing (denial of due process); for its part, the local board steadfastly claimed that the teachers had been transferred, not fired, and therefore no formal charges or hearings were required. In the materials that follow in this chapter, both sides agree that the existing system of transferring teachers against their will is a violation of due process. Where they disagree—and sometimes vehemently—is whether they believe the local board sought a confrontation in order to establish a power it did not have (control over personnel in the district), or whether they feel the union belatedly opposed the existing involuntary transfer system in order to discredit the local board in particular and decentralization in general. Critics of Ocean Hill, notably Maurice Goldbloom and Martin Mayer, have charged that Rhody McCoy and the local board deliberately provoked the confrontation. According to these critics, McCoy spurned Superintendent Bernard Donovan's offer to transfer the teachers quietly, and, thus, these transfers were not routine, and the union was justified in its reaction. Ocean Hill supporters counter that there never was any offer to transfer the teachers as a group; rather, Donovan proposed to transfer the teachers one at a time. Because Donovan had on other occasions stated that he would not transfer more than four or five teachers at a time, Ocean Hill estimated that individual transfers would take years; hence, the sincerity of the offer was questioned. Insisting that the transfers were routine, supporters of Ocean Hill point out that the union had no history of opposing involuntary transfers and, indeed, had no contractual clause covering such transfers. Therefore, they argue, if a confrontation was provoked, it was the union that was the prime mover. In any event, Judge Rivers, while acknowledging the right of administrative involuntary transfer stressed in the Ocean Hill legal brief, refused to apply it in the cases before him. Hence, the Rivers decision—the first document in this chapter—was to turn on the question of due process; to this end, testimony was taken in evidence on both sides, although, lacking the full force of the legal system, the Rivers hearing did not include subpoena power and witnesses were under no obligation to attend.

One month after the Rivers decision was submitted to the board, the Niemeyer Committee report was released. Speaking to the same question of involuntary transfer, the committee noted that it was an entrenched practice, and then went on to review the events in the Ocean Hill case. Excerpts are included in this chapter.

In early October, the New York Civil Liberties Union released its report on the Ocean Hill controversy. The report, which is also included in this chapter, exerted major impact on public opinion. In it, the UFT is accused of using due process as a smoke screen to discredit the local board. Involuntary transfers, states the report, are common and are sanctioned by the Board of Education bylaws. While involuntary transfers violate due process, they have never before been opposed by the union and, in fact, are not covered under the terms of the union contract. The report chastised the union for turning transfers into "firings."

Before the release of the NYCLU report, the due process issue had been separated from the issue of decentralization. Late in September, the Ad Hoc Committee to Defend the Right to Teach had issued an advertisement condemning the violation of due process involved in the dismissals and stating emphatically that decentralization was not the issue. The committee position was challenged by Nat Hentoff and, indirectly, by Maurice Berube. Each, in turn, was challenged: Hentoff by Michael Harrington, co-chairman of the committee, and Berube by Sandra Feldman, UFT special representative. Their exchanges are included in this chapter; taken together, they illuminate the positions of the two sides, with their opposing interpretations of events.

The response to the NYCLU report charging that the UFT was using due process in order to mask its hostility to decentralization was swift and explosive. Three signers of the original advertisement on the right to teach resigned publicly from the Ad Hoc Committee. Attacks on the NYCLU report came from several quarters, including the UFT itself. Reprinted here are the advertisement of the Ad Hoc Committee for Justice in the Schools, which summarizes the case for the UFT, and the response from the NYCLU. In the advertisement, the committee claims that involuntary transfers were subject to the union contract grievance machinery and rested on unsatisfactory rating hearings according to Board of Education bylaws. The NYCLU responded that, in the majority of cases, transfers were made involuntarily and without recourse to grievance procedures or unsatisfactory ratings hearings.

Underlying the due process issue was the sensitive question of what was to be done about unsatisfactory teachers. In the previous five years, only twelve teachers from a teaching staff of approximately 60,000 had been dismissed from the New York school system; yet, ghetto parents apparently find some teacher attitudes most objectionable. A study of Bedford-Stuyvesant conducted by the Center for Urban Education found that, although parents revealed little desire to control the schools or have a voice in selecting school personnel, they did want power to transfer teachers and principals; much of the unrest in the schools was focused on the desire of ghetto parents to remove a particular teacher or principal. Since the teaching staff is over 90 per cent white and the student body is predominantly black and Puerto Rican, these tensions are racially accentuated. They are likely to continue unless some mechanism is developed to deal with all sides fairly and reasonably.

DOCUMENTS

The Rivers Report

The questions presented here are whether Superintendent of
Schools Bernard E. Donovan should grant the request of Rhody
A. McCoy, unit administrator of Ocean Hill–Brownsville district,
to transfer out of that district any or all of the following teachers:
Richard Douglass (PS 271), David Bergen (PS 144), Barry Goodman (JHS 271), Abraham Olener (IS 55), Paul Satlow (PS 137),
Theresa Galano (PS 137), Burton Landsman (PS 137), Daniel
Goldberg (JHS 271), Cliff Rosenthal (JHS 271), Frederick Nauman (JHS 271), pursuant to his power under Article II §101.1 of
the bylaws of the Board of Education regarding the transfer of
teachers.

The fact that the proceedings against these teachers are to be
deemed in the nature of requests for transfers results from it having been stipulated between the parties at the May 31 hearing;
since before that time the relief sought had been as follows: May
9, 1968, all of the teachers were removed from their teaching assignment by the unit administrator, and on May 27, he preferred
formal charges of misconduct against some of them and stated
that they were suspended immediately.

By a resolution adopted by the Board of Education of the city
of New York on May 14, 1968, the matter of hearing these charges
and requests for transfer of these employees was transferred to
Francis E. Rivers, Esq., as special counsel to the Board of Education, who was to serve in the capacity of trial examiner and make
recommendations thereon to the superintendent of schools.

In addition to the cases of the ten teachers named above being
so referred to Francis E. Rivers, Esq., as trial examiner, there were
also referred to him at the same time the matter of Devorrah
Gelb, teacher, PS 144, and the matters of Sylvia M. Shaffer, Larry

---

ORIGINALLY TITLED *Board of Education of the City of New York, Administrative Hearing into Complaints of Rhody A. McCoy, Unit Administrator of
Ocean Hill–Brownsville, Requesting Transfer of Teachers: Report and Recommendations of Francis E. Rivers, Esq., August 26, 1968.*

Greenberg, Joseph F. Lightcap, Paul Hirschfield, Isidor Gordon, and Josephine Burnieri, each of whom was either principal or assistant principal, and a member of the Council of Supervisors' Association (CSA).

Upon the consent, the matter of Devorrah Gelb was adjourned without date since efforts to locate and produce her were futile.

All the members of CSA named above signed on May 21, 1968, a request for temporary reassignment to board headquarters until final disposition of the proceedings against them; and on June 10, 1968, each of them, except Isidor Gordon, signed a statement to the effect that they had been administratively reassigned on a temporary basis to board headquarters and were to be transferred to other special service schools for the fall term, or schools where appropriate positions become available, and that all proceedings pending, initiated by or through Mr. Rhody A. McCoy were withdrawn and terminated.

Hearings in the matter of these ten teachers took place at the Board of Education, 65 Court Street, Brooklyn, New York, before the special trial examiner on the following days: May 21, May 31, June 20, June 26, July 3, and July 15, 1968.

The charges that are presented in support of the request for transfer will be summarized for each respondent below and can be classified into these main classes: (1) sins of omission, that is, failure of a teacher to perform properly a duty, particularly failure to control his pupils, which is charged against teachers Douglass, Bergen, Olener, Satlow, and Galano; (2) sins of commission, that is, the intentional doing of a wrongful act, such as opposing openly the demonstration project (charged to Goldberg, Goodman, Nauman, and Rosenthal), or inflicting corporal punishment on a student (charged to Landsman).

Governing Principles

The fact that counsel for the demonstration school district argues that true decentralization requires that the governing board have the independent powers to transfer teachers out of its district, or, failing that, that its transfers be presumed legitimate so as to put the burden of proof on the accused teacher, makes it necessary to state some basic principles deemed controlling in deciding these matters.

Perhaps if the unit administrator had sent to the superintendent

of schools a simple request to transfer the teachers, without assigning any supporting charges, he (the superintendent) may have been
able to do so without a hearing by virtue of Article II §101.1 of
the bylaws of the Board of Education.

But here the unit administrator of the board requests that transfer be made by the superintendent upon the ground that the respondent, in each instance, has rendered unsatisfactory services
as a teacher. Each request by Mr. McCoy therefore presents two
questions: (1) Does the evidence prove that the respondent teacher
breached his duty as charged in the complaint and as amended
by the proof submitted? (2) If the teacher has been found by competent evidence to have breached his duty as a teacher, does it
justify his involuntary transfer as requested as a consequence?

If it is held that wrongful conduct by the teacher is so serious
as to justify his involuntary transfer, then the decision would be
potentially effective to deprive him of his property rights (a lower-
ing of his rating as a teacher and consequent lessening of salary
or other benefits, or injury to his reputation as a teacher or otherwise) and hence could not be upheld unless it was arrived at in
accordance with "due process of law."

This conformity to due process is required not only by the Constitution of New York State, but also by the Fourteenth Amendment. Furthermore, since such decisions of the governing board
of the district would be state action, they must be nondiscriminatory in order to conform to the "equal protection" mandate of the
United States Constitution.

Hence, although its being an administrative hearing excuses a
strict application of the rules of evidence, nevertheless, in the steps
taken in connection with the initiation, prosecution, and deciding
of the case, the respondent teacher must have the protection of the
relevant procedural and substantive constitutional guarantees that
exist to secure one's rights. Particularly applicable here are these
constitutional guarantees: right of the respondent to be informed
of the nature and cause of the charge against him; to be confronted with the witnesses against him and be able to cross-examine
them; the right to call witnesses in his defense and to be represented by counsel; to be presumed innocent of the charges until his
accuser has proved them by a fair preponderance of the credible
evidence; and to be accorded equal and nondiscriminatory treatment.

The bylaws of the Board of Education contain provisions (105a) calculated to insure scrupulous observance of these constitutional mandates in hearings that may affect rights of the teacher to non-discriminatory treatment and/or his property rights.

Determination of whether nondiscriminatory treatment has been accorded a respondent must be made in the light of the evidence as to the performance of the mutual obligations existing between teacher and the school administration. These mutual obligations can be summed up as duty to the administration to perform his services in a manner equal to that of the averagely competent teacher under similar circumstances, and the administration is under a duty to the teacher to furnish him with the assistances required by law, by regulations, and by custom.

Hence, in the case where failure to attain standard performance is charged, the complainant must submit a preponderance of the credible evidence to show that the teacher has failed as charged to perform in a manner equal to that of the average performance of a teacher under like circumstances and also to show that the administration has afforded the teacher the duly required opportunities for help in his teaching. In both of these instances, the complainant must produce a preponderance of the credible evidence in order to sustain the burden of proving that the request for transfer should be granted.

Showing that the teacher has given substandard performances under the circumstances can be shown by the testimony of a professional who qualifies as an expert, like a principal, or by evidence of the performance of teachers in a number of similar classes having a similar caliber of pupil.

What aid must be shown to have been furnished to the teacher in order for the administration to prove having fulfilled its part of the contract was testified to by Assistant Superintendent Abraham Wilner as follows:

> If evidence is presented to a principal of the inability of a teacher to control the class to such an extent as to permit fights between pupils and other disorderly actions, the principal normally would take the following steps: study the roster of the class to ascertain whether there are more than an average number of children of more than average difficulty in the class; get the school's guidance and behavior counsellors to assist with individuals or groups in the class; visit and observe the teacher in action and make suggestions as to how to handle disorderly and inattentive children; send for the par-

ents of the children involved and discuss with them the behavior of the children in the classroom; and remove those children who are disorderly to such an extent as to prevent the class from operating in a normal fashion.

In addition to Mr. Wilner's oral description of the aid normally given by the principal to the teacher, the fact that such activities to aid the teacher are required is shown by the provisions of Article X §9 of the bylaws of the Board of Education.

The five cases involved here of Douglass, Bergen, Olener, Satlow, and Galano were all of the type where failure to perform adequately was the essence of the charge. In appraising hereafter sufficiency of the evidence in each of these cases, due weight has been given to the fact that the unit administrator's proof lacks in each instance any showing as to how the average teacher performed under similar circumstances and also lacks any showing as to what assistance was furnished to the teacher by the principal to aid him to handle his problems.

The evidence in each of these cases will now be appraised in the light of these guiding principles and recommendations made.

Richard Douglass. The nature of the complaint against Richard Douglass as amended to conform to the proof as shown by a letter (Unit Administrator Exhibit 1) signed by Rhody A. McCoy, unit administrator of the district to Richard Douglass dated May 27, 1968, is as follows: failure to maintain such control of his class and such order as to permit proper teaching and learning and to allow the safety of the children to be placed in jeopardy.

Richard Douglass testified that he holds a license as a substitute teacher of fine arts at Junior High School 271, which he received about two-and-one-half years ago, since which time he has taught for two years in elementary schools—at PS 120, for which service he was rated satisfactory and superior, following which he served for about six months at per diem work at PS 56, where he received "S" rating. He said he had never received a formal observation from any superior at JHS 271.

The unit administrator produced three witnesses against Mr. Douglass as follows: John Mandracchia, assistant principal of JHS 271, supervisor of art and the immediate supervisor of Richard Douglass; Claire DeVine, acting assistant principal at JHS 271, and charged with overseeing the department of art and music; and Cecil Bowen, substitute teacher and third floor controller at JHS 271, having commenced work in that capacity about the middle of May, 1968.

Of these three witnesses, it was Cecil Bowen who gave testimony relevant to the charge made in the complaint and said that on one occasion he observed the students in the classroom of Mr. Douglass walking in and out of the room; observed Mr. Douglass exercising very poor control over them such that he had to go into the room to break up a paint fight in which the youngsters threw paint at one another at a time when Mr. Douglas was present; that there were several pupils engaged in the paint fight and three or four were throwing the paint; that the rest of the class was in complete disorder; that they were between thirteen and fifteen years of age and that there were girls as well as boys. He said that he admonished them and managed to bring order into the classroom. He said that there were forty-two classes on the third floor, of which about one-fourth had incidents of disorder at various times as a result of which the teachers had called him in to assist them.

Since May 9 was the last date for Richard Douglass to serve there, Bowen's observation of him (said to be in the early part of May) must have been just before Douglass ceased his services there.

Douglass said that Mrs. DeVine, one of the witnesses who testified against him, had suggested that he use pencils instead of paint in the classroom because it would be simpler to give pencils instead of paint brushes and that this caused him to ask Mrs. DeVine about per diem work because he felt he could not do much good for the students in teaching them art if he could not use paint and that there was a great need for per diem teachers. He said further that he had told Mr. McCoy that he enjoyed his pupils so much and they enjoyed him that he hoped when the whole matter was over it would be possible for him to come back, maybe in September.

Even if the one instance of failure to maintain order in his class by Mr. Douglass occurred, there is no evidence to show that committing disorder on one occasion during the school year manifested below-average performance as a teacher, and this is particularly true where the witness for the complainant testified that such instances of disorder occurred at various times in at least one-fourth of similar classes on the same floor.

Findings. The evidence submitted by the unit administrator fails to show that the performance of the respondent Richard Douglass failed to measure up to the average competent performance of a teacher at that school of similar status and under similar conditions and hence the complainant unit administrator has failed to sustain the burden of proof as to the charge that the respondent teacher failed to maintain such control and order in his class as to permit proper teaching and learning; and thereby failed to show that involuntary transfer of this respondent was justified.

David Bergen. The charge presented by Rhody A. McCoy, unit administrator of the Ocean Hill–Brownsville district, against David Bergen as contained in a letter dated May 27, 1968 (Unit Administrator Exhibit 2), and amended to conform to the proof is as follows: failure to maintain order and control in his classroom; excessive lateness in arrival at school in the morning and in picking up his class after lunch.

The unit administrator presented as witness in support of this charge against Mr. Bergen Ralph Rogers, principal of PS 144 at which David Bergen was a teacher. Mr. Rogers had become principal in October, 1967, after having been appointed provisionally without taking a competitive examination and on March 4, 1958, the Supreme Court of Kings County rendered a decision holding his appointment invalid, which decision has been appealed to the Appellate Division and is still pending undecided.

Mr. Rogers testified that Mr. Bergen allowed children to be in the hallway.

There was marked in evidence (Unit Administrator Exhibit 12) the absence and lateness record of David Bergen showing latenesses incurred by Bergen during the period from October, 1967, to May, 1968, on twenty-two separate days and totaling 220 minutes.

Mr. Rogers stated further that he never discussed these latenesses with Mr. Bergen. He said that on occasions Bergen would be late in picking up his class after lunch, which made it necessary for a cluster teacher to be in the classroom until the teacher showed up, during which time the whole discipline of the class would be lost. He stated no dates as regards the lateness in picking up the class, nor did he ever file an observation report. There was marked in evidence (United Federation of Teachers Exhibit B) an observation report dated February 29, 1968, signed by J. Lightcap, assistant principal, which Mr. Rogers said amounted to a rating of "good" as to the performance of Mr. Bergen.

There was also marked in evidence (United Federation of Teachers Exhibit C) a letter dated February 8, 1968, signed by J. Lightcap, principal, and addressed to Mr. Bergen congratulating him on the fine way he handled his class a day before during the visit of student teachers.

Mr. Bergen, the respondent, explained the following as excuses for his latenesses: the fact that at the beginning of the school year the car he drove to work broke down so that he had to take the train and it took him some time to get adjusted to the train schedule; that, as to the longer latenesses, he had overslept.

He said that some of the latenesses in picking up his class after lunch resulted from his playing ball with the pupils in the yard and being unwilling to refuse their request to have "one more out," for fear of destroying the rapport built up between himself and his pupils. He denied that Mr. Rogers had ever actually circulated in his classroom, but would just come in the door and then go out.

The evidence of excessive latenesses testified to here cannot be held against Mr. Bergen as evidence of substandard performance in view of the fact that the principal, Mr. Rogers, admitted that he had never discussed these latenesses with him and thereby failed to give the guidance and leadership required of a principal. Furthermore, no evidence was given to show that the latenesses were more than those suffered by a teacher of similar status to Mr. Bergen and under similar circumstances.

The one instance testified to of Mr. Bergen permitting students to be in the hallway and also his lateness in picking up his class after lunch are not sufficient evidence to show that Bergen did not measure up to average teaching competence under the circumstances in view of the fact that he had good ratings and in view of the fact that his lateness in picking up his class was caused by activities important to his relationship with his pupils and in view of the failure by the unit administrator to show by competent testimony what would be the standard performance under the circumstances. In fact, although the principal testified, he was not asked whether he could say as an expert that Mr. Bergen had not performed with average competence under the circumstances.

Findings. The unit administrator has failed to sustain the burden of proving that David Bergen failed to perform as an average competent teacher under the circumstances and has failed to show that the administration provided him with the assistance duly required to be afforded him and that therefore the administration has failed to prove that Mr. Bergen should be transferred.

Abraham Olener. The nature of the complaint against Abraham Olener as contained in the papers filed by the unit administrator with the Board of Education on May 27, 1968, and marked (Unit Administrator Exhibit 5) in evidence, is as follows: failure to maintain order of pupils in class; permitting excessive numbers of pupils to be improperly out of the classroom and in the halls; failing to submit cutting cards of students cutting classes; failing to decorate the classroom properly and excessive use of the blackboard.

Testimony was given by Abraham Olener that he has held a regular license as a teacher of social studies regular junior high schools since 1962 and during the four years before that held a substitute high school license of social studies. At present, he teaches at JHS 178, which, since February 1, has been numbered IS 55.

Witnesses testifying on behalf of the Ocean Hill–Brownsville school district versus Abraham Olener were: Percy W. Jenkins, acting principal of IS 55, and Robert Ferlauto, assistant principal of IS 55.

The net of their testimony as regards the ability of Abraham Olener to maintain order in his class was as follows: that on various occasions when they went into Olener's classroom they witnessed confusion and sometimes fights and that on various occasions they found in the halls pupils who had left Olener's class without being given proper permission. No number of times or when this occurred was furnished by the witnesses nor were any dates of the occurrences furnished. Acting Principal Jenkins testified further that fights were not uncommon and occurred in other classrooms and that the general level of disorder was a problem. He testified that Olener was deficient in putting decorations in his classroom and failed to send in cutting passes for students having cut his class.

No evidence was given of the principal or the assistant principal conducting a conference with Olener regarding his conduct of the classroom nor was any evidence given of the acting principal having studied the roster of the class to ascertain whether there were more than [the] average [number of] children and more than average difficulty in the class; nor was evidence given of the principal or acting principal having taken the other steps to help Abraham Olener to perform to their satisfaction as required by Article 10, Section 89, of the bylaws of the Board of Education and as was testified by Assistant Superintendent Abraham Wilner was the customary procedure for principals and/or acting principals to follow to help the teacher perform satisfactorily. No observations or rating regarding Abraham Olener that had been prepared by the witnesses for the District were submitted in evidence.

A letter signed by Percy W. Jenkins and dated May 27, 1968, and a confidential report signed by Robert Ferlauto and dated May 27, 1968, were submitted (Unit Administrator Exhibit 5), but are without evidentiary value since they were prepared after the date when Olener's services were in fact stopped by the unit administrator; hence, the documents are simply an attempt of the witness to corroborate his oral testimony by his own written declaration.

Abraham Olener, in his testimony, presented an observation report dated May 6, 1968, and signed by N. July, acting chairman of social studies, regarding himself (Olener), which Olener appraised as giving him a "good" rating, and in addition Olener had marked in evidence a rating report for the year ending June 30, 1967, a report dated May 17, 1963, and a report dating from 1962, each of which rated him satisfactory, and a letter dated June 29, 1966, from his principal expressing pleasure to have him in the social studies department, and a letter dated June 26, 1967, signed by Jack Feld, assistant principal, praising his work. In addition to these commendations, Robert Ferlauto, assistant principal, testified that Olener was a hard-working teacher.

In view of the fact that the evidence of the complainant shows that the general level of disorder was a problem and that fights were not uncommon, there is a failure to prove that the order maintained by Abraham Olener in his classroom was not equal to the average control maintained by other teachers under similar circumstances, and as no authenticated documentary evidence was produced to show that Mr. Olener was deficient in his performance otherwise, and as documentary evidence was submitted attesting to satisfactory performance by Mr. Olener, it must be considered that charges of inefficient performance by him in matters other than maintaining control have not been proved.

Findings. The evidence produced by the unit administrator against Abraham Olener fails to sustain the burden of showing that he did not perform as a teacher with the average competence of a teacher under similar circumstances, and hence, justification for his transfer has not been established.

Paul Satlow. The nature of the written complaint made by Rhody A. McCoy, unit administrator of the district, against Paul Satlow by letter dated June 3, 1968, (Unit Administrator Exhibit 11) is as follows: complete inability to control his class.

The testimony regarding this complaint was received at the hearing held on July 3, 1968.

The testimony revealed that Paul Satlow holds a license issued by the Board of Education as a substitute in accounting and business subjects; that he began teaching in September, 1966, and, at the end of the year, received "S" grade; began teaching at PS 137 in September, 1967, and was assigned a class designated "OP-4" which was located on the second floor of PS 137.

The witnesses testifying on behalf of the unit administrator were: Eduardo Braithwaite, assistant administrative director of curriculum in the school district; Clara Marshall, chairman of the personnel committee and vice president of the governing board of the Ocean Hill–Brownsville School District; Ethel Parham, president of the Parent-Teachers Association of PS 137.

The net of the testimony that is relevant to the question of control exercised by Paul Satlow over his class is as follows:

1. That on one occasion in either December, 1967, or January, 1968, three pupils had the audio-visual equipment, playing it on the ceiling and on the walls; that two boys and one girl came out of one of the closet doors; that the pupils were running around; and that Satlow tried to get the pupils in order but that they paid no attention to him.

2. That in the latter part of October, 1967, two pupils standing in the hallway and making noise stated that they had been put out of Mr. Satlow's classroom; that, about the middle of November, Mrs. Marshall, upon finding a little girl crying in the hall, entered the room of Mr. Satlow and asked what was wrong with

the little girl, to which he (Mr. Satlow) did not reply and that subsequently, after the principal, Mr. Gordon, came down, the little girl was admitted back into the classroom; that on one occasion, in April, 1968, Mr. Satlow had his pupils in the yard and failed to stop some of them from running across the street to a store.

3. That on one occasion, in November, 1967, the pupils in Mr. Satlow's class were observed to be throwing chairs around and stopped only after being ordered to do so by Mrs. Parham, that Paul Satlow did nothing to stop it. There was marked in evidence (United Federation of Teachers Exhibit K 7–15–68) a letter from the director of the bureau of maintenance stating that the fixed furniture was not taken up from the floor in this (Satlow's) classroom until the period beginning April 10, 1968.

Paul Satlow testified that, in view of his short time as a teacher and his short time with PS 137, his experience was limited; that many of his pupils had discipline problems and some of them were "hold-over students"; that he locked the door at times because many of the pupils had relatives and friends in the upper grades who would try to break into his classroom and pull various of his pupils out in order to fight with them.

An observation report signed by Paul Hirschfield, assistant principal, and dated March 21, 1968, which was marked in evidence, contained at paragraph III, eight commendations of Satlow's teaching performance and, in paragraph IV (Suggestions), there were eleven suggestions, none of which related to improving his methods of controlling the behavior of the students.

The evidence submitted by the complainant describes three separate occasions when Mr. Satlow had trouble maintaining order in his classroom but submits no evidence of the situation in other classrooms to be used as a standard for determining whether Mr. Satlow's performance was below the average performance under the circumstances. Furthermore, no showing is made on behalf of the unit administrator as to what assistance was furnished by the principal to the teacher in order to help him with his problems as a teacher.

Findings.   The unit administrator has failed to sustain the burden of proving that Paul Satlow failed to perform as an average competent teacher under the circumstances and has failed to show that the administration provided him with the assistance duly required to be afforded a teacher; and therefore has failed to prove that Mr. Satlow should be transferred.

Theresa Galano. The nature of the complaint against Theresa Galano made by Rhody A. McCoy, the unit administrator, in a letter dated May 27, 1968 (Unit Administrator Exhibit 4), as amended to conform to the proof is as follows: conduct prejudicial to good order [and] inefficient services, where suspension is made necessary in order to maintain a safe atmosphere in the school and to prevent the safety of the children from being placed in jeopardy.

Theresa Galano holds a teacher's license in social studies and, when the complaint was made in May, 1968, was serving at PS 137, where her assignment was to teach children of the ages of seven and eight years to read. She had, prior to May, 1968, been employed at JHS 271 during the year 1967–68, where she had two social studies classes and three science classes. She had been assigned to PS 137 about three days when the complaint and request for transfer was made regarding her.

The evidence on behalf of the unit administrator was made up in one part by testimony given by Eleanor Axon, who was assigned to PS 137 as an educational assistant in mathematics and who holds no license from the Board of Education. She testified to having heard Mrs. Galano use profane language to her pupils in her class, something Mrs. Galano denies. I find that testimony incredible and hence give it no weight in this instance.

The other testimony was the letter of Mr. J. Mandracchia, assistant principal, dated March 27, 1968 (Unit Administrator Exhibit 12), [which] complains that Mrs. Galano [at] many times had been unable to control the behavior of the pupils in her class.

Regarding this, Mrs. Galano said that Mr. J. Mandracchia spoke to her about control of her class a number of times, that he "did not help me teach a class, so I went to the principal and I got his statement that he would help me. He would get the science head of the school to help me; and I said, wonderful! great! I will do a very good job. No one helped me and I was still floundering so I decided that if I could not help the children and could not do a good job I had to transfer out of the school, which is exactly what I did. I went to an elementary school and I was much better off, because I could not control the science class and I just transferred out."

After she had been transferred from JHS 271 to PS 137 and had been there for three days, the unit administrator stopped her from teaching and requested her transfer.

No evidence was presented by the unit administrator as to her performance during the three days at PS 137. Counsel for the unit administrator admitted that they had no experience tables on Mrs. Galano's performance at PS 137 and that the complaint against her was based upon her prior experience at JHS 271.

The unit administrator has therefore failed to prove that the respondent teacher has not performed with average competence as a teacher under the circumstances at PS 137 nor has any evidence been presented sufficient to prove that she could not render services of the required competence at that school.

Findings. The evidence produced by the unit administrator against Mrs. Theresa Galano fails to sustain the burden of showing that she did not perform at PS 137 with the average competence of a teacher under similar circumstances, and hence, a justification for her transfer has not been established.

Burt Landsman. The nature of the complaint against Mr. Landsman as contained in the papers filed with the Board of Education on June 3, 1968, and as amended at the trial on motion of counsel for the district, and marked (Unit Administrator Exhibit 10) for identification, is as follows: that Mr. Burt Landsman inflicted corporal punishment upon Alfonso Berry and has made inappropriate remarks to girl students.

Testimony was given by Mr. Landsman that he was employed by the Board of Education as a teacher at PS 137, holds a regular license, common branches, and had been teacher at PS 137 for three years; and that he is teaching "6-OP-3," which is known as a difficult class and contains students who either are underachievers or have been left back once or twice. He testified that he has had a total of four-and-one-half years teaching experience.

Testimony was offered on behalf of the district in support of the charges against Landsman by Albertha Loftin, a teacher at PS 137, which was excluded since it related to her 1966–67 year; by Ethel Parham, president of the Parent-Teachers Association of PS 137, which was excluded because it was hearsay on top of hearsay, as Mrs. Parham could only testify to what Mrs. Boone had told her she was told by her daughter; and by Vera Wright, which was excluded because it related to her 1966 and 1967 year [sic]. Hence there was no competent evidence relating to any improper remarks made by Mr. Landsman to any of his pupils that could be received.

The testimony offered by the district to support the charge of Mr. Landsman's having inflicted corporal punishment upon Alfonso Berry was given by Ethel Parham, who told what Alfonso Berry had told her, which was as follows: that Landsman, before lunch, had taken from him (Berry) his ball, which he had in the classroom, and said that he would return it to him at lunchtime; that, upon his not getting back the ball, Berry went to the teachers' room, where he found Landsman, but that Landsman punched him in the stomach, used karate on him, and dragged him downstairs to the office of the acting principal, Mr. Hirschfield.

On behalf of Landsman, the following witnesses testified: Evelyn Paris, employed by the Board of Education as acting guidance counsellor; Michael Rothstein, a cluster teacher at PS 137; Steven Mofshin, a licensed teacher in the sixth grade at PS 137. Each of these witnesses stated that they knew Berry, and some of their testimony was as follows: that Berry had formerly been at PS 26 where, because of improper behavior and truancy, he had been suspended and committed to Creedmoor; that upon his release from Creedmoor it was arranged for him to go to PS 137, which he did not want to attend and wanted to go back to PS 26; that he had no interest in school, liked to wander around the building; that he was a discipline problem, which included fighting frequently with other pupils in the school and having no respect for authority; that Berry would be very destructive, would call out loud in class and bang on the desk, and leave his seat and the classroom and not return for a period of time; that he had fought with a girl in Landsman's classroom and had to be restrained by Landsman and Steven Mofshin and several times had chased girls into Mofshin's room.

Burton Landsman's testimony was to the effect that he has never spoken to any girl in his class about her sexual life and had never used corporal punishment on any student. He said that Alfonso Berry was throwing the ball against the wall in his class on a day in February, 1968; that he took it from him, telling him that he would give it back to him at lunchtime; that at 11:00 A.M. he went to the teachers' room; that Berry came there about ten minutes later and began hollering for his ball; that he told Berry to go to his room and that he would tell the teacher named Rifshin to give him his ball at 12 o'clock when he went to lunch; that

Berry would not leave and picked up a wastebasket and started swinging it at him, Landsman; that he grabbed the basket from him and took him outside the room, during which time Berry kept kicking and throwing his feet; that he grabbed him by the arm and told him to stop, which he did not do, and so he took him to the principal's office, where Berry tried to throw a typewriter at him; later, he said, Berry apologized to him.

He denied having punched Berry in the stomach or having used karate on him.

Findings. The evidence produced on behalf of the Ocean Hill–Brownsville district is insufficient to prove that Burton Landsman committed the offense of inflicting corporal punishment upon Alfonso Berry as charged in the complaint, and the evidence on behalf of the respondent that he did not so act being credible and believable, it is hereby found that the complaint of any wrongdoing by Burton Landsman has not been sustained.

Daniel Goldberg. The nature of the complaint against Daniel Goldberg as shown in the papers filed with the Board of Education dated June 3, 1968, and marked (Unit Administrator Exhibit 8) for identification as amended to conform to the proof is in substance as follows: Daniel Goldberg was hostile to the program of the Ocean Hill–Brownsville demonstration school district and had attempted to instill in the minds of his colleagues anxieties about their participation in the program.

Daniel Goldberg testified that he is employed by the Board of Education as a teacher of social studies and is acting social studies chairman at JHS 271 and holds a license for teaching regular junior high school social studies, which license he has held for five years.

In support of these charges, the district offered one witness, Marvin Holland, English teacher at JHS 271, who testified that, on one occasion, at a Christmas party, Goldberg, in speaking only to him, said in substance the following: he felt the way things were going at the school that he should not teach there; that he wanted to see if they could possibly iron out some kind of problem or get together something that would create a better circumstance at the school; that the way things were, the substitutes would all leave.

Mr. Holland testified further that the teachers wanted a free and open transfer plan which allowed them to go to schools other than those considered to be special service schools, but that many of the teachers objected to that and wanted to go wherever they wished.

Mr. Kalodner, counsel for the unit administrator, stated that the specifications would show that Mr. Goldberg was a competent teacher and that the governing board made no complaint against him on the basis of competency. The fact that Daniel Goldberg is a competent teacher was further evidenced by the introduction in evidence of UFT exhibits (L to P inclusive), each of which was a written statement by persons in a position to know attesting to Mr. Goldberg's outstanding ability as a teacher.

Mr. Goldberg said that he was the membership chairman of the [UFT] chapter that year as well as treasurer, and his duties included the collection of dues and handling of any grievances. He said the transfer plan had been discussed at the open UFT meeting, which he attended and which had 100 people present. The teachers wanted an arrangement whereby any teacher who desired to transfer out of the district would be allowed to do so, which was the situation when the administrative districts were set up in August, 1967. Later, a plan was evolved whereby 5 per cent of the teachers would be transferred out under the regular plan and another 5 per cent could be transferred out in February. There was an additional element in the plan that made it so that 20 per cent of the teachers in one year could transfer out under a voluntary plan. Mr. Goldberg stated that the teachers wished for a larger percentage of teachers who could transfer out and in fact wanted a 100 per cent transfer plan.

He testified that at a Christmas party on December 23, 1967, he spoke to Mr. Holland in reference to certain problems they were having in the school and that Holland asked him "what do the majority of the teachers want?" to which he replied that "they want a full written dismissal plan from this district and a satisfactory plan for the district, that is, a transfer plan that would be satisfactory to Mr. McCoy and the governing board as well as to the teachers in the district." Mr. Goldberg said that he never at any time made statements seeking to subvert or hostile to the entire demonstration project but was making statements that he considered permissible criticisms as to how the system could be improved; that he never made statements to teachers or supervisors that were intended by him to discourage them from coming to JHS 271, but, on the contrary, urged Miss Burnieri to go there as an assistant principal.

An appraisal of what Marvin Holland stated he had said to him as well as of what Goldberg said he stated to Holland and his statement of what he meant by these remarks shows that Goldberg was actually attempting to give constructive criticism of the project so as to enable it to hold the substitutes. It would appear that what Goldberg actually said to Holland, even if it were credible, was protected both by the First Amendment freedom of speech prerogative and by the privileges adhering in a union official under the Fair Labor Practice Provisions.

Findings. It is hereby found that upon this evidence the unit administrator failed to sustain the burden of providing the charges it made against Daniel Goldberg and therefore has failed to present competent evidence to support its request for transfer of Daniel Goldberg from the Ocean Hill–Brownsville district.

Dismissal of the Cases of Cliff Rosenthal, Barry Goodman, Frederick Nauman. The nature of the charge against each of them is substantially as follows: that they have expressed opposition to the project and contributed to the growing hostility between the Negro and white teachers.

These charges against them are contained in three separate letters each dated June 3, 1968, signed by Rhody A. McCoy and marked for Identification as follows: Unit Administrator Exhibit 6 (Rosenthal), Unit Administrator Exhibit 7 (Goodman), Unit Administrator Exhibit 9 (Nauman).

When the case of Barry Goodman was called on June 26, 1968, the counsel for Ocean Hill–Brownsville stated that he was not prepared to go forward with any witnesses against Mr. Goodman, and he did not present any evidence against him.

The application of the counsel for Mr. Goodman to dismiss the charges against him was therefore granted.

When the cases of Cliff Rosenthal and Frederick Nauman were called on July 15, 1968, Mr. Kalodner [counsel] stated that he was not prepared to present evidence against them due to lack of witnesses being present.

Mr. Kaufman then moved to dismiss the charges against them, and this motion was granted.

Findings. No evidence having been produced against Cliff Rosenthal, Barry Goodman, or Frederick Nauman, and the charges against them having been dismissed, there is nothing to support the request for their transfer out of the district, and hence the request should be denied.

Recommendations

Upon all the evidence herein and due deliberation having been had, and it appearing that Rhody A. McCoy, unit administrator of the Ocean Hill–Brownsville demonstration school district, has requested the superintendent of schools to transfer out of his district the teachers named below because of certain charges made by him (McCoy) against each of them, and evidence concerning these charges as to each of these teachers having been heard before Francis E. Rivers, Esq., the duly appointed special trial examiner, who has found that this evidence is insufficient in each case to sustain the necessary burden of proof,

Now, therefore, it is hereby recommended by the undersigned as follows:

That the request made by Rhody A. McCoy, unit administrator, to the superintendent of schools to transfer out of the Ocean Hill–Brownsville demonstration school district each of the following teachers: Richard Douglass, David Bergen, Barry Goldman, Abraham Olener, Paul Satlow, Theresa Galano, Burton Landsman, Daniel Goldberg, Cliff Rosenthal, and Frederick Nauman, be denied.

Respectfully submitted,

Francis E. Rivers
Special Trial Examiner

Excerpts from the Niemeyer Report

In May, 1968, the project board sent notices of termination of service to nineteen professionals (one principal, five assistant prin-

EXCERPTED FROM the final report submitted to the New York City Board of Education by its Advisory and Evaluation Committee on Decentralization (Niemeyer Committee) on July 30, 1968; chap. III, pp. 94–97.

cipals, and thirteen teachers) on grounds of what the project administrator called "intolerable conditions and a general worsening of the situation between certain professionals and the people in the community." The nineteen were referred to the Board of Education headquarters for reassignment. This move was interpreted by the professional staff, the community at large, and the press as dismissal. The project board has steadfastly denied these allegations, arguing that they simply requested that the staff members be transferred out of the district. This request was rejected by the superintendent; the UFT demanded written charges, thus placing the request for transfers (for which no charges are required) into the realm of dismissal. Initially, no formal charges were filed against the nineteen professionals. The project administrator stated that school safety was a factor in the "ouster," charging that those involved had allowed "hazardous conditions" to exist, which set an "unhealthy tone" for the schools. Formal charges have been filed against six professionals; two have voluntarily requested transfers; one has been reinstated by the project board. In addition, the project board has even prepared formal charges against a substitute teacher, a procedure not required by normal administrative regulations.

The project administrator regards the strict interpretation of his action by the Board of Education as an attempt to diminish his authority as district superintendent. He claims that, as the administrative head of a school district, he has the power to reassign personnel. Although this is true to the extent that a district superintendent operates within his own jurisdiction, the lines of authority are not formally delineated nor do they extend when a district superintendent attempts to reassign personnel, via central headquarters, to another area.

The direct confrontation in Ocean Hill–Brownsville made it a focal point of controversy. Under normal circumstances, the demonstration project might have been able to accomplish the transfer of "unsatisfactory" personnel informally, but a larger struggle was being waged in the New York State Legislature over a general proposal to decentralize the entire school system. Thus, the events in Ocean Hill–Brownsville became a precursor of what could happen under community control of the schools. The project became a looking glass, and any likelihood of working out informal arrangements in such a sensitive area as professional performance and transfer became most difficult. Parenthetically, it should be noted that the project administrator had tried to reassign teachers *within* the school project, a move that was within his authority according to oral information he had received. The Board of Education attempted to resolve this impasse but failed when certain teachers refused to transfer.

In any event, the children in the Ocean Hill–Brownsville project have lost fifty-two school days. These include the April 10 and 11 boycott of the schools by the parents to support the community call for meaningful control; the boycott by parents and the walkout by teachers over the "dismissal" controversy, when a substantial proportion of students lost thirty-six days of schooling in May and June; and the fourteen-day city-wide teachers "strike" at the beginning of the school year (September, 1967).

A proposal for binding arbitration to resolve the dispute was suggested and accepted by the Board of Education and the UFT. The project board rejected this approach and suggested mediation instead. They recommended that Commissioner Allen establish a panel, of which he would also be a member, to come forth with a settlement acceptable to all parties. The union rejected this idea, mainly because they considered that Allen's support of the Regents Plan before the state legislature would be prejudicial. The project board, anticipating the union's response, then sought to have Allen exercise his authority to remove the Board of Education. Allen rejected any involvement in the mediation effort, a response that seems to rule out more drastic action on his part. He also suggested that the project board avail itself of the services of Theodore Kheel, a lawyer and prominent labor mediator.

Both sides agreed on Kheel as mediator. He, in turn, made several recommendations, including the suggestion that all teachers involved, with the exception of those six formally charged, return to school pending the outcome of the mediation. The project board rejected this recommendation.

The school year ended in a stalemate; the teachers were not in school; the children were not being taught; the battle for community control still raged and may well be carried over into the next fall term.

The Burden of the Blame: NYCLU Report on the Ocean Hill–Brownsville School Controversy

The current school dispute in New York City has yielded no revenue; it has yielded nothing but discontent, disorder, disobedience. It has been a dispute with no heroes and many villains.

Summary of Conclusions

The New York Civil Liberties Union supports school decentralization as a means of giving ghetto communities equal access to the process of making decisions vitally affecting the education of their children. We are also deeply committed to due process of law and academic freedom. We do not find any inconsistency in our support for decentralization and our commitment to due process and academic freedom. Indeed, we find the charge that existing standards of due process are seriously threatened by community control unfounded, both in theory and in fact. NYCLU is issuing this statement at this time because we believe that it is crucial to set the record straight regarding the causes of the chaos in Ocean Hill–Brownsville. Our examination of the record has persuaded us that *the chaos was not a result of local community control*. On the contrary, we are persuaded that *the chaos resulted from efforts to undermine local community control* of the schools.

Specifically, our research leads us to the following basic conclusions:

1. That from the beginning, *the central Board of Education attempted to scuttle the experiment in Ocean Hill-Brownsville* by consistently refusing to define the authority of the local governing board.

2. That *the United Federation of Teachers has used "due process" as a smoke screen* to obscure its real goal, which is to discredit decentralization and sabotage community control;

WRITTEN BY Associate Director Ira Glasser and approved by the New York Civil Liberties Union Board of Directors, *The Burden of the Blame* has been further footnoted by Mr. Glasser since its first issuance and appears in full here by permission of the NYCLU.

3. That there are serious shortcomings in existing Board of Education standards of due process, which have long permeated the entire school system; and that to the degree that the Ocean Hill–Brownsville board violated due process, it did so only by following normal standards and procedures of the Board of Education.

4. That the major burden of blame for the chaos in Ocean Hill–Brownsville must fall on the central Board of Education and the UFT.

These conclusions are entirely supported by public documents that have been generally available but largely ignored or distorted. These include: the Niemeyer Committee's Report to the Board of Education, the Report and Recommendations of special trial examiner Francis E. Rivers after the administrative hearing of charges brought by Rhody McCoy against ten Ocean Hill–Brownsville teachers; a special pamphlet on decentralization published by the UFT; the contract between the UFT and the central board; and the official bylaws of the Board of Education.

The Role of the Board of Education

Ironically, the demand for decentralization or, more properly, community control of the schools, began with the failure of the central board to effectively implement integration. In explaining their failure, Board of Education administrators often said that they could not and would not "tell the principals how to run their schools."[1] Integration failed at least partly because it was resisted by many principals and because the system was already administratively decentralized to the point where recalcitrant principals were not forced to comply with board policy on integration.[2]

The growing sense of betrayal among ghetto leaders who had been repeatedly promised integrated schools came to a head during the IS 201 controversy. Intermediate schools, embracing grades five or six through eight, were specifically designed to further integration by getting children out of elementary schools a year or two earlier and into intermediate schools, which would

[1] Jason Epstein, "The Politics of School Decentralization," *The New York Review of Books* (June 6, 1968).

[2] See generally David Rogers, *110 Livingston Street* (New York: Random House, 1968).

draw their students from a wider community to produce a greater racial mixture. To do this, the intermediate schools were supposed to have been built in areas that bordered on both black and white communities and built to accommodate large numbers of children.

IS 201 fulfilled neither condition. It was built in the middle of Harlem and its capacity was no larger than a normal junior high school. As a UFT pamphlet published early in 1968 said:

> Having been promised by the Board of Education that the school would be integrated, parents of children there soon found they had been betrayed, and that the school would remain segregated. Mounting frustration coupled with the increasingly obvious fact that children were not learning soon led to a translation of the original demand for integration into one for "local control."[3]

Disenchanted black parents decided that since they were once again stuck with a segregated school, they might at least run it themselves. Thus was born the movement for community control of black schools. It is crucial to remember that integration was not abandoned by black parents but by the Board of Education, which consistently failed to deliver on the promise of integrated schools. It is also crucial to remember that the demand for community control was a direct response by ghetto residents to the lack of access to decision-making processes that vitally affected the lives of their children. In that respect, "community control" came to symbolize the struggle for democratic power just as "no taxation without representation" symbolized a similar struggle by the founders of the American republic.

In the wake of the disorders that followed, the Board of Education, with financial assistance from the Ford Foundation, established IS 201 as part of a somewhat autonomous experimental school district in Harlem. At the same time, two additional "somewhat autonomous" experimental districts were launched, one in lower Manhattan and the other in Brooklyn in an area known as Ocean Hill–Brownsville.

From the start, no one knew what "somewhat autonomous" meant. Certainly the board never said. For whatever reason, the

---

[3] Eugenia Kemble, *New York's Experiments in School Decentralization: A Look at Three Projects* (United Federation of Teachers, 1968).

board simply never defined the powers of the local governing boards of the experimental districts.

According to the Niemeyer Report,[4] a broad spectrum of the Ocean Hill–Brownsville community began to meet in February, 1967, to plan "for some means to participate more directly in school affairs."[5] For five months, the group continued to meet, was in contact with the mayor's office, and held exploratory discussions with the Board of Education's administrative staff.[6]

In early July, 1967, the Ford Foundation gave the local planning group $44,000 for the specific purpose of completing the planning phase of the experiment according to a twenty-six-day timetable.[7] On July 29, 1967, at the end of the twenty-six days, the Planning Council produced a written set of proposals, which was submitted to the Board of Education in August.[8] These proposals clearly defined specific powers, responsibilities, and functions of the local- governing board. Among other things, the proposals provided that the local governing board would be directly responsible and answerable to the New York City superintendent of schools and the state commissioner of education.[9]

Thus it is clear that, although the Planning Council was asking for effective community control, it was by no means demanding complete independence. Indeed it was merely seeking powers

[4] The Niemeyer Report was the final report of an advisory committee appointed on July 1, 1967, by the Board of Education to study school decentralization with particular emphasis on the three experimental districts. The committee's full title was the Advisory and Evaluation Committee on Decentralization of the Board of Education of the City of New York. It functioned from July 1, 1967, to June 30, 1968. Its final report, entitled *An Evaluative Study of the Process of School Decentralization in New York City*, was submitted to the board on July 30, 1968, and released in September, 1968. Its chairman was John H. Niemeyer, president of Bank Street College of Education, and its other members were Mrs. Lillian Ashe, former president of the United Parents Association, Dr. Charles R. DeCarlo, director of Automation Research for I.B.M., James Marshall, former president of the New York City Board of Education, Frederick O'Neal, president of Actors Equity, and Mrs. Celia Vice, chairman of local school board 14, Brooklyn. The staff executive director was Dr. Bert Swanson, director of the Institute for Community Studies at Sarah Lawrence College. (Hereinafter referred to as Niemeyer Report)

[5] Niemeyer Report, p. 72.

[6] *Ibid.*

[7] *Ibid.*

[8] *Ibid.*, p. 74.

[9] *Ibid.*

already possessed by every suburban or rural township in New York State.

The Planning Council's proposals also included the following provision:

> (8) The [local] board shall make provisions for periodic evaluation of the total program. Such evaluations will include the project administrator, principals, teachers, community workers, etc. *This is not to be construed as meaning the [local] board will do the evaluating. Existing Board of Education procedures for evaluating teachers will remain intact* [emphasis added].[10]

This provision makes it clear that the Planning Council did *not* contemplate bypassing existing procedures and substituting for those procedures arbitrary standards of its own. Indeed, at this point the Planning Council did not see any conflict between existing standards of due process and effective community control. But as events would soon make clear, the Board of Education had little intention of going through with a genuine experiment in community control.

The first indication of this came when the Planning Council attempted to elect parent representatives to the local governing board. According to a recent study of the Ocean Hill–Brownsville dispute,[11] the Planning Council needed the names and addresses of students in order to register the parents who were eligible to vote. The Planning Council asked the Board of Education for help. But the board refused:

> The board told them the community groups could get the necessary names and addresses only by hiring two Board of Education secretaries to go into the files. When the community leaders agreed to do this they were informed that the two secretaries had gone on vacation and that no one else was available. The Ocean Hill leaders were dismayed, but they got sympathetic teachers to canvass students for their addresses. Then, by going from door to door, they finally got 2,000 parents registered by August.[12]

10 *Ibid.*, p. 75
11 Richard Karp, "School Decentralization in New York: A Case Study," *Interplay* (August–September, 1968).
12 *Ibid.*

Although this patchwork approach produced several unorthodox practices in the election that followed, the Niemeyer Report concluded that "no charges were made or misdeeds observed" and that "there was no evidence of coercion during the nominating process or during the election period itself."[13]

By August, 1967, the local governing board had been elected and, in addition, Rhody McCoy, an acting principal with eighteen years of experience in the New York City School System, had been selected as the project administrator.

As the opening of school approached, the Board of Education had still not acted on the Planning Council's proposed delineation of the specific powers, responsibilities, and functions of the local board. As September grew closer, no one yet knew who was going to run the schools, who had the power to do what, and exactly what the content of the experiment was supposed to be. Despite repeated urgings by the local governing board that it simply could not operate much less conduct a valid experiment unless it knew what its powers and responsibilities were, the central Board of Education consistently refused to define those powers. In fact, according to the Niemeyer Report, "both parties [were] still awaiting the specific delineation of powers and authority to be granted" as of July 30, 1968, when the Niemeyer Committee concluded its work.[14]

Apparently, *once the Board of Education understood that what Ocean Hill–Brownsville really wanted was an experiment in genuine community control, it backed off even before it had begun.* Almost immediately, the board began to talk about community *involvement* as opposed to community *control.*[15] And then, in January, 1968, more than five months after the Planning Council had submitted its proposals, and four months after the "experiment" had "begun," the central board suggested its own guidelines.[16] These guidelines completely emasculated the experiment in community control by stripping the local governing board of virtually all of its substantive powers. Moreover, it left blurry and vague the lines of authority between the local board and the central board. The local board met with the central board and again asked for more specific delineation of authority

13 Niemeyer Report, p. 77.
14 *Ibid.*, p. 91.
15 Karp, *op. cit.*
16 Niemeyer Report, p. 91.

and for the restoration of significant powers. But the central board refused to act.[17]

Thus, as the school year passed its midpoint, it became clear that the Board of Education had, in effect, scuttled the experiment. It had refused to delegate significant powers, and it had refused to specifically define administrative authority. *It is an abiding mystery how an experiment in community control is supposed to proceed when no control is given and no authority is defined.*

As the Niemeyer Report noted, the ambiguity about operational powers raised the critical question of who has authority to run the schools.[18] It is a question the Board of Education has never answered.

Vacuums created by the absence of clearly defined lines of authority are usually filled by individual discretion, arbitrary action, and administrative abuse. Only chaos can then result, as it has in Ocean Hill–Brownsville. The burden of blame for that chaos must fall on the Board of Education for leaving lines of authority undrawn and governing powers undefined. If the central board had deliberately set out to discredit decentralization by insuring chaos, it could not have done so more effectively. It freely predicted that decentralization would be chaotic, and by its actions it made certain that its predictions came true.

The Role of the United Federation of Teachers

In the beginning, teachers were involved cooperatively with the Planning Council. At the time of the Ford grant, teachers were participants in the planning of the Ocean Hill–Brownsville experiment and, according to a statement by the teachers quoted in the Niemeyer Report, they were quite happy with the Planning Council.[19]

At some point in September, the teacher representatives began to complain that they had been bypassed in the planning stage and no one was listening to them.[20] At first, the teachers' annoyance seemed to be directed primarily at the Ford Foundation and the central board for having initiated the planning phase in

[17] *Ibid.*, pp. 93–94.
[18] *Ibid.*
[19] *Ibid.*, p. 73.
[20] *Ibid.*

early July when most teachers would have left for summer vacation.[21] Soon, however, the focus of teacher complaints was the Planning Council itself for having "begun expanding on the plan without our presence."[22] As disagreements grew between the teachers and the Planning Council, open, bitter, and hostile exchanges apparently took place. In the context of previous grievances between the teachers and the community, it did not take much to develop the disagreements into hostile mistrust on the one side and mounting fear on the other.

On September 2, 1967, the new local governing board held its third meeting and appointed five new principals for their schools. The appointments were made necessary when five incumbent principals left the district at the beginning of the experiment. Although the five new principals all had state certification, they were not chosen from the approved "waiting list." As Richard Karp put it:

> What irked [the teachers] and what frightened a large number of union members was the fact that the principals chosen by the community were not on the approved Civil Service list. No one denied the merit of the elected principals.* but the sight of educators chosen with no regard for bureaucratic procedures seemed to strike symbolically at every teacher's job security.[23]

The next week, the UFT called a city-wide strike. Although the union claimed that the strike was designed to extract city-wide pay increases and smaller classes, the local governing board perceived the strike as a show of power aimed against Ocean Hill–Brownsville and specifically in reaction to its hiring of the five principals. The UFT asked the local governing board to support the strike but was refused. At this point, the teacher repre-

---

[21] Kemble, op. cit.

[22] Ibid.

* There were rumblings about the politics of one appointee, Herman Ferguson, who never actually functioned as a principal in Ocean Hill–Brownsville. Mr. Ferguson at the time faced criminal charges. He was since convicted, but his conviction was appealed and at this writing a new trial has been ordered. In any case, the opposition of the CSA and UFT was not limited to Mr. Ferguson. They opposed any bypassing of the approved waiting list quite apart from the merit of the individual involved.—I.G.

[23] Karp, op. cit.

sentatives resigned from the local board, never to return. It was this incident that marked the beginning of the escalation of rhetoric between the Ocean Hill–Brownsville board and the UFT and exposed the deep fears and hostility that existed between the white, middle-class educational establishment and the black community.[24] The community began to accuse the teachers of scuttling the experiment, and the teachers, having resigned from the local governing board, began to talk about black extremists and black racism.

Given the enormous social and psychological pressures inherent in the situation and given also the Board of Education's refusal to clearly define the powers of the local governing board, it is difficult to sort out the equities in the dispute between the teachers and the local board up to the September, 1967, strike. It is enough for the purposes of this report to note that at some point late in September, 1967, the UFT grew very fearful of community control and determined to block it, discredit it, and, if need be, defeat it.

In the months that followed, the UFT began to fan the flames of racial fears as it increasingly harped on "extremism," "the militants," and "black power." This much is a matter of public record.[25] The UFT was soon joined by the Council of Supervisory Associations, which sued to remove the five principals appointed in September and which encouraged its members to abandon the experiment. To be sure, on November 1, 1967, all eighteen assistant principals left Ocean Hill–Brownsville.

Then, in the December 20, 1967, issue of the *United Teacher*, a periodical publication of the UFT, it was announced in an article on Ocean Hill–Brownsville that:

> The UFT has been negotiating with the [central] Board of Education for a transfer plan which will enable teachers to leave, although the union has encouraged them not to leave their schools. . . . The transfer plan being settled upon would give teachers the option of transferring at two points during each school year for as long as the experiment continues.[26]

[24] *Ibid.*
[25] Kemble, *op. cit.* See also generally *The New York Times* from September, 1967, to the present.
[26] Kemble, *op. cit.*

It must be pointed out that transfers are not ordinarily available to teachers on such an easy basis. The procedures and regulations are complicated and require twelve pages of the contract between the UFT and the board to explain.[27] In general, the normal contractual procedures are designed to discourage teachers from fleeing ghetto schools. According to the Board of Education, "the present contract with the UFT provides that teachers must serve five years on regular appointment before being eligible for transfer; after this, their names are listed in order of seniority."[28] There are other limits as well, including an absolute prohibition against transfers at teacher initiative of more than 5 per cent of the teachers at any one school during any one year.[29]

Yet, in Ocean Hill–Brownsville, the UFT sought to ignore all these procedures and gained the right for unlimited numbers of teachers to transfer out at will for the duration of the experiment, to abandon the experiment for as long as it continued and then to be free to return, presumably when "normal" conditions had been reinstated. Apparently, the UFT was not very concerned about the disastrous consequences to the experiment that might occur if large numbers of teachers were allowed to leave. Significant numbers of teachers did leave, sometimes in groups large enough to cause serious shortages.

Months later, when the Ocean Hill–Brownsville local governing board attempted to exercise a similar unilateral right of transfer, the UFT cried foul. Yet quite apart from the issues of due process raised by the manner in which the local governing board attempted to transfer nineteen teachers and administrators, the UFT appeared to take a position of startling inconsistency. On the one hand, the UFT claimed that due to special conditions in Ocean Hill–Brownsville, teachers should be allowed to bypass all the contractual procedures and transfer out at will. On the

[27] Agreement between the Board of Education of the City of New York and United Federation of Teachers, Local 2, American Federation of Teachers, AFL-CIO, pp. 20–32.

[28] *Tentative Proposals for Decentralization* (Board of Education, August, 1968), p. 2.

[29] UFT contract, *op. cit.* See footnote 27.

* This was overstated in the first edition. Actually, the agreement finally reached allowed a maximum of 20 per cent of the teachers in any one school in Ocean Hill–Brownsville to transfer out at will. This was four times the usual maximum and in practice gave teachers a virtually unlimited right to leave Ocean Hill–Brownsville.—I.G.

other hand, when the local governing board made the same claim (that due to the special conditions of the experiment, it should be allowed to transfer teachers to another district) the UFT expressed indignation and pleaded for strict fidelity to established procedures.

In trying to appear to the public as if it was only seeking fair procedures for teachers, the UFT has consistently claimed that it is in favor of decentralization. Yet it is a matter of public record that during the last session of the state legislature, the UFT carried on intensive lobbying activities against the Board of Regents Plan to implement decentralization and institute community control.

When school opened on September 9, the UFT went out on strike. NYCLU supports the right of teachers to strike. Unfortunately, the UFT chose to use the strike not only to demand the reinstatement of the transferred teachers but also as an extension of its lobbying efforts to defeat decentralization. By this time, the UFT was predicting that local community control would lead to chaos. By striking, the UFT proved its point by creating chaos.

The Due Process Issue

By early spring, 1968, the following was clear:

1. The Board of Education, by refusing to delegate power or define authority to the local governing board, had ruined the experiment and set itself squarely against community control.

2. The UFT, by its special agreements involving transfers and by its emerging lobbying position against the various proposed plans, had set itself squarely against community control.

3. The CSA, by its suit challenging the appointment of non–civil service principals and by encouraging assistant principals to leave Ocean Hill–Brownsville, had set itself squarely against community control.

4. The $44,000 of Ford planning money, which had run out in the fall of 1967, was not going to be followed up by the previously promised $250,000 to fund substantive programs until the local board was formally recognized by the central board.

Thus, by the spring of 1968, without funds, without power, without authority, and with serious opposition in the ranks of its teachers, the Ocean Hill–Brownsville board was virtually unable to run its schools or conduct its experiment.

It is against this background that in April the Ocean Hill–Brownsville board decided to transfer nineteen of what it called the "most uncooperative" teachers and administrators.

At first—and this appears to be a fact that is not generally known—McCoy tried to reassign the nineteen *within* the experimental district. According to the Niemeyer Report, McCoy had the authority to do that based on oral information he had received.[30] Yet when some of the teachers refused to be transferred, the Board of Education refused to back up McCoy's authority.[31] Apparently it was clearly within McCoy's authority to transfer personnel *within* his district until he actually tried to exercise it.

Next, McCoy requested that the nineteen be transferred to another district entirely. This request was denied by Superintendent Donovan.[32] Finally, early in May, 1968, the local governing board sent notices of transfer to' the nineteen, referring them to Board of Education headquarters for reassignment.[33] This transfer was interpreted by the professional staff, the community at large, and the press as dismissal.[34]

In attempting to understand why the attempted transfer was so widely perceived as an attempted firing, it is important to examine the distinction between transfer and dismissal in the Board of Education bylaws.[35]

Dismissals must be accompanied by the requirements of due process, including written notice of charges, right to a hearing, right to confront witnesses, right to call witnesses, right to introduce evidence, right to receive transcript, right to appeal, etc.[36] The bylaws mandate these requirements for regular teachers, and the UFT contract extends the requirements to substitute teachers.[37] *But neither the bylaws nor the contract mandate the requirements of due process for mere transfers.* Article II, section 101.1 of the bylaws says: "Transfers of members of the teaching and supervising staff from one school to another shall be made by the superintendent of schools, who shall report immediately

[30] Niemeyer Report, p. 96.
[31] *Ibid.*
[32] *Ibid.*, p. 94.
[33] *Ibid.*
[34] *Ibid.*
[35] Bylaws of the Board of Education of the City of New York.
[36] *Ibid.*, section 105a.1.
[37] UFT contract, article IV, section F, paragraph 15b, c.

such transfers to the Board of Education for its consideration and action."[38]

The purpose of this provision is apparently to allow the superintendent maximum flexibility to move teachers around for a variety of reasons. Implicit in the provision is the assumption that the right to a job does not include the right to choose your assignment within the system. In fact, many hundreds of such transfers take place during every school year, apparently without the UFT's objection. Why then did the UFT make such a fuss in this case and insist on due process when it knew that due process was not required under existing procedures?

The answer is clear: the UFT demanded due process because it wished to create the impression that the teachers had been fired and because it wished to discredit the local governing board. This conclusion is hardly speculative. In many of its advertisements, the UFT has used the word "fired." Furthermore, the Niemeyer Report bluntly states the UFT motive: "the UFT demanded written charges, thus placing the request for transfers (for which no charges are required) into the realm of dismissal."[39]

Thus, at least by existing standards, the entire due process issue has been from the beginning a myth created by the UFT and swallowed whole by practically everyone. Eventually, McCoy yielded to the pressure to bring charges. As a final irony, it must be noted that, in exonerating the teachers of the charges, trial examiner Francis E. Rivers noted in his opinion that:

Perhaps if the unit administrator [McCoy] had sent to the superintendent of schools a simple request to transfer the teachers, without assigning any supporting charges, he (the superintendent) may have been able to do so without a hearing by virtue of article II, section 101.1 of the bylaws of the Board of Education.[40]

Which is, of course, precisely what McCoy had done.

It is by now not difficult to guess what the motives were behind the game being played by the central board and the UFT. The Niemeyer Report makes it clear: "Under normal circumstances

[38] Bylaws, article II, section 101.1.
[39] Niemeyer Report, p. 94.
[40] Report and Recommendations of Special Trial Examiner, Board of Education, City of New York, Administrative Hearing into Complaints of Rhody A. McCoy, p. 5.

the demonstration project might have been able to accomplish the transfer of "unsatisfactory" personnel informally, but a larger struggle was being waged in the New York State Legislature over a general proposal to decentralize the entire school system."[41]

For almost precisely at the time that the UFT decided to create the due process myth, UFT representatives were in Albany lobbying against community control. It certainly seems abundantly clear that the due process issue as used by the UFT was nothing but a smoke screen behind which the effort to discredit and destroy community control could go on.

The Future

It is clear that under present standards, the superintendent of schools has the power to transfer teachers without due process. If the superintendent's powers are transferred to unit administrators under decentralization, as they should have been in the experimental districts, then the unit administrator would have the power to transfer teachers without due process. *There is no question that under present standards, the United Federation of Teachers created the due process issue out of thin air.*

But, in looking toward the future, the New York Civil Liberties Union urges the adoption of stricter standards than those that exist today. We admit that whoever the administrator is, he ought to have the flexibility to transfer personnel administratively. But we also know that in many instances this power is used punitively. And since the Ocean Hill–Brownsville board admits that at least four of the teachers it wished transferred were guilty of "opposing openly the demonstration project,"[42] the power to transfer appears to have been used punitively in Ocean Hill–Brownsville.

We cannot condone such action. We insist that those who exercise power do so with full respect for due process of law and the right to dissent. "Due process of law" is not a mere technicality unrelated to the substance of power. On the contrary, it goes to the very heart of the procedures by which free men regulate their affairs. Freedom is truly indivisible; if the Ocean Hill–Brownsville dispute proves anything, it proves that unless decisions are made and disputes resolved through fair, honest, and equitable pro-

41 Niemeyer Report, p. 95.
42 Trial Examiner's Report, p. 4. See footnote 40.

cedures that respect individual rights, everyone will suffer. We are firmly and unbendingly committed to this view.

But we are also committed to the view that, while fair procedures are necessary, they are not sufficient. The main goals of decentralization must be to provide black and Puerto Rican children with equal access to quality education and black and Puerto Rican parents with equal access to the process of making decisions that affect their children's lives.

As of now, the Board of Education's decentralization plan makes no mention at all of specific grounds for transfer. Standards for evaluating teacher performance in ghetto schools must be spelled out specifically and known in advance by administrators, teachers, and parents. If such standards are not set, we can expect to see charges made against teachers by local boards that, even if substantiated, will be considered illegitimate by the central board on appeal. Fair procedures will be useless if what those procedures are supposed to determine is irrelevant.

The achievement of those goals may well inconvenience many of us. Teachers and administrators may have to be transferred for reasons that seem to them improper or unusual. Yet it is entirely possible that a teacher may be competent to teach in a white, middle-class school and incompetent to teach in a black or Puerto Rican ghetto school. Recent studies have clearly shown, for example, that a student's achievement is directly related to his teacher's expectations. The effect of teacher expectations of the academic achievement of black and Puerto Rican children thus appears to be a crucial factor in assessing the effectiveness of ghetto schools.[43] It may be necessary, therefore, to re-evaluate the criteria for transfers to include the legitimate grievances of ghetto communities. If teachers who are otherwise competent are ineffective with black or Puerto Rican children, then perhaps such ineffectiveness should be seen as a legitimate reason for transfer to another school.

In order to avoid chaos in the future of the sort that we have suffered in the recent past while proceeding with decentralization, NYCLU calls upon the Board of Education to take the following steps:

1. Make the adoption of a plan for effective community control its first priority. Such a plan should precisely set forth the powers

[43] Robert Rosenthal and Lenore F. Jacobsen, "Teacher Expectations for the Disadvantaged," *Scientific American* (April, 1968).

and responsibilities of local governing boards and the rights of administrators, teachers, and students.

2. Spell out the criteria for transfer and expand such criteria to include standards of effectiveness and establish, for the first time, standards of due process for punitive transfers.

3. Appoint an educational ombudsman to serve as an independent office of review of all local and central board decisions under decentralization. The ombudsman, who must have impeccable credentials of integrity and impartiality, should have the power to receive complaints from students, teachers, administrators, or parents. He should have the power to subpoena witnesses, inspect records, and hold hearings. His powers of action, however, should be limited to recommendation and publicity. In view of the dishonesty and duplicity that characterized the recent dispute, an office of ombudsman would seem to be a useful mechanism to provide the public with independent information and analysis.

If the due process standards suggested above are clearly spelled out for the future, all legitimate fears of the UFT should be ended. If the powers and responsibilities of local boards are clearly spelled out for the future, then all legitimate fears of the local communities should be ended.

Finally, we suggest that intensive meetings be held with representatives of the three local experimental districts, the UFT, the central board, and such civic organizations as the NAACP, the UPA, the Citizens Committee for Children, and NYCLU to work out standards for due process *and* community control. We need a massive act of good faith on the part of all parties to the dispute. Certainly we have had enough bad faith to last a century. How long must we continue to "wade up to our eyes in blood"?

VIEWPOINTS

The Freedom to Teach /
AD HOC COMMITTEE TO DEFEND THE RIGHT TO TEACH

The terrible conflict in the New York City public school system is a matter of grave concern to us all. The turmoil and tensions generated in recent days threaten severe damage to the education of children. Moreover, they endanger the very fabric of community in New York City.

If catastrophe is to be averted, we believe that the real issues of this dispute must be clearly understood.

Decentralization is *not* the issue. Decentralization of the city schools is under way. The United Federation of Teachers has pledged its full cooperation to make the reorganization succeed and to make whatever modifications it deems necessary through the democratic legislative process.

The real issue now is job security. It is the right not to be fired arbitrarily by your employer because he doesn't like the color of your skin, or the way you wear your hair, or the political opinion you hold.

It is the right to a contract that protects the interests of both the employer and the employee—not a contract that can be violated or torn up by the employer whenever he feels like it.

It is the right to due process on the job. If an employee is to be fired, he is entitled to a list of specific reasons, and he is entitled to answer the charges against him. If those charges are dismissed by a court of law, he has the right to be reinstated.

It is the right of freedom from harassment, intimidation, and violent assault on the job. Which of us goes to work every day expecting anything less?

These are not subtle or disputable rights. They are elementary.

THIS ADVERTISEMENT appeared in *The New York Times* and the *Daily News* on September 20, 1968. Co-chairmen of the Ad Hoc Committee were Michael Harrington and Tom Kahn, and the address given was 112 East 19th Street, New York City.

They are enjoyed as a matter of course by every worker who belongs to a union. Incalculable sacrifice has gone into securing these rights, and the struggle continues to extend them to every citizen regardless of race, color, or creed.

These rights were to be protected under decentralization. But then, on May 9, 1968, ten teachers in the Ocean Hill–Brownsville district were fired by the local governing board. The vague charges against them were subsequently dismissed by Judge Francis E. Rivers. The local governing board refused to abide by this decision, and a city-wide teachers' strike was the result.

The strike was seemingly ended after two days when Mayor Lindsay promised that the teachers would be allowed to return to their duties. When school opened the following day, however, the teachers, including more than 100 others who had supported them, were barred from entering the schools by groups of shouting, shoving "community representatives" with the obvious support of the local board. Because of these incredible events, the union had to call the teachers out again.

There is good reason to doubt that these "community representatives" are in fact representatives of the Ocean Hill–Brownsville community. Their core appears to be a group of 50 to 100 individuals who turn up at one school after another throughout the city to harass and intimidate teachers.

Some people have urged the UFT, in the interest of peace, to yield on this issue. We believe that they fail to understand that more than a matter of abstract principle is at stake. The future of teacher unionism is at stake and so is the very governability of New York City.

We believe that the UFT is correct in perceiving that if the ten teachers of Ocean Hill–Brownsville can be fired without cause, teachers' rights and union membership will be eroded in one decentralized school district after another. It happens, for various reasons, that this problem has arisen first in the ghettos, but it can spread to predominately white areas, where local reactionary forces will attack black and white teachers who hold liberal political and racial views. We notice that these forces have not spoken out against the Ocean Hill–Brownsville events. They are eagerly waiting in the wings for *their* turn.

This danger is understood by black and white teachers alike— which explains their strong solidarity in the most effective strike in teacher union history.

The destruction of the UFT would mean placing teachers at the mercy of local groups throughout the city. It would mean liquidation of the most effective organized force for improved quality education.

It is precisely this concern for quality education—the absence of which in the ghettos and *barrios* of New York has been scandalously documented again and again—that motivates our strong support for both parent participation and teacher unionism. We know that genuine parent participation and teacher unionism will *both* collapse if the freedom to teach and the freedom to learn are snuffed out by mob rule.

If this happens, it would mean that in New York City relatively small groups of demagogues and self-appointed community vigilantes can make and break people, institutions and laws—and do so with the frightened or politically calculated acquiescence of the city administration.

We urge Mayor Lindsay not to allow this to happen. And we support the United Federation of Teachers in its determination that it shall not happen.

Ad Hoc Committee on Confusion / NAT HENTOFF

It's all perfectly clear. There's only one reason the UFT has been on strike—"The Freedom to Teach." That's the title of a nearly full-page ad in the September 20 *Times* sponsored by the Ad Hoc Committee to Defend the Right to Teach, 112 East 19th Street. Co-chairmen of this instantaneous committee are Michael Harrington and Tom Kahn. It's a rather awkward title they chose for the committee. Why not call it the League for Industrial Democracy? That used to be a grand old name. Anyway, there are twenty-five signatories of the ad. Most are prominent intellectuals, men of independent judgment. How they are able to support the remarkably simplistic language of this document is inexplicable to me. And that language is worth examining.

"The real issue now is job security," we are instructed. This

REPRINTED FROM *The Village Voice*, September 26, 1968, by permission of the author.

strike is all about due process. Nothing more. Let me say again, as one who spends some time on the affairs of the New York Civil Liberties Union, that there is no question in my mind that the ten teachers were not given due process. But to claim that this is the sole reason for the strike and to sign a document that makes the UFT appear to be virtuous innocents in this battle puts the signatories in a strange position. It is as if they have all just returned from a five-year space flight.

This is what they signed: "Decentralization is *not* the issue. Decentralization of the city schools is under way. The United Federation of Teachers has pledged its full cooperation to make the reorganization succeed and to make whatever modifications it deems necessary through the democratic legislative process."

As if the UFT has not been trying to kill real decentralization in each of the three experimental districts. As if the UFT has evidenced the slightest comprehension of what real decentralization consists of. In an interview in the September 20 *Times*, Albert Shanker states once more that the hiring and firing of teachers should be done by the central Board of Education under any reorganization of the school system. Would anyone of the signatories tell us how decentralization is possible under that condition?

This strike was called because a blunder by the Ocean Hill–Brownsville governing board gave the UFT a chance, it thought, to fully discredit community control not only in Brooklyn but in the IS 201 and Two Bridges districts.

Again, it is one thing to sign a statement affirming the right to due process, but to ignore the total context of the dispute is an extraordinary action.

They also back this statement: "There is good reason to doubt that these 'community representatives' are in fact representatives of the Ocean Hill–Brownsville community. Their core appears to be a group of 50 to 100 individuals who turn up at one school after another throughout the city to harass and intimidate teachers." A serious charge. How many of the twenty-five signatories checked out the facts, or do they simply support on faith this incredible misreading of the feeling in ghetto communities?

The signatories tell us, in addition, that there is "strong solidarity" between black and white teachers "in the most effective strike in teacher union history."

How do they explain the organization of the Black Caucus within the UFT, a caucus which has accused Shanker of "calling a strike against the community"? An organizer of that caucus is Richard Parrish, assistant treasurer of UFT, whose labor credentials are impeccable. How do they explain the opposition to the strike by most of the young white teachers in the Ocean Hill–Brownsville and IS 201 districts? Not only the entirely new teachers, but those at 201 who have now had some experience in working within an actually decentralized situation? Intimidation is Shanker's explanation. Since they have already put themselves on the line in this ad, why don't the signatories go up to 201 and talk to the white teachers there who have been working throughout the strike?

Nor is there any mention in the "Freedom to Teach" ad of the need to define the criteria of teachers' performance so that due process does not mean the continued retention of teachers who have failed in the classroom. This is going to be an essential issue in the battles to come, and I would hope these signatories, having come into the battle, will address themselves to *that* problem. Because it is crucial. A teacher may be perfectly decent and not a racist but unable to reach black and Puerto Rican kids. How do you transfer him under due process? I suggest the signatories consider this report by Fred Hechinger in the September 9 *Times*: "Quite apart from the current dispute, the fact is that in a recent five-year period only twelve teachers with tenure were removed for reasons other than retirement or resignation. In a system of 60,000 teachers, this indicates a low degree of quality control, especially since there is no effective system of probationary weeding out."

Has the UFT ever expressed concern with this problem of quality control for those of its members who have achieved tenure, for those of its members who have failed to educate black and Puerto Rican children year after year and cannot be removed in due process under present regulations?

Shanker himself continues to talk as if there were no Harlem street academies, as if Herbert Kohl (*36 Children*) and Larry Cole of LEAP had never existed. He keeps quoting the Coleman Report (*Times*, September 20) to underline his own self-fulfilling prophecies about who can be educated: "The influencing factors on children's achievements," he said, "appear to be 'the socio-economic class of the parents' and 'the amount of integration in a classroom.'" What about the quality of the teachers? They're "inadequately trained," Shanker says. As if attitude and expectation were not central to performance. Let me emphasize again what time spent in most ghetto schools will tell any of the signatories—there are many teachers in those schools who are trained but wrong, harmfully wrong, for the children in those schools. Is the Ad Hoc Committee to Defend the Right to Teach going to continue to be involved in school affairs and work on setting up criteria of performance, or was this just a one-shot to help the cause of trade unionism?

In a letter (*New York Post*, September 17), John E. Traube, UFT chapter chairman and UFT chairman, District 5, writes of community activists: "It is further distressing to us to see these same people join in an effort to break the union by crossing picket lines and attempt to keep the schools open in spite of the knowledge that no real education can go on in a school without the presence of licensed teachers." How much "real knowledge" is absorbed in New York schools when all the members of the UFT, including the fully licensed ones, are at work? A recent report by the Lincoln Hospital/Albert Einstein College of Medicine Mental Health Services discloses that a survey of fifty-three public schools in the South Bronx ghetto shows that 83.5 per cent or 26,624 of 31,871 students scored below their grade level in reading. The schools have an enrollment of 59 per cent Puerto Rican and 37 per cent black. Furthermore, "a far greater ratio of ghetto students are further behind in number of years than non-ghetto students. For example, of those tested in the eighth and ninth grades, six ghetto students were found four or more years behind for every one student in the non-ghetto schools."

Is it the license he has or the nature of the teacher that helps explain those scores? Of course, there are other factors—overcrowding, inadequate budget, et cetera. But Shanker and his distillation of the Coleman Report notwithstanding, ghetto children *can* learn if teachers are convinced they can learn. In the unlikely event the Ocean Hill–Brownsville experimental district is at peace for the next two years, I would expect a substantial rise in achievement in those schools because of the staff that has been there from the beginning of this school year. I have no idea how many of them are fully licensed, and I don't think it matters in view of their attitude toward the children.

By the way, the twenty-five signatories attack in the ad what they term "relatively small groups of demagogues." Have they anything to say about Shanker's public statements of the past two years, in particular his deliberate use of the specter of anti-Semitism? Yes, there is some, but anti-Semitism is not a substantive

issue. Even Arnold Forster of the Anti-Defamation League, otherwise unaware of the total context of the strike, admitted that on
Channel 13's "Newsfront" last week. And as Nancy Hicks of the
New York Post (September 19) and others have pointed out, 70
per cent of the teachers who have been working in the Ocean
Hill–Brownsville district during the strike are white, and of them
50 per cent are Jewish.

Now let's get back to due process. The twenty-five signatories
have signed an ad which asserts the UFT's high, consistent concern with due process. There is no indication of their awareness
that the UFT's concern with this fundamental principle is rather
late in its manifestation. There have been many cases in the city
schools in which due process has been denied students—the handling of "disruptive" children, political and other demonstrations,
the right to leaflet. Where has the UFT been?

A reader writes: "In the white neighborhood where I live, the
junior high school teachers—all white—picketed boldly. Last year
when my daughters sought to organize a peace march they were
forbidden and threatened by administration and teachers and told
'They had no right to do this on school time.' So my daughter rode
over on her bike and faced one of the picketing teachers with this.
He said, 'Well I was wrong last year.' " There are civil libertarians
on that list of signatories. Mike Harrington is one of them. Perhaps they might discuss the entire issue of due process for students
with the UFT and stimulate the UFT to support due process for
everybody. In the months ahead, the issue of civil liberties for
students in the public schools is going to be unprecedented in
scope and degree. Where will the UFT be?

Another element in the due process issue is the whole question
—which is currently being researched—of the degree and con-
sistency of concern the UFT has shown in certain principals' transfers of teachers, and due process in the transfer procedure in general.
Do the twenty-five signatories have the knowledge to state so surely
that this intense effort now by the UFT to focus on due process in
Ocean Hill–Brownsville can be considered without reference to
decentralization? ("Decentralization is *not* the issue," says the ad.)

Again, I consider it impossible to deny that due process is indeed
an issue here, but I am astonished that these twenty-five men permitted their names to be used for a statement which does not
present the entire context and thereby distorts rather than clarifies.
I asked one of the signers about this. He answered: "It's proper

to take one issue at a time." I don't know what he means by "proper," but it is unreal to approach the battle of the schools without discussing all the pertinent issues simultaneously.

Let's go back to last May when this particular stage of the battle became so intensified in the Ocean Hill–Brownsville district. A statement was issued at the time by the Brooklyn chapter of the American Civil Liberties Union, and I would hope the twenty-five signatories will read that statement and then contrast it with what they signed:

> Due process under law is the bulwark of the rights of individuals in a free society. Just laws and the capacity of the people to change laws which no longer serve them well are the foundations upon which a popular respect for due process is built. The protection of the rights of employes of the Board of Education under existing laws may be the first line of defense of the rights of future employes which may vest under new laws. But it is abundantly clear that the existing laws under which present rights have accrued do not achieve the educational conditions which best serve the people of the communities in Ocean Hill and Brownsville in Brooklyn.

"Having agreed to experimental efforts in behalf of the decentralization of the schools in these communities," the Brooklyn chapter of the ACLU continued,

> it is an obligation of the Board of Education and the United Federation of Teachers to honor the spirit as well as the letter of that to which they have agreed. Where present law must be changed to achieve the experimental goals, the enactment of new laws promptly is the soundest way to insure due process for and the protection of the vested rights of the employes of the board and the members of the UFT.
>
> It is unfortunate that effective steps have yet to be taken to terminate the ambiguous and confused administrative conditions fostered by the Board of Education in the school districts designated "experimental" in the pursuit of decentralization. We urge that such steps be taken now.

Nothing changed from May to September to make the Ocean Hill–Brownsville governing board feel any less besieged or in a less ambiguous position. There has been much talk of trust. I ask the twenty-five signatories: If you can project yourselves into being members of that governing board, would you trust the UFT? Would you believe that all the UFT is concerned about is due process?

While you're role playing, I also call to your attention this statement by a group of UFT members who have refused to support the strike:

Although the UFT claims to fight for improved education—for smaller class sizes, remedial and psychological services, et cetera— it has consistently compromised on the basic educational issues as it has not consistently compromised on the issue of salaries. The union poses as the defender of minority rights, but it refused to support the integration boycott. While the union claims to be fighting for quality education for all, it has neither recognized nor defended the civil liberties of students. Although the union claims that it favors decentralization, it sent a contingent to Albany to kill any measures that supported local control. . . . The UFT leadership has not provided intelligent and responsible leadership that might have drained the color out of the school issue. When the union inflames racial tensions and places teachers in opposition to community aspirations, when it denies parents recourse against its pose of infallibility, and when Shanker calls community members diseased and criminal elements, the union drives the community to desperate acts and makes a climate for due process impossible.

I don't feel due process can ever be abandoned, no matter what the climate, but to sign a statement which ignores the climate— and the role of the UFT in creating that climate—is to be of no use at all to anybody. Except perhaps the UFT. And I ask the twenty-five signatories that if they are not wholly uncritical of the UFT, this is the time for them to say so and to work on ways in which due process can apply to everybody involved in the schools. And to recognize that the corollary of the freedom to teach is that schools have to be accountable to the communities in which they exist.

If the UFT remains resistant to real decentralization, I see only three eventual likelihoods. The UFT will become a nearly all-white union in constant battle with community boards. Or, as more young whites and more black people become teachers, they will gather the strength to end city-wide bargaining and have each local bargain with each board. Or they will gather the strength to create another union which will win bargaining rights away from the UFT.

The twenty-five who signed that ad are correct, in my view, that the ten teachers did not get due process; but when they go on to say that "the UFT is the most effective organized force for improved quality education," the burden of proof is on them. And it's a huge burden, getting huger all the time. There are many more than "50 to 100 individuals" who believe quite the opposite. Not only black people and Puerto Ricans, but whites, including many of the new young white teachers entering the system. They believe the Board of Education is changing; the level of expectation of new teachers is changing; and that leaves the UFT and its new allies, the Council of Supervisory Associations, as the primary organized obstacles to improved quality education in this city.

That is also an issue. And the twenty-five signers didn't say one word about it.

The Freedom to Teach: Beyond the Panaceas / MICHAEL HARRINGTON

In the ghetto schools of New York there are poor children whose very desire to learn is subverted by the school system. That would have been a tragedy at any point in this country's history, but it has become even more unconscionable in this age of advancing technology. For since economic opportunity increasingly is a function of education, these innocents are effectively being sentenced in childhood to adult lives of poverty and despair.

That is the huge intolerable fact, the reality which confronts the twenty-five signatories of the "Freedom to Teach" ad, which I helped initiate, and Nat Hentoff, who criticized us in the last issue of *The Voice*. In replying to Hentoff it will be necessary to take up some specific charges he made. However, my main purpose is not to make debater's points but to illuminate some heartbreaking,

REPRINTED FROM *The Village Voice*, October 3, 1968, by permission of the author.

impossible problems which must be solved at once. In the process I assume the *bona fides* of Nat and the twenty-five signatories and assume that we share a common concern—the lives and minds of impoverished children whom the society grievously wrongs—but have significant differences on how to proceed.

I shall not, therefore, attempt an item-by-item refutation of Hentoff's critique. And I shall certainly not attack the idea of decentralization, for I am for it. I am, however, against the decentralization panaceas; the various "radical" plans which would formally institutionalize segregation *and* inferior schooling; the theories which charge that it is the callous, unconsciously racist teacher who is responsible for the systematic economic, social, and political iniquities which a slum visits upon its children. And yet I honestly hope that I—and though I cannot speak for them, the other signatories of the "Freedom to Teach ad—will be able to work with Hentoff, with parents in the community, and with others who seek a really workable, democratic transformation of education in New York.

But first, a technical matter which must be set straight for the record. Why, Nat asks, did we not sign the ad in the name of the League for Industrial Democracy? ("That used to be a grand old name," he adds, in an unworthy ironic aside which suggests that we were hiding something.) The reason is simple: the LID did not sponsor, nor endorse, the statement. The initiators and some of the signatories are associated with the League; quite a few of the signers are not. We took the honorable, straightforward tack of an ad hoc committee precisely because we did not want to limit ourselves to, or commit, a particular organization.

I am sure that Nat has been on an ad hoc committee or two; I am puzzled that he makes this an issue. Moreover, I should make it clear that, in what follows, I speak for myself, not for the LID or the signatories to the ad. Now let me turn to the substantive issues.

Hentoff chides us for saying that "the real issue is job security" and that decentralization is not basic to the strike. He holds that we have no right to pick on the isolated question of due process— that teachers were arbitrarily fired—and affirms that we had a positive responsibility to deal with the total context of the conflict.

There is a strike at this writing (Sunday). It has closed the schools and exacerbated racial tension in New York City to a terrifying degree. It has turned unionists and some black and

Puerto Rican parents into antagonists when the only real hope for educational reform lies in a united front of organized teachers and parents. It is in the interests of practically everyone that the strike be resolved. There is one issue which prevents this resolution. It is not the question of decentralization in any way, shape, or form. The strike will end when, and only when, the due process guarantees provided for teachers under the Bundy Plan, the Regents' proposed law, the existing law, and affirmed by the mayor's office are observed.

A bit of chronology might make this point even more clear.

The teachers whom the local board in Brooklyn did not want could have been quietly transferred. The Board of Education, as Jason Epstein, an enthusiastic champion of decentralization, recounted the incident in the *New York Review of Books*,

> would get the teachers out of the neighborhood if the local board did not also insist that it was within the right of any community to fire and hire teachers at its own discretion, a right which clearly conflicted with the principles of collective bargaining and job security on which not only the UFT but unionism itself depend. The decision by the local board to elevate the conflict to the point where the UFT was left with no choice but to intervene on behalf of its general membership was anything but whimsical [emphasis added].

The basic purpose of the local board, then, was not to free children from the alleged incompetence of certain teachers, but to assert a right to fire without statutorally mandated due process. It was thus Mr. McCoy and company, not the signatories to the ad, who abstracted this problem from the over-all context.

When school was to begin, the union struck on this, and other issues. That dispute was resolved, and the teachers went back to work. Demonstrators in Ocean Hill–Brownsville used physical force and threats to veto the agreement and did so with the tacit, moral support of the local board. It was at this point that the second strike began and there was one, and only one, matter in bitter contention: the question of job security and due process. To quote Epstein again: "the Brooklyn group had obviously decided not to await the orderly transfer of power which the new board promised" (the central board of education with Lindsay's new majority). In citing Epstein, I should make it clear that he does not share my interpretation of the facts.

Now under these circumstances, where there is a single unre-solved dispute which keeps schools closed, I think it proper and quite responsible for twenty-five individuals with a long record of concern for the problems of ghetto education to make a clear state-ment on the decisive issue. None of us were, I am sure, unaware of the complicated chain of causation which led up to the impasse, but the local board itself had made the question of due process overriding. And Nat's insinuation that we were involved in "a one-shot to help the cause of trade unionism" is hardly fair to people who have been politicking, picketing, speaking, and writing to get decent education for all for years.

So due process is the issue, and Nat agrees with us at least on the rights and wrongs on that count.

But then, why don't we have a heart? Why doesn't the union, whose members are after all more privileged than the children of the ghetto, magnanimously concede on this point? There are two relevant answers. First, as Epstein rightly observed, the conflict is over "principles of collective bargaining and job security on which not only the UFT but unionism itself depend." A union which cannot defend the job rights of its members, particularly when they are theoretically protected both by law and a binding contract with the employer, will simply cease to exist.

Second, and more important, the right of an organized minority to annul public, democratic agreements by the threat or use of physical force is inimical to democracy itself and particularly to those in the society who have the least *force majeure* in the long run: the poor, whether black or white. If vigilantism can triumph in Ocean Hill–Brownsville today for organized black powerites, it can win for reactionaries or fascists on Staten Island or in Queens tomorrow. This is particularly important in a year when there is a fascistic leader who coyly advocates violence by deploring it (that is what George Wallace was doing when he said that, unless the police contain and control "anarchy and violence," "you are going to have a movement that's not going to be on the left. It's going to be on the other side and it's going to stop all of this").

Hentoff is disturbed that the ad mentioned the professional militancy of some of the people involved in the unilateral, forceful abrogation of the collective-bargaining agreement. He asks if we checked out the charge. I did. I am convinced that there are many minority group parents sincerely, honestly concerned; I am sure that many more have come to support the local board since the strike began because of the general racial polarization which has taken place. I am also convinced that there are demagogues, confrontationists, and street pols involved who care less for the children and more for the issue. But beyond my own impressions, there are some elements of hard data. In June, the Board of Education released a poll of the Center for Urban Education showing that a majority of parents in Bedford-Stuyvesant were not for the community right to hire teachers and principals; there have been petitions in the Ocean Hill–Brownsville area calling for new elections and challenging the representative character of the old; and there have been PTAs at variance with local board leaders.

But even if the board represented the community 100 per cent, even if there were no questions, that would not provide an excuse for the violent veto of public policy. Indeed, it is a paradox that, unless the UFT prevails on the due process point, there will be no decentralization. For if the destruction of the union and the affirmation of the sovereign power of an organized group in a given neighborhood are the pre-condition of decentralization, it will never take place. As Fred Hechinger wrote in the September 29 *Times*, the Ocean Hill–Brownsville tactic has already threatened the entire future of decentralization. It is the local board, not the union, which endangers reform.

In short, the due process issue is not simply a matter of union self-interest (it certainly is that) but of the profound common interest of a democratic society committed to nonviolent change. And if there is a general breakdown and disputes are settled by superior force in the streets, the repressive forces of this society—including the police—are much better prepared for the moment than the poor, the Black Panthers included.

Finally, I would like to make a few comments on the more basic point of the decentralization panacea.

The union has a long history of fighting for quality education, as in its struggle for More Effective Schools. It has also defended the civil liberties of its own critics, as when it fought for the job rights of Ralph Poynter, a black separatist. It has not been perfect —I think it overemphasized its criticisms of decentralization to the detriment of its advocacy of it when the issue was first raised— but I believe that its actions on this issue have been basically motivated by a concern for children. For it is not, to my mind, a proved fact that centralization is the fundamental cause of, and decentralization the decisive remedy for, the fantastic inadequacies

of schooling in the slums. That proposition has reactionary implications which the union rightly challenged.

The most effective advocates of decentralization were originally
upper-class Republicans like Bundy and Lindsay. (More generally,
Epstein refers to a coalition between well-off New Yorkers who
send their children to private schools and the racial minorities.)
At times, I think that the social class origins of the extreme-
panacea versions of the idea are not without significance.

From the day he took office to this very moment, John Lindsay
has not once given the slightest hint that he has any sympathy for,
or understanding of, unionisn. He has botched every negotiation
he has handled, in part because he is so obviously contemptuous
of organized workers. He is capable of a charismatic relationship
to the underorganized ghetto, but not of any on-going participation
in collective bargaining. Indeed, when he confronts blacks and
Puerto Ricans as union members, his compassion relaxes.

I am not, therefore, surprised that Lindsay would like a program
which threatens the very existence of the union. More broadly,
and less on an individual level, it is not a shock to me that some
sophisticated Republicans esteem an analysis of the problem of
slum education which requires changing administrative structures.
That approach avoids the uncomfortable point that there must be
a social investment of billions of dollars in physical plant, in up-
grading facilities, and, above all, in replacing the tenements with
decent housing, both in New York and in new towns around the
country. WASPdom, I am suggesting, does not mind being radical
(a) so long as it does not involve a massive expenditure of dollars
in a democratic fashion, and (b) if the program is carried out
through *noblesse oblige* rather than collective bargaining.

I think Nat Hentoff is, in part at least, taken in by this ploy.
Talking of the incredibly low levels of education in the ghetto,
Nat asks, "Is it the license he has or the nature of the teacher
that helps to explain those scores? Of course, there are other factors—overcrowding, inadequate budget, et cetera. But Shanker and
his distillation of the Coleman Report notwithstanding, ghetto
children *can* learn if teachers are convinced they can learn." The
"other factors" are the massive social and economic determinants
which impinge upon the daily life of the slum. And, in essence, the
insensitive teacher is made the scapegoat for the organized system
of injustice which the society imposes upon the poor.

Now I think there are such inadequate teachers—and some time ago the union proposed an independent civilian review board with power to remove them—but they are only a part, and not the most important part, of an outrage built into the very structures of our late capitalist society (I tried to document this statement in *Toward a Democratic Left*). I am sorry to see Nat, and others on the left, adopt this conservative angle of vision because of their sincere, genuine passion to change the schools.

A case in point is Jason Epstein. In his *New York Review* article, Epstein essentially accepts a Milton Friedman "free market" solution in which, in essence, vouchers are given to school districts to bid competitively for teachers and education (that is Epstein's Friedmanesque interpretation of the current decentralization scheme). But, without going into the dreary economic documentation, doesn't everyone know that this pretended equality of sovereign consumers—or school districts—in a supposedly "free" market is, and always has been, a rationalization for the actual inequality of the real world? But more specifically, in the long run, public schools in middle-class and wealthy areas would, under such a system, purchase better segregated education with public funds because they are economically, politically, and socially stronger than poor schools. That trend might be initially offset, or even somewhat modified, by the tendency of idealistic middle-class youth to go to the poorest districts precisely because of their poverty, but, given the absence of the massive social investments and changes which are required, money would eventually, as it always does, out.

But in saying this, I am not arguing against decentralization. I am for decentralization because I indeed believe that there is a scleriotic bureaucracy which bears at least part of the responsibility for the present crisis, and I am for opening up new channels of innovation and popular participation. But there can be no decentralization in New York City based on breaking the union; there can be no effective decentralization apart from a long-range program to end the slums.

Most of the decentralization panaceaists are, like Nat Hentoff, devoted partisans of social justice. But it should give them pause that a George Wallace has similar ideas about local control in order to build white power, or that the economics of their scheme can be so easily reconciled with the theories of Barry Goldwater's old adviser Milton Friedman. For I do not think that segregation and "free" market competition are the answers to our educational crisis. And I believe that both principles are unwittingly, and for the best of reasons, implicit in the more extreme versions of community control of the schools.

When the strike is over, there is going to be an enormous task of reconciliation and reconstruction. I believe that the decentralization which I advocate—and, as I understand the matter, it roughly corresponds to what the union has in mind—is not that distant from Hentoff's position. Democratic community participation through due process in districts large enough to be integrated and politically diverse is a positive good, and I hope that many of the men and women of good will who are on different sides in this bitter conflict—organized teachers, community, and public as a whole—will be able to work together to that end.

It would indeed be sad if, as Hechinger wrote in the September 29 *Times*, the actions of the local board drove their honest critics into the reactionary camp of "law and order." All of us, in this fearful year, must fight that.

The Unschooling of New York's Children / MAURICE R. BERUBE

New York City's teacher strike may prove to be a watershed in the black struggle over control of urban schools. The strike reflected the fear of leaders of the UFT, the most vigorous opponent of community control, that school decentralization is inevitable.

Last spring, few would have thought so. New York's state legislature, under UFT pressure, discarded the Bundy and Regents plans for decentralization. Instead, the legislature empowered a hostile city school board to try its hand at devising a decentralization scheme for consideration at the spring session. Careful not to humiliate fellow Republican Mayor John Lindsay, sponsor of the strong plans, the legislature permitted the mayor to increase the city board from nine to thirteen members. Despite this token gesture, the odds were heavily against a repeat performance of last spring's bitter school decentralization battle.

REPRINTED FROM *Commonweal*, October 25, 1968, by permission of the author and Commonweal Publishing Co., Inc.

But by summer's end all had changed. After Miami, Mayor Lindsay was no longer worried over jeopardizing a national reputation for keeping the racial peace. The mayor let it be known through an exclusive interview on the front page of *The New York Times* that he considered community control of the schools to be the "Number 1 tension in our poor neighborhoods" and the first order of business this year.

It took the unexpected to give the mayor his chance to make good on his new determination. Two key resignations tipped the balance of control of the city school board to the Lindsay forces. When Board of Education President Alfred Giardino, an implacable foe of decentralization, quit in despair and disgust, the anti-decentralization forces of the "old" board were left with a mere one vote advantage (one "old" board member had joined the Lindsay camp). The turning point came when Clarence Senior, finding it difficult to honor his board commitments, surprised everyone by resigning. The Lindsay people were now in command.

They wasted little time in giving a preview of what may come. Early in September, the "new" board transferred sweeping powers, in an "interim" plan, to the thirty existent local school boards and to the three experimental "decentralized" boards. Each local board would possess powers over personnel, budget, and curriculum—pending approval of the interim plan by the state Regents. Except for the fact that the thirty local boards had been previously appointed (in the three experiments, however, parents had elected governing boards), New York City's schools were decentralized and under community control. No doubt this interim plan will furnish the basis for the draft to be submitted in mid-December. School decentralization emerges once again as a live option for improving the education of the urban black poor.

And once again the teacher's union, reading the handwriting on the wall, took drastic action. The UFT struck all city schools over the transfer of ten teachers (originally nineteen, but one case was dropped and the other eight decided not to press the matter) from the experimental Ocean Hill–Brownsville district last May and the replacement of some 300 sympathetic strikers. It was a bold gamble that stood the teacher's union the chance of making major contract gains in a nonbargaining year, while thwarting school decentralization.

Technically, the union had no clear-cut case of due process. Under Board of Education bylaws, administrative involuntary transfers are proper and are commonplace; nor did the UFT contract cover involuntary transfers. However, one could overlook the letter of the law in the spirit of giving the teachers the benefit of the doubt. Certainly, if there was no protective clause *there should have been*. And the UFT, mindful of its past negligence in this respect, was anxious to obtain such a clause, now that the prospects for school decentralization were improved.

The union nearly gained all its objectives. After a short two days, the UFT negotiated a settlement, without the Ocean Hill–Brownsville governing board, that returned the teachers, and gave the union the contract guarantee it lacked. All case of involuntary transfers were to be submitted to arbitration; furthermore, the union was to have an agency shop (a condition whereby nonunion members pay a service charge to the bargaining unit whose benefits it enjoys but does not support through membership fees).

The Ocean Hill–Brownsville governing board, having raised the issue of the self-determination of the experimental boards, stood fast, but did not "prevent" the return of the teachers. However, after community activists bitterly protested the teacher's return, the UFT went back on strike and frittered away its hard won gains. Three weeks later the teachers returned, still officially resisted by the local governing board, which felt its integrity violated should it rescind its order transferring the teachers.

The union strategy backfired. Not only did the union fail to extend job protection but the UFT inadvertently provided the three experimental districts with an opportunity to prove themselves. While the rest of the schools were shut down, the ghetto schools in the three districts functioned smoothly for the first time. It is doubtful whether the teachers' union can long maintain its unrivalled power in school affairs. The black ghettos that kept open its public schools successfully challenged that power.

The strike raises some hard questions. Can the gulf separating teachers and parents, whites and blacks, be bridged? If the strike was any indication, the answer may not be hopeful. Clearly, the strike accelerated and crystallized problems to be anticipated later under a decentralized system. How can black parents remove teachers who are detrimental to their children's well-being? How can teachers be assured of job security?

Recent research, along with the firsthand testimony of such former teachers as Jonathan Kozol and Herbert Kohl, attests to the widespread and deleterious effects of self-fulfilling prophecies of middle-class teachers. Too many teachers expect poor, black students to fail, and their expectations influence the performance of the children so that they do fail. It is this low opinion teachers have of black children that infuriates ghetto parents. They feel that bad teaching can be corrected much easier than the more nebulous effects of poverty. And when one considers that only twelve teachers out of a staff of 60,000 were dismissed in the last five years in New York schools, one can understand the anxiety of ghetto parents for community control.

The conflict in New York has national implication. Already, urban school decentralization movements have begun in various states, notably New Jersey and Michigan. And the parent body of the UFT, the American Federation of Teachers, finds itself racially split over school decentralization. In pitting itself against the desires of the black community for self-determination the UFT alienated all of its black leaders who supported the Ocean Hill governing board rather than their union. In contrast, the Washington teacher's union, predominantly black, endorses community control.

But the AFT, at last summer's convention, elected a former UFT organizer, David Selden, as its president, on a platform disavowing community control and merely advocating "increased parent participation" in the schools. Selden's opponent was a black caucus candidate for strong school decentralization. This is a precarious policy for a union whose strength is in the heavily black urban areas of the nation.

The teacher's union is fighting a desperate, last ditch battle that may destroy it.

An Exchange of Views: Challenge and Reply

Sandra Feldman for the UFT

To the Editors: We were surprised and chagrined to read the report by Maurice Berube on the current school crisis in New

REPRINTED FROM *Commonweal*, December 6, 1968, by permission of the author and Commonweal Publishing Co., Inc.

York. Several points he makes are simply contrary to fact and ought to be corrected.

1. Speaking of the United Federation of Teachers strike, Mr. Berube says: "It was a bold gamble that stood the teachers' union the chance of making major contract gains in a nonbargaining year, while thwarting school decentralization. Technically, the union had no clear-cut case of due process."

First of all, the only demand made regarding the contract was that it be upheld and maintained in a decentralized system. The one extra-contractual demand made was that all dismissals of tenured teachers be subject to outside impartial arbitration, and that was part and parcel of the major issue, which indeed *was* due process. Why did Mr. Berube neglect to mention the decision regarding the ten teachers which had been made by the distinguished Judge Francis Rivers? In a sweeping decision indicting the inept administration of the district, Judge Rivers completely exonerated all ten of the accused teachers.

Some of the teachers had been charged with "expressed opposition" to decentralization. Even if this were true, surely teachers in this day and age have a right to opinions and to the expression of them. But in fact that opposition was never established. Those who made the charges brought forth no witnesses and no evidence to substantiate them.

One teacher was accused of having no control over his class. The children, a letter from an assistant principal asserted, were observed to be throwing chairs around the classroom. But investigation revealed that the chairs and desks in that particular classroom on the date of the alleged observance of the incident were of the stationary sort, fastened to the floor. . . .

One could go on and on with a recitation of the Rivers' decision. But anyone can read it. Mr. Berube should. Mr. Berube certainly knows that the union had always fought the involuntary punitive transfers of teachers, and that, in fact, the arbitrary "termination of services"—as the governing board stated it in the identical letters sent to nineteen people in the middle of a working day, without warning or reason—was completely unprecedented.

Certainly the Board of Education, the mayor of New York, and the New York state commissioner of education agree that there was an issue of due process involved, for all have stated that the disputed teachers belong back in their jobs. Even the New

York Civil Liberties Union said the governing board's action could not be condoned.

2. Mr. Berube states that the union won an "agency shop" as a result of the first strike. This is simply not true. The Board of Education offered the union an agency shop in exchange for the transfer of all of its teachers out of Ocean Hill–Brownsville. The UFT turned that "offer" down.

3. "After community activists bitterly protested the teachers' return, the UFT went back on strike and," says Mr. Berube, "frittered away its hard-won gains." This is a rather simplistic statement of the event which triggered the second strike. On the day that the teachers returned, they entered their schools without difficulty. Only Sonny Carson, chairman of Independent Brooklyn CORE, and a few of his followers were on the steps of JHS 271, and they stepped aside at the request of the police. But Mr. McCoy and the governing board had laid careful plans. The principals made no attempts to assign teaching duties. They waited instead for a call, which came, from Mr. McCoy, summoning the returned teachers to an "orientation" session in the auditorium of IS 55. They were kept there for more than two hours, while Mr. Carson, members of Brooklyn CORE, some governing board members, and a number of young adults filed into the room. They were then subjected to taunts, vilification, verbal abuse (especially the returning black teachers in the group), and threats upon their lives and the lives of the children. The lights in the windowless room were turned off and on while people screamed at them, "You're going out of here in pine boxes." When they returned to their schools after that session, many of them were subjected to the same treatment again. The Board of Education did nothing. The mayor did nothing. And so the union was forced to act again. No union decides to strike easily. The implication that accompanies the words "frittered away" is that what the union did was in some way whimsical. Faced with this kind of threat not only to the job security and dignity but to the very lives of its members on the one hand and the inaction of the Board of Education and Mayor Lindsay on the other hand, the 50,000 teachers of New York City had no other choice.

4. "While the rest of the schools were shut down, the ghetto schools in the three districts functioned smoothly for the first time." First, the district in Ocean Hill–Brownsville was fully staffed with scab teachers who had been hired over the summer to

replace boycotting union teachers. Second, attendance in the district since the firing of the nineteen had been and continues to be down to somewhere between one-third and one-half, and so classes are unusually small. Third, on the first day of the second return, UFT teachers found more often than not their "buddy" teacher was floundering and anxious for help. The more experienced returning teachers began preparing lessons and classroom aids—until non-UFT teachers were called to a separate meeting with the principal. When they emerged, they had stopped talking, stopped fraternizing, stopped asking for help. What does "running smoothly" mean? Schools reduced to half their pupil population because parents are filled with fear and mistrust? Teachers who toe the anti-union line despite their need and desire for advice from more experienced union teachers? Why is it that despite the fact that IS 201 hired its own staff of eighty teachers last September only sixteen returned this September? Could it have something to do with the fact that teachers—teachers "chosen" by the community—are kept so tightly reined they may not dissent under community control? Could it have something to do with the fact that teachers in IS 201 and in the Two Bridges district who are committed to the project but supported the union and struck were "fired" by their local boards?

5. "How can black parents remove teachers who are detrimental to their children's well-being?" So far, none of the decentralization plans gave either this right or very much voice at all to parents. It is the UFT which came up with the only idea that would enable parents to have their complaints against teachers effectively heard. Last spring, our delegate assembly overwhelmingly endorsed the establishment of a "Teacher Review Board" similar to the Civilian Complaint Review Board which had been proposed for the Police Department and which the UFT also supported.

6. Mr. Berube completely mistakes what happened at last summer's AFT convention. It is true that David Selden's opponent was a black caucus candidate who was for, as he puts it, "strong school decentralization." But it is also true that the decentralization position the AFT adopted was carried *unanimously* by the convention after having been amended by Ed Simpkins, the leader of the opposition caucus and supported on the floor of the convention by Albert Shanker.

The actual language, which endorsed "effective community responsibility and involvement through elected representation in the operation of schools in the black, Puerto Rican and other minority communities . . ." was in fact written by Simpkins and supported by his caucus.

The UFT is not opposed to decentralization; the AFT is not split on this issue; and every teacher union in the country is solidly behind the teachers of New York in their present struggle for due process and job security.

Maurice Berube Replies

What has been at stake in the teachers' strike? Nothing less than the future of public education in the nation's cities and race relations in New York City.

I am convinced that Albert Shanker and the United Federation of Teachers are intent on impairing both. Despite the casuistry of union spokesmen, the UFT *is* determined to put an end to the concept of community-controlled schools. And the outcome of the strike will determine what happens in cities throughout the nation who normally follow the New York lead.

Mrs. Feldman, the UFT and its defenders, would have us believe otherwise. According to them, the strike is merely one of insuring due process for teachers. The UFT does not oppose decentralization, just "extremism" and "union-busting." The cry for community control, reactionary in thrust, echoes George Wallace's demand for local state control. In short, the UFT is saving the schools, preserving civil liberties, and steering a moderate racial course.

This is newspeak. The due process issue is a ploy, designed to undermine what the UFT most fears: limiting its power and transferring power to the public—and a black public at that.

The UFT is "for decentralization" in much the same fashion as the backlash Parents and Taxpayers said they were for integration a few years back. The union has ardently campaigned against strong decentralization plans, while "for decentralization," just as PAT opposed busing, school pairings, and education parks, while "for integration." Only recently have school activists discarded the ambiguous term. They now speak of community control to signify the Bundy idea of public power over budget, curriculum, and personnel. And make no mistake about it, the UFT is dead set against community control.

As I thought I made clear in my earlier piece, the union's due process argument developed as an afterthought. No, Mrs. Feldman, read your contract again; no clause provides for involuntary transfers. The UFT gained that in the strike through revising state bylaws. And UFT practice had never been to defend individual teachers on involuntary transfer. As a former UFT staff member, I recall no such defenses (although the union opposed massive transfers of experienced teachers to ghetto schools, another racial matter), and in one instance where I interceded in behalf of an involuntarily transferred teacher I was told that nothing could be done.

The union case rests on establishing a clear-cut violation of due process. They claim that the contract was violated. Not true. They claim that the teachers were fired. Not true. The teachers did not lose their licenses or job rights but were transferred for reassignment elsewhere.

And that was the standard operating procedure. The Ocean Hill–Brownsville board did not do anything out of the ordinary. I wrote my piece before the New York Civil Liberties Union issued its report "condemning the UFT for using due process as a smoke screen to obscure its real goal," to "sabotage community control."

Both the NYCLU and Judge Rivers acknowledged that involuntary transfers were the normal procedure. Rivers: "Perhaps if the unit administrator had sent to the superintendent of schools a simple request to transfer the teachers, without assigning supporting charges, he (the superintendent), may have been able to do so without a hearing by virtue of Article II 101.1 of the bylaws of the Board of Education." Precisely what Rhody McCoy, Ocean Hill–Brownsville administrator, was preparing to do until the UFT and the superintendent requested hearings.

Does that procedure violate due process? I believe so. And I have written to that effect in these pages. So does the NYCLU. Until a predominantly black governing board used this ordinary procedure, however, the UFT had never challenged it. The NYCLU report is emphatic on that point: "Why then did the UFT make such a fuss in this case and insist on due process when it knew that due process was not required under existing procedures? The answer is clear: the UFT demanded due process because it wished to create the impression that the teachers had been fired and because it wished to discredit the local governing board."

It is the familiar white man's tactic of changing the rules of the game when they no longer suit his purpose. As long as white educators transferred teachers, there was no complaint. But let a black governing board try, then, it's time to revise the rules.

Mrs. Feldman is correct in saying that the union did not gain an agency shop (point 2), although it was a bargaining issue. But, the idea for a teacher review board (point 5) came from the American Civil Liberties Union a year and a half ago, and was opposed by Albert Shanker. The plan would siphon off some parental discontent but more far-reaching provisions would still have to be made in state education law.

From all accounts (such as Fred Hechinger of the *Times*, state and national educational leaders), the demonstration school districts displayed an uncommonly enthusiastic educational climate (point 4). Last year the programs were hampered by teacher dissent and the inexperience of the governing boards. In Ocean Hill–Brownsville, at least a half dozen exciting educational programs have been started, including the only use of the Bereiter-Engelmann method in the city and the teaching of Puerto Rican pupils to read first in Spanish.

Although Mrs. Feldman admits of the black caucus opposition in the AFT for strong school decentralization, she fudges over the divisions within the national union (point 6). The unanimous plank adopted at the convention was preceded by an intense racial caucus infight.

However Mrs. Feldman may wish it differently, racial tensions in the AFT exist. In recent conversations with black AFT leaders outside New York, they have privately condemned the strike as a "disaster" and the UFT's role in it. Bill Simons, the black president of the Washington Teachers' Union and an AFT vice president, told me, for public consumption, that the WTU "doesn't look upon community control as a threat, but as a sound approach to benefit children" and that they preferred to say that they "did something right in supporting community control than say that somebody did it wrong." I'm sorry, Mrs. Feldman; there is a difference of opinion in AFT councils.

Did any of the occurrences in Ocean Hill–Brownsville justify a strike? On the matter of involuntary transfers couldn't the union have initiated court action? And did they have to close the schools a third time for alleged browbeating, curses, and threats made by other teachers in one school? Mr. Shanker and Mrs. Feldman would have us believe that an entire school system was struck to protect the safety of teachers although, as Jimmy Breslin reported, "when the supposed death threat was made, there were enough police inside the school to calm Chicago" and yet, "no threat was reported."

At this writing the UFT has rejected all peace formulas, including the Ocean Hill governing board's final concession to willingly readmit all teachers, rescinding their previous stand. It appears that Mr. Shanker hopes that a special session of the state legislature, hostile to community control, will settle the matter finally in his favor.

He refuses to accept any proposal to end the strike save the dismissal of McCoy and the governing board. As Murray Kempton pointed out, it is cruel irony that the man who raised the issue of "firings" should request that others be "fired." I'm especially disturbed by the removal of a friend and former colleague, UFT Vice President John O'Neill, from his paid staff position, through a reorganization, because he has consistently opposed the UFT's recent confrontations with black ghettos. John O'Neill many times helped stay the union leadership from rash actions. The assault by Shanker on O'Neill's character is reprehensible; the least that he deserved was due process. But Mrs. Feldman knows this as well as I.

Clearly the union is promoting racial strife. It has reprinted and distributed anti-Semitic and anti-white literature throughout the city, (some of it a year old), written by warped individuals. Mr. Shanker refers to black opponents as "black gangsters," "Nazi types"; to moderates like board president John Doar, formerly in charge of federal efforts to integrate in the South, as an "extremist"; and to Mayor John Lindsay as a "racist."

The UFT's actions have precipitated an unimaginable racial polarization. Even blacks who once criticized the Ocean Hill–Brownsville governing board (excepting Bayard Rustin who moved from his uptown Harlem offices into UFT quarters) rallied to their support. As for whites, Shanker boasted that, "All of New York is against the blacks."

Who are the militants for community control that so worry the UFT? An old integrationist activist core, (Rev. Milton Galamison, Annie Stein, Rev. Herbert Oliver, Ellen Lurie, Preston Wilcox, to name a few) is joined with younger black and white activists.

True, some black anti-Semites have latched onto community control, but they are not representative and have been disowned.

Who supports the UFT? A few prominent social democrats and liberals like Michael Harrington, Jewish groups who are rightfully anxious over black anti-Semitism, others who are plainly anxious about blacks, and that anti-Semitic, anti-black white constituency (many Catholic) who supported PAT. Quite a coalition. Certainly the larger segment would most probably support local control in the white South, but not the urban black North. This is the audience Shanker addresses himself to, in a tone, Jimmy Breslin observes, that is but "an accent away from George Wallace."

There are not many alternatives to improve the schools. Community control constitutes the most relevant. Coleman, in his study, found that the most important factor in a black student's achievement was the extent to which he felt he had some control over his destiny. That feeling of powerlessness would, to a large extent, be dispelled under community-controlled schools. Furthermore, Greeley and Rossi, in their study of Catholic school achievement, inferred that Catholic students did well because of the security generated by the ghetto atmosphere of Catholic schools. In short, that is the black-power thesis in educational terms.

Much of the educational debate revolves around the deep and abiding belief that children can learn, white and black, rich and poor. In recent years, Albert Shanker has privately and publicly questioned that belief.

He is not alone. Consider, for example, Bayard Rustin's statement: "Every year there has been a new gimmick (in New York schools). First it was buses; the next year it was the Allen plan. Now these are forgotten. The following year it was talk about education parks. Last year it was the More Effective Schools policy. This year it's decentralization. Next year it will be still another gimmick. The fundamental reasons educators have become involved in this gimmickry is that they do not seem to understand that unless there is a *master plan* to cover housing, jobs, and health, every plan for the schools will fall on its face. No piecemeal strategy can work."

I can't believe that the Irish poor, the Jewish poor, or even my own French-Canadian poor, had to wait until better houses were built and more jobs created before they could learn in the schools. And, of course, no one questioned whether they were "educable."

Certainly, the black (and white) activists advocating community control do not take such a defeatist view. They hold that schools *can* make a difference and share educational psychologist Jerome Bruner's conviction: "We begin with the hypothesis that *any* subject can be taught *effectively* in some intellectually honest form to *any* child at *any* stage of development . . . No evidence exists to contradict it; considerable evidence is being amassed that supports it [emphasis added]."

I concur. The tragedy is that the Shankers and the Rustins do not.

Due Process, Civil Liberties, and the Public Schools / AD HOC COMMITTEE FOR JUSTICE IN THE SCHOOLS

The following statement was prepared before the teachers' strike was settled. Nonetheless, the issues it discusses are of long-range significance. They must be understood by all New Yorkers if we are to avert a recurrence of turmoil in our schools and pave the way for a creative reconciliation of all citizens who are striving to build a better school system.

As the teachers' strike enters its fourth week, charges and counter-charges fill the air. In the crossfire, the real issues may be confused in the public mind. If that happens, the strike will be prolonged, demagogues will have a field day, and an atmosphere of hate and fear will flourish in our city.

To avert such a disaster and to lay the groundwork for ultimate reconciliation, the citizens of New York must understand the obstacles to a settlement of the strike.

Unfortunately this understanding has not been advanced by recent advertisements in *The New York Times* attacking the United Federation of Teachers or by the "Report on the Ocean Hill–Brownsville School Controversy" issued by the New York Civil Liberties Union.

What are the real issues?

THIS ADVERTISEMENT appeared in *The New York Times*, November 24, 1968.

Due Process

The NYCLU insists that due process is not an issue because the Ocean Hill–Brownsville teachers were only transferred, not fired. But here are the facts:

The letter received by the teachers said: "The governing board of Ocean Hill–Brownsville demonstration school district has voted to end your employment in the schools of this district . . . This termination of employment is to take effect immediately."

Rhody McCoy, unit administrator of the district, said: "Not one of these teachers will be allowed to teach anywhere in this city. The black community will see to that." (The New York Times, May 16, 1968)

An anti-UFT ad cites, as a source of its facts, an article by Richard Karp in Interplay *magazine. But here is what Mr. Karp wrote: "On May 10 the governing board formally dismissed nineteen teachers and supervisors in Ocean Hill–Brownsville, charging them with having attempted to 'sabotage' the demonstration project."*

The argument that the teachers were merely transferred rests flimsily upon this sentence in the letter of dismissal: "You will report Friday morning to Personnel, 110 Livingston Street, Brooklyn, for reassignment."

By any accepted definition, "transfer" means movement from one job to another by prearrangement. Yet the Personnel Bureau knew nothing of these alleged transfers and had no jobs waiting for the "transferred" teachers. Nor had the teachers been forewarned of this action.

Nonetheless, the NYCLU insists not only that the teachers were transferred but that Rhody McCoy, the unit administrator, had the power to transfer them without due process. Here is what the NYCLU says: "The superintendent of schools has the power to transfer teachers without due process. If the superintendent's powers are transferred to unit administrators under decentralization, as they should have been under the experimental districts, then the unit administrator would have the power to transfer teachers without due process."

But here are the facts:

The superintendent can transfer teachers without due process only in cases of voluntary transfer. (Obviously the Ocean Hill–

Brownsville teachers were not voluntary transfers.) Involuntary *transfers are another matter, as we shall see.*

Even if the superintendent had the power to transfer without due process, his powers are not transferred to the unit administrators under present law—whether the NYCLU thinks they should be or not.

Even if, under decentralization, a unit administrator had all the powers within his district that the superintendent has within the city, he could no more transfer a teacher to another district by unilateral action than the superintendent can transfer a teacher to Yonkers!

As for involuntary transfers, there are certain procedures to be followed—procedures that not even the superintendent can violate and which have never been ignored or challenged before in our city. (They were challenged in a Mid-west city that attempted a mass transfer of black teachers, and the union stood up for the teachers.)

Indeed large sections of the teachers' contract make sense only if one assumes the unchallenged existence of such procedures. For example:

The section dealing with seniority rights specifically explains the basis on which teachers can be involuntarily transferred.

The section on the rights of regularly assigned substitutes specifically provides them with protection against arbitrary transfer without due notice, written charges, hearings, etc. This would make no sense if tenured teachers had less.

Punitive transfers involve a U rating, and this requires specific charges that can be appealed to a board hearing, and finally to Commissioner Allen or to the courts.

These procedures were not observed in Ocean Hill–Brownsville precisely because the governing board was not interested in getting the teachers transferred. According to Mr. John Niemeyer (whose report the NYCLU repeatedly cites), the Board of Education had promised last spring to transfer quietly any teachers who were unacceptable to the governing board. But, as Mr. Niemeyer asserted, "the governing board was determined to prove it had control of the schools by circumventing normal procedures . . ." (*The New York Times*, September 14).

Even Jason Epstein, who signed an ad attacking the UFT, wrote in *The New York Review of Books* that there could have been an arrangement whereby the Board of Education would get the teachers out of the neighborhood if the local board did not also insist that it was *within the right of any community to hire and fire teachers at its own discretion*, a right which clearly conflicted with the principles of collective bargaining and job security on which not only the UFT but unionism itself depends. The decision by the local board to elevate the conflict to the point where the UFT was left with no choice but to intervene on behalf of its general membership was anything but whimsical.

Sabotage

The teachers were accused of "sabotage." But when Rhody McCoy was compelled to bring specific charges, they were dismissed by Judge Rivers. One of the anti-UFT ads, not satisfied with this decision, states:

> What the governing board found wanting in these teachers was a genuine desire to teach the children in their charge. . . . And it is a very difficult charge to prove in a court of law. How do you document a sneer? How do you prove a tone of voice? How many witnesses are needed to convict teachers of the failure to love their children?

Difficult indeed. And how do you refute a sneer, disprove a tone of voice, or plead not guilty to the charge of not loving? How would you go about defending yourself against the charge of witchcraft? How do we protect ourselves against malicious gossip, or innuendo, or the revenge of grudge-holders?

Are we to conclude that teachers can have no rights, no protection against extremely subjective personal judgment? Or, conversely, are we to conclude that there is no way to remove a teacher who is deficient in these intangible qualities that make for effective teaching?

Bad Teachers

An anti-UFT ad argues that: "Under due process, exactly twelve teachers have been fired in the last five years. Impartial men must come to the conclusion that the UFT's version of due process does not work in a school system of over 60,000 teachers when only twelve miscreants are found in five years."

The fact is that under the prevailing practice—and this is not "the UFT's version of due process"—most poor teachers are not fired in hearings but are weeded out by principals in face-to-face meetings. The teachers are customarily given the option of leaving before charges are brought against them. In addition, many poor teachers simply quit when they realize that they cannot do their job.

This procedure is not satisfactory; nonetheless the same percentage of poor teachers is let go in New York City as in the decentralized local districts throughout the country.

The UFT has stated, and we agree, that there are teachers who should be removed from the school system. Moreover, the union believes that teachers—and supervisors, administrators, and all public officials—should be held accountable to the public for their performances. Accordingly, the union has proposed:

1. A public review board to which parents can bring complaints and charges against teachers on nonprofessional matters (e.g., abusing a child, using racial epithets, etc.).

2. The development of objective tests to compare teachers' performances with children of various socio-economic backgrounds. These tests need not be exercises in mystification or in mass psychoanalysis of teachers; they need not rest upon vague impressions of personal radiance. They can be fair and effective, and we can begin work on them immediately.

3. Additional training and supervision of those teachers who consistently fall below par in the teaching of children from disadvantaged socio-economic backgrounds. If those teachers do not consequently improve, they should be removed from the system.

4. An internship program that would give new teachers a real probationary period. Right now they are thrown into classrooms with full teaching loads, to sink or swim. A new teacher should carry only half a load the first year, spending the rest of his time working with experienced teachers. The load should gradually be increased to a full load in the third year, at the end of which tenure would be determined.

Motives

The NYCLU has charged that "the United Federation of Teachers has used 'due process' as a smoke screen to obscure its real goal, which is to discredit decentralization and sabotage community control."

For years the Civil Liberties Union has defended the rights of those with whom it disagrees—Fascists, Communists, and Klansmen, for example. It never inquired into their motives. It asked only whether their rights had been violated.

When the New York Civil Liberties Union defended George Wallace's right to speak in Shea Stadium, did it ask whether his motive was to spread fear and hate?

We are saddened and distressed that the NYCLU, upsetting a long and revered tradition, has chosen to dismiss the legitimate due process claims of the teachers and instead attacks the motives of the UFT.

Why does the report of the NYCLU say not one word about the systematic and sadistic harassment, intimidation, and humiliation of teachers, which are a matter of record in Ocean Hill–Brownsville —and this treatment encouraged by the local governing board after it had promised not to obstruct the return of the teachers?

We do not deny the right of the NYCLU or anybody else to speak out on the decentralization controversy. But we do deny that decentralization is a civil liberties issue.

Decentralization

The undersigned are not prepared to unite in a judgment of the UFT's past positions on decentralization. Nor does this seem to us the issue now.

At this moment it is Mayor Lindsay and the Board of Education whose policies most endanger the future of decentralization. If they persist in evading their lawful responsibility to protect the rights of teachers, decentralization will be construed as abrogating due process, granting local groups the right to hire and fire teachers arbitrarily, and surrendering the schools to demagogic extremists.

Decentralization will become synonymous in the public mind with all of the ugliness we have seen on television. The original misgivings over decentralization will be intensified, and decentralization may be struck down by the legislature.

But if due process and teacher unionism are upheld, earlier misgivings will be proven groundless and decentralization can be made workable.

Where We Stand

We agree that the school system of New York is not meeting the needs of our children, especially those of low income and minority groups in the ghettos. We share the indignation of the parents in Ocean Hill–Brownsville—and Harlem and every other ghetto—whose struggle for quality education for their children has again and again run up against a brick wall of bureaucratic indifference and poverty of imagination.

We do not proclaim these sentiments to be diplomatic—this is not the time for cheap talk—but because we feel them sincerely. And we believe the UFT does too.

The terrible tragedy is that, while urban education deteriorates, forces that should be working together in a vigorous fight for better schools are fighting each other.

For the sake of our children, for the sake of our schools, for the sake of our city, there must be a reconciliation.

A genuine and lasting reconciliation, we believe, is only possible within a framework of school decentralization that respects the rights of all parties. This means:

1. *There must be an authentic community voice in the schools regarding curricula and other matters of educational policy.*

2. *There must be central certification and placement of teachers to ensure minimum professional standards and adequate distribution of personnel to meet the needs of the entire city.*

3. *Dismissal of teachers should be a local function, based on due process and subject to review procedures.*

4. *There must be objective procedures for spotting teachers who cannot effectively teach children of minority groups. Such teachers should get additional training or be weeded out—with due process.*

5. *There must be an end to vigilantism in the schools. Threats and intimidation must stop—now and without question. Our schools must be cleansed of all forms of racism.*

If decentralization is to succeed, and we earnestly hope that it will, these principles must be implemented forthwith in Ocean Hill–Brownsville—and the mayor and the Board of Education must see that they are. The important thing is that the teachers' strike be ended through a fair and equitable settlement and that all of the parties join together to make decentralization work.

Even then our problems will not be solved, for decentralization is no panacea—though it is frequently offered as one. It is no substitute for massive social investments of billions of dollars to provide remedial programs, improve physical plants, upgrade faculties, construct new schools—in short, to give our children the best education possible.

Beyond this, we must work at every level for the elimination of slums and poverty, for the rebuilding of our cities, and for the eradication of all those conditions of social and economic inequality that now weigh so crushingly on the education of our children.

To achieve these goals, parents, teachers, and community groups will have to forge a strong alliance. They will have to organize and stand together, black and white, overcoming the bitterness and frustration that now separate them.

To this end we pledge our help and ask yours.

NYCLU Reply to the Ad Hoc Committee for Justice in the Schools

On November 24, 1968, a group calling itself the Ad Hoc Committee for Justice in the Schools published a full-page advertisement in *The New York Times* entitled "Due Process, Civil Liberties, and the Public Schools." This advertisement attacked other advertisements in *The New York Times* published by various groups and also attacked NYCLU's statement of October 9, entitled "The Burden of the Blame: A Report on the Ocean Hill–Brownsville School Controversy."

We will not undertake to defend advertisements placed in the *Times* by other organizations. The sponsors of those advertisements are perfectly capable of defending themselves. However, we do feel obliged to issue this statement to correct the distortions and misstatements contained in the Ad Hoc Committee's advertisement that specifically concern NYCLU's report.

1. The Ad Hoc Committee's advertisement states: "The NYCLU insists that due process is not an issue because the Ocean Hill–Brownsville teachers were only transferred, not fired."

Response. From first to last, the NYCLU report insists that due process is an issue. NYCLU's difference with the UFT is that NYCLU argues "that there are serious shortcomings in existing Board of Education standards of due process, which have long permeated the entire school system" and that it is necessary to

USED BY permission of the New York Civil Liberties Union and Associate Director Ira Glasser. The reply was issued on November 25, 1968.

spell out the criteria for transfers to establish "for the first time, standards of due process for punitive transfers." The UFT and its suporters have taken public positions designed to convey the impression that the abuse of due process in Ocean Hill–Brownsville was unique and a peculiar outgrowth of that experiment in local community control.

2. The Ad Hoc Committee's advertisement states that "the argument that the teachers were merely transferred rests flimsily upon this sentence in the letter of dismissal: 'You will report Friday morning to Personnel, 110 Livingston Street, Brooklyn, for reassignment.' "

Response: This evidence is hardly so flimsy. Section 101 of the Board of Education bylaws is headed "Assignments and Transfers of Teachers, Etc." The words "reassignment" and "transfer" are used interchangeably in the school system. This differentiates them from "Resignations, Retirements, Removals, Etc." which are discussed in sections 102 to 105 of the Board of Education bylaws.

Beyond what the letters plainly said, the only other information that seems relevant to an interpretation of them is what the Ocean Hill–Brownsville local governing board and its project administrator intended to convey in sending the letters. Referring to the attempt to interpret these letters as dismissals, the Niemeyer Committee (an official advisory committee to the Board of Education on decentralization) stated at page 94 of its report that "The project board has steadfastly denied these allegations, arguing that they simply requested that the staff members be transferred out of the district." Even the attempt to transfer the teachers out of the district was only made after a previous attempt to transfer the teachers within the district had failed. At page 96 of its report, the Niemeyer Committee states that "the project administrator had tried to reassign teachers *within* (emphasis not added) the school project, a move that was within his authority according to oral information he had received. The Board of Education attempted to resolve this impasse but failed when certain teachers refused to transfer."

How is it in the interests of a union to interpret transfers of some of its members as dismissals? It isn't, unless, as in this instance, there are other considerations operating. At page 95 of its report, the Niemeyer Committee sheds light on this subject. "Under normal circumstances," the report states, "the demonstration project might have been able to accomplish the transfer of 'unsatisfactory' personnel informally, but a larger struggle was being waged in the New York State Legislature over a general proposal to decentralize the entire school system." Thus we see that the adverse publicity that "dismissals" would give to decentralization in the legislature became determinative in the public interpretation of the letters by the UFT.

3. The Ad Hoc Committee argues that, even if the teachers were only transferred, it had to be done with due process. According to the advertisement, "The superintendent can transfer teachers without due process only in cases of *voluntary* transfer. (Obviously the Ocean Hill–Brownsville teachers were not voluntary transfers.) Involuntary transfers are another matter, as we shall see."

Response: Neither the Board of Education bylaws, state Education Law, the UFT contract, past practice, nor anything else provides for due process in transfers. At page 94 of its report, the Niemeyer Committee states that "no charges are required" for transfers. The Board of Education's trial examiner, Judge Francis E. Rivers stated at page 5 of his decision that a simple request to transfer teachers could be made without assigning any supporting charges.

The Ad Hoc Committee's attempt to create a distinction between "involuntary" and "voluntary" transfers is misleading. No matter how involuntary they are, almost all transfers in the school system are called "voluntary." A principal threatens a teacher with an unsatisfactory rating and to avoid that rating, and to avoid having to continue working with an unfriendly principal, the teacher agrees to a "voluntary" transfer. These transfers are no more or no less "voluntary" than the transfers of the teachers in Ocean Hill–Brownsville would have been if they had agreed to the transfers—that is to say, they are not at all "voluntary." In fact, some of the teachers in Ocean Hill–Brownsville did not contest the transfers. Under this nomenclature, those transfers became "voluntary" even though, like hundreds of other transfers that take place in each school year, they were, in fact, coerced.

In a handful of instances each year, a teacher refuses to go along with a transfer and the transfer thereby becomes "involuntary." The only way that a teacher can contest an "involuntary" transfer is through the grievance procedure, in which the teacher bears the burden of proof, and not through due process, where the school administrator would have to bear the burden of proof. The fact is that the UFT ignored the grievance procedure in Ocean Hill–

Brownsville. The transfer letter sent to the teachers by the Ocean Hill–Brownsville governing board and its unit administrator stated: "In the event you wish to question this action, the governing board will receive you on Friday, May 10, 1968 at 6:00 P.M., at Intermediate School 55, 2021 Bergen Street, Brooklyn, New York."

In order to set the grievance procedure in motion, the teachers who received the transfer letters should have done either of two things: (1) appeared at IS 55 at the designated time; (2) asked for a more convenient time to meet with the governing board or its unit administrator.

None of them did either of the things they could have done to set the grievance procedure in motion. Under the terms of the UFT contract, the failure to take such a step is "deemed to be acceptance of the decision rendered at that step."

Again, it may be appropriate to ask why the UFT did not set the grievance procedure in motion. The answer is provided by the Niemeyer Committee's reminder (cited above) that "a larger struggle was being waged in the New York State Legislature."

4. In support of its contention that due process is required in cases of involuntary transfer, the Ad Hoc Committee states that "large sections of the teachers' contract make sense only if one assumes the unchallenged existence of such procedures." The committee then cites the following sections of the contract:

a. "The section dealing with seniority rights specifically explains the basis on which teachers can be involuntarily transferred."

Response: Here is the only statement that appears in the contract on this subject (page 21 of the UFT contract): "In the case of teachers excessed [an administrative form of involuntary transfer] into a school, seniority shall be determined by including length of service in the previous school." In other words, a teacher transferred involuntarily does not lose his seniority rights. How is that relevant to the Ocean Hill–Brownsville dispute?

b. "The section on the rights of regularly assigned substitutes specifically provides them with protection against arbitrary transfer without due notice, written charges, hearings, etc. This would make no sense if tenured teachers had less."

Response: The only provision for hearings for regular substitutes that appears in the UFT contract states (page 47 of the contract): "Regular substitutes and teachers on probation shall be entitled to the review procedures prescribed in section 105a of the bylaws of the Board of Education." Section 105a of the Board of Education bylaws is headed and deals exclusively with "Hearings Related to Probationary Period, Salary Increments, Ratings, and Disability Retirement." How is that relevant to the Ocean Hill–Brownsville dispute?

c. The advertisement states that: "Punitive transfers involve a U rating, and this requires specific charges that can be appealed to a board hearing, and finally to Commissioner Allen or to the courts."

Response: Ratings are not dealt with in the UFT contract. There is an appellate procedure dealing with ratings spelled out in section 105a of the Board of Education bylaws. There is nothing in either the Board of Education bylaws or the UFT contract or in past practice to indicate that a U rating or any other rating must be a precursor to any kind of transfer.

In practice, school administrators and teachers have traditionally circumvented the procedures for giving unsatisfactory ratings by coercing transfers as indicated in the response to (3) above.

5. The Ad Hoc Committee's advertisement states: "Even if the superintendent had the power to transfer without due process, his powers are not transferred to the unit administrator under present law—whether NYCLU thinks they *should* be or not."

Response: The largest section of NYCLU's report is devoted to setting forth the wholly ambiguous situation within which the Ocean Hill–Brownsville board and its unit administrator had to function. As the report stated: "Vacuums created by the absence of clearly defined lines of authority are usually filled by individual discretion, arbitrary action, and administrative abuse. Only chaos can then result. The burden of blame for that chaos must fall on the Board of Education for leaving lines of authority undrawn and governing powers undefined." NYCLU believes that if specific powers of the superintendent had been explicitly delegated to the unit administrator, it would have been possible for the unit administrator to know the outer limits of those powers and, thereby, to have helped avert the problems arising out of Ocean Hill–Brownsville.

6. The Ad Hoc Committee's advertisement states: "Even if, under decentralization, a unit administrator had all the powers within his district that the superintendent has within the city, he could no more transfer a teacher to *another* district by unilateral action than the superintendent can transfer a teacher to Yonkers!"

Response: That is one of the reasons why the NYCLU report

insists that, in conjunction with the adoption of any plan for decentralization or local community control, standards of due process in transfers must be established. They have not existed in the past. If the UFT and the Ad Hoc Committee are interested in the question of transfers under decentralization, let them join with NYCLU in proposing specific guarantees of due process. (A copy of NYCLU's statement of October 30 is attached).

7. The Ad Hoc Committee's advertisement states:

> For years the Civil Liberties Union has defended the rights of those with whom it disagrees—Fascists, Communists, and Klansmen, for example. It never inquired into their motives. . . . We are saddened and distressed that the NYCLU, upsetting a long and revered tradition, has chosen to dismiss the legitimate due process claims of the teachers and instead attacks the motives of the UFT.

Response: The signatories of the advertisement are apparently not very familiar with the "long and revered tradition" of the Civil Liberties Union.

Over the entire course of its history, the Civil Liberties Union has been concerned with motives. The Civil Liberties Union was an outgrowth of efforts during World War I to protect the rights of conscientious objectors. In seeking special treatment for those motivated in their refusal to serve in the armed forces by religion or conscientious beliefs, the Civil Liberties Union had to be concerned with motivations. Some more recent examples of our concern with motivations include: (1) our opposition in 1966 to the Patrolmen's Benevolent Association's effort to prevent civilian review of complaints against police. We said the PBA wanted police to be a law unto themselves. (2) our opposition in 1967 to efforts to substitute First Amendment language for the explicit prohibition in the state constitution on aid to religious schools. We said the proponents of this substitution, such as Citizens for Educational Freedom, wanted massive public funding of religious schools. (3) our argument earlier in 1968 that the U.S. Supreme Court should strike down the law against draft-card burning. We argued that in passing the law, Congress had been motivated by a desire to curb dissent over the war in Vietnam.

Since intent or motivation is such an important element of law, it is ludicrous to suggest that an organization that functions as much in the courts and the legislatures as the Civil Liberties

Union is "upsetting a long and revered tradition" when it inquires into motives.

As for defending the rights of those with whom we disagree, we have made clear to the UFT's counsel our willingness to participate, as a friend of the court, in support of Albert Shanker's right not to be sent to jail for leading the recent strikes.

8. The Ad Hoc Committee's advertisement asks, "Why does the report of the NYCLU say not one word about the systematic and sadistic harassment, intimidation, and humiliation of teachers, which are a matter of record in Ocean Hill–Brownsville—and this treatment encouraged by the local governing board after it had promised not to obstruct the return of the teachers?"

Response: It is a matter of record that the UFT has charged over and over again in public statements that such incidents took place on a systematic basis. It is *not* a matter of public record that the incidents actually took place.

It is also a matter of public record that the UFT has distributed hundreds of thousands of fraudulent leaflets designed to exploit racial fears by portraying Ocean Hill–Brownsville as a haven for extremism. The distribution of these leaflets impugns the credibility of the UFT substantially and is one of the factors that makes us unwilling to accept as credible the UFT's charges until such time as they are proven. At this writing (November 25), charges are pending against four teachers. It is our understanding that a number of the more serious charges against these teachers have already been dismissed as unfounded or unsubstantiated and that, as yet, nothing has been proved.

Therefore, we find no basis, at this time, for accepting the UFT public statements as truths.

9. The Ad Hoc Committee's advertisement states that: "We do not deny the right of the NYCLU or anybody else to speak out on the decentralization controversy. But we do deny that decentralization is a civil liberties issue."

Response: Since the qualifications of the Ad Hoc Committee to determine what is or is not a civil liberties issue are not obvious, we will respond only briefly to this statement.

Equality is a civil liberties issue and one of the central concerns of the Civil Liberties Union. We view decentralization or local community control as a promising means of moving toward equality within the New York City School System. We have supported, previously, such other efforts to bring about equality of education as school pairings and educational parks. The failure of these efforts to bring about equality has been extensively documented in the recent Random House book by David Rogers entitled, *110 Livingston Street*. Mr. Rogers' research confirms our own view that these failures were a product of bureaucratic sabotage within the New York City School System. Perhaps the most promising aspect of the movement toward decentralization is that it is specifically designed to cut through this problem of bureaucratic sabotage.

We do not regard local community control as a panacea. But we firmly believe that, with the failure of every other effort to bring about equality of education, experiments in local community control must be given a chance to prove their worth. The fact that, with all the vicissitudes of the past year, there continue to be signs that the experiment in local community control is bringing about substantial improvements in education in Ocean Hill–Brownsville is an encouraging sign that a real breakthrough may be made in bringing about educational equality.

3. Anti-Semitism and Racism

Perhaps the most disturbing effect of the strike was the polarization of black and white, in particular, black and Jew. Most studies indicate less anti-Semitism among blacks than among whites, but the strike significantly increased black hostility to the Jewish community. It did not create black anti-Semitism but crystallized it in New York. As Jews have increasingly gained acceptance in American society, their reformism has tended to diminish. Black resentment at the lessening of the traditional reformism of their Jewish allies has been growing stronger for some time. Only half the city's Jews supported the proposed civilian review board that would have checked police brutality in the ghettos, and some Jews have opposed the building of low-income housing for blacks in Jewish neighborhoods. Still, Jewish reformism persists; a recent poll revealed that Jews are the largest white group supporting school decentralization in New York.

In part, the racial tension can be viewed merely as the result of an out-group's resentment of those in power. In New York, both the teaching and the supervisory staffs are predominantly Jewish. Their interest in maintaining the *status quo* was seized upon by black extremists who produced leaflets attacking not the staff or teachers but the Jews. In turn, the UFT and the CSA distributed copies of those leaflets in an attempt to gather support for their own positions. At this point, the leadership of the Jewish community overreacted.

Black anti-Semitism was not the product of community control. The Ocean Hill board and unit administrator clearly disavowed anti-Semitism, and the board pointedly noted that it had hired a predominantly white, predominantly Jewish teaching staff to fill the classrooms of striking teachers. These new teachers, estranged from the union because of the decentralization issue, eventually took a newspaper advertisement in order to deny publicly the existence of anti-Semitism in the district's schools.

The racial antagonisms unleashed by the strike made it the most racially polarizing event in the city's history. When Mayor Lindsay, until then one of the city's most popular mayors, spoke at a Brooklyn synagogue during the strike, he was jeered and humiliated. And, though an apology was offered and it was argued that the synagogue was filled with noncongregants on the occasion, very much the same thing greeted the director of the New York Civil Liberties Union shortly afterward. When he appeared to speak at a Manhattan synagogue, he was told the talk had been canceled for fear of violence.

The documents reprinted in this section represent the extant record of black anti-Semitic and anti-white feeling. The validity of a circular signed by well-known Harlem teacher and black militant Ralph Poynter and purporting to have been issued by the JHS 271 Parents Community Council was challenged on the ground that the school has no such council. Similarly, a reprint from *Education News*, purporting to relate an anti-white lesson taught by a teacher in an Ocean Hill school during the strike was misleading; the incident allegedly occurred in the autumn of 1967 (not 1968) in a school that was not then and is not now a part of the Ocean Hill district. The magazine subsequently sued the UFT for composing and distributing the reprint.

To mitigate the prejudicial effects of the strike, Mayor Lindsay appointed a Special Committee on Racial and Religious Prejudice. The committee, chaired by retired Judge Bernard Botein, noted the outbreaks of black anti-Semitism and the more subtle forms of white racism, but was exceedingly general in its comments. It advocated the creation of a new city agency to handle matters in this delicate area, suggesting that such an agency have the power of subpoena—something the Botein committee lacked.

The viewpoints in this section deal with all the elements in the confrontation, but particular stress is given to anti-Semitism and racism. Sol Stern, an editor of the radical magazine *Ramparts*, views the union's action as white backlash. The result, he writes, was an increase in anti-Semitism in the black ghetto. Stern regards the teachers' union, once a model of progressive reform, as a conservative extension of the old radical left, with which it has many deep and personal ties.

How did classroom teachers view the struggle? One cannot read two more disparate accounts than those reprinted here. For Charles Isaacs, a teacher in the district (JHS 271), community control represents no anti-Semitic threat; rather, in addition to being educationally beneficial, community control represents the only means of improving relations between the races. His article, describing the mood at JHS 271, stresses the healthy independence of the new black militancy.

On the other hand, Patrick Harnett, a New York City school teacher (though not based in Ocean Hill), presents a very different picture of teachers, unions, and the school system. The teacher, Harnett writes, is just barely out of poverty, and he reflects the racial prejudices of a white lower-middle class threatened by school boards composed of the black poor. The supporters of community control—a white Protestant upper class, a handful of liberal intellectuals, and a black and poor substratum—fail to understand the plight of this lower-middle-class teacher.

The path to reconciliation between blacks and Jews has yet to be explored. Probably, only when both blacks and Jews feel secure and unthreatened will such reconciliation occur. Hopefully, community control will serve as one means to this end and will provide a meeting ground for both groups.

DOCUMENTS

Hate Literature*

CITIZENS, PARENTS, TEACHERS: The following are excerpts from "educational literature" placed in the teachers' letter boxes and posted on pupils' bulletin boards in the Ocean Hill–Brownsville schools:

We demand that only black or Puerto Rican teachers are employed in our schools. We demand that we have the right to hire and fire

* The three pieces of hate literature contained in this segment are reprinted in their entirety and without editorial comment.—Eds.

all personnel. All outsiders-teachers (baby sitters) must be released as soon as Negro or Puerto Rican educators are available. Any teacher who belongs to the UFT or any other hostile group must be discharged. We demand that only locally controlled police can enter our schools. All supplies, wherever possible, must be purchased locally from friendly sources. All repairs must be given to black or Puerto Rican contractors. All "whitey" textbooks must be burnt and replaced by decent educational material. "Whitey" art and John Birch–type social studies must be replaced by African arts and crafts and African history.

> Some supervisors and we know who you are
> Plotting and scheming well you've gone too far
> We didn't ask you here and we don't want your kind
> One thing we learned and we learned it from you
> And it's screw the next man before he can screw you
> So here Judas pimps we'll give you a clue
> Shape up or ship out before this "Fall"
> Or all you mothers against the wall

If African-American History and Culture is to be taught to our Black Children it Must Be Done by African-Americans Who Identify With And Who Understand The Problem. It is Impossible For the Middle East Murderers of Colored People to Possibly Bring to This Important Task The Insight, The Concern, The Exposing of the Truth That is a *Must* If The Years of Brainwashing and Self-Hatred That Has Been Taught To Our Black Children By These Bloodsucking Exploiters and Murderers Is to Be Overcome. . . . Get Out, Stay Out, Staff Off, Shut Up, Get Off Our Backs, Or Your Relatives In The Middle East Will Find Themselves Giving Benefits To Raise Money To Help You Get Out From Under The Terrible Weight Of An Enraged Black Community

FLASH! The Board of Education last night approved an evening adult program at JHS 271 in Ocean Hill–Brownsville that features courses on revolution, how to stage demonstrations, and "self-defense."

A course on "The History and Examination of Revolutionary Struggle" will be taught by Herman Ferguson, convicted of conspiracy to murder moderate civil rights leaders. Since Mr. Ferguson is currently in jail, the opening session of the course last night

was taught by Oliver Leeds, former chairman of the Brooklyn chapter of the Congress of Racial Equality.
IS THIS THE KIND OF TEACHING MATERIAL WE WANT IN AMERICAN PUBLIC SCHOOLS?

Council of Supervisory Associations
186 Joralemon Street
Brooklyn, N.Y. 11201
October 17, 1968

This is a verbatim text of a leaflet distributed by the Parents Community Council of JHS 271 and phoned to a UFT representative:

Tentative Plan: Parents Community Council, JHS 271, Ocean Hill–Brownsville
Ralph Poynter, Chairman

The schools in this community were built using Our money. The schools at the present time are operated by an unfriendly outside board. The teachers in Our school are supplied by this unfriendly outside board. The teachers wages are paid using our taxes. The equipment in Our school was purchased with money belonging to African-Americans. The supplies used in our schools were bought with Our money. The children attending these schools are Our children.

We demand that we have absolute control over our schools.
We demand that only black or Puerto Rican teachers are employed in Our schools. We demand that we have the right to hire and fire all personnel. All outsiders-teachers (baby sitters) must be released as soon as Negro or Puerto Rican educators are available. Any teacher who belongs to the UFT or any hostile group must be discharged. We demand that only locally controlled police can enter Our schools. All supplies, wherever possible, must be purchased locally from friendly sources. All repairs must be given to black or Puerto Rican contractors. All "whitey" textbooks must be burnt and replaced by decent educational material. "Whitey" art and John Birch–type social studies must be replaced by African arts and crafts and African history.

All future school construction funds must be given to the local community. All future building plans must be made by companies that employ a certain per cent black or Puerto Rican personnel.

The following was placed in teachers' mailboxes at JHS 271 and PS 144 in Brooklyn:

If African American History and Culture is to be taught to our Black Children it Must be Done By African Americans who Identify With And Who Understand The Problem. It Is Impossible For The Middle East Murderers of Colored People to Possibly Bring To This Important Task The Insight, The Concern, The Exposing Of The Truth That is a *Must* If The Years Of Brainwashing And Self-Hatred That Has Been Taught To Our Black Children By Those Bloodsucking Exploiters and Murderers Is To Be OverCome. The Idea Behind This Program Is Beautiful, But When The Money Changers Heard About It, They Took Over, As Is Their Custom In The Black Community, If African American History And Culture Is Important To Our Children To Raise Their Esteem Of Themselves, They Are The Only Persons Who Can Do The Job Are African-American Brothers and Sisters, And Not the So-Called Liberal Jewish Friend. We Know From His Tricky, Deceitful Maneuvers That He is Really Our Enemy and *He* is Responsible For The Serious Educational Retardation Of Our Black Children. We Call On All Concerned Black Teachers, Parents, And Friends to Write To The Board of Education, To the Mayor, To The State Commissioner of Education To Protest The Take Over Of This Crucial Program By People Who Are Unfit By Tradition And By Inclination To Do Even An Adequate Job.

The Black Community Must Unite Itself Around The Need To Run Our Own Schools And To Control Our Own Neighborhoods Without Whitey Being Anywhere On The Scene. We Want To Make It Crystal Clear To Your Outsiders And You Missionaries, The Natives Are On The Move!!! Look Out!!! Watch Out!!!! That Backfire You Hear Might Be Your Number Has Come Up!!!! Cut Out, Stay Out, Stay Off, Shut Up, Get Off Our Backs, Or Your Relatives In The Middle East Will Find Themselves Giving Benefits To Raise Money To Help You Get Out From The Terrible Weight of An Enraged Black Community.

IS THIS WHAT YOU WANT FOR YOUR CHILDREN?
THE UFT SAYS NO!

Preaching Violence Instead of Teaching Children in Ocean Hill–Brownsville: An Observation of an Actual "Lesson" in JHS 271. This excerpt is one example of what the Ocean Hill–Brownsville governing board feels is suitable curriculum for the children in that district.

What Black Power Teaches*

During the New York City teachers' strike, . . . a reporter [from] *Education News* visited the eighth-grade class taught by Leslie J. Campbell, a leader of the African-American Teachers Association. . . . These are excerpts from [his] account of the class session.

Mr. Campbell: Now, class, ask Timmy questions about our Afro-American heritage and black power.

Pupil 1: We have leaders like Martin Luther King, and he tells us to be peaceful, and then we have leaders like Malcolm X and Rap Brown and they tell us to use violence. Who is right?

Mr. Campbell: Timmy, tell him what you learned.

Timmy: Well, I think Martin Luther King is not so good. Whitey don't want to give us anything, so we got to fight for it.

Pupil 2: Why do we have to fight? Why can't we just demonstrate peacefully like Dr. King?

Mr. Campbell: Whitey doesn't listen. The only thing he understands is when we get up and start throwing bricks and Molotov cocktails.

Pupil 3: What is black power?

Mr. Campbell (*writing on the blackboard*): Black power is control by Afro-Americans of three things. The first is political power, the second is economic power, and the third part is social. We have 12 per cent of the people. There are 100 senators. How many are black? One, and he [Edward Brooke, R. of Mass.] is an Uncle Tom. Now, Timmy, would you like an Afro-American state?

Timmy: Well, I don't know. Sometimes I do and sometimes I don't.

Mr. Campbell: Think! Our own state for black people.

Timmy: Yeah, I guess that would be good.

It Is Time For Citizens To Know The Truth! Leslie Campbell is still on the staff at JHS 271, "instructing" and "organizing."

* *Education News,* the magazine from which this was taken, subsequently sued the UFT for composing and distributing the reprint in a misleading way.—Eds.

Write to Mayor Lindsay today. Demand an end to *all* racism in our schools.

Anti-Semitism?—A Statement by the Teachers of Ocean Hill–Brownsville to the People of New York

This statement, prepared by the teachers of the Ocean Hill–Brownsville demonstration school district now teaching there, is designed to clarify some issues with respect to racism and particularly anti-Semitism. At first, we thought that only the several hundred Jewish teachers in the district should sign it, but then we realized that, in view of the persistent charges of racial polarization, all of us, Jewish and non-Jewish, white and black, should join to set the record straight about the scurrilous charges that have been leveled against our board.

It is time to scotch the rumors and hysteria about anti-Semitism, racism, and revolution being the underlying causes of the problems of Ocean Hill–Brownsville. Statistically, 70 per cent of the 541 teachers teaching the 8,500 youngsters in Ocean Hill–Brownsville are white, 50 per cent of this percentage are Jewish, and all are certified by the Board of Education. What we want to do is to teach the children entrusted to us without having to live and work behind a wall of fear and mistrust that Mr. Shanker has helped to build around us.

The UFT Wall of Fear

In an effort to tag the Ocean Hill–Brownsville governing board with anti-Semitism, the UFT is engaged in a massive publicity campaign and is distributing UFT reprints of anti-Semitic literature. The most talked-about is the one that refers to "Middle Eastern murderers."

This is actually a composite reprint of two separate leaflets. One, signed by the purported chairman of fictitious "JHS 271 Parents Community Council," is anti-UFT and urges the exclusion of whites from teaching black or Puerto Rican children.

THIS ADVERTISEMENT appeared in *The New York Times*, November 11, 1968.

The other section, with its anti-Semitic references, is reproduced from a different, anonymous leaflet surreptitiously inserted in some teachers' mailboxes during the May walkout (strike) that followed the involuntary transfer of the nineteen teachers.

Blending these two leaflets together in this fashion is intended to imply that the demand for community control of education in a black community means: (1) firing all white teachers, (2) virulent anti-Semitism, (3) support for these doctrines by our board.

What the New York Civil Liberties Union Says

On the basis of its own study of this piece of propaganda, the New York Civil Liberties Union has concluded: "The UFT is trying to pin responsibility for the anti-white and anti-Semitic sentiments in these leaflets on the Ocean Hill–Brownsville decentralization program. This is a smear tactic reminiscent of the days of Senator Joseph McCarthy."

Mr. Shanker is using propaganda of this type to win the support of white teachers and parents in this battle against our governing board.

We, the undersigned teachers, are living proof that such charges are false on all counts.

What Has This to Do with Our Governing Board?

We state unequivocally that by their words and actions they have shown that they will not tolerate any form of anti-Semitism. Furthermore, we resent the continued allegations that are being made against the governing board when we know that they are untrue.

Here are the words of the Ocean Hill–Brownsville governing board on this matter:

The Ocean Hill–Brownsville governing board, as well as the entire Ocean Hill–Brownsville demonstration school district, has never tolerated nor will it ever tolerate anti-Semitism in any form. Anti-Semitism has no place in our hearts or minds and indeed never in our schools.

While certain anti-Semitic literature may have been distributed outside our school buildings, there is absolutely no connection between these acts and the thoughts and intents of the Ocean Hill–

Brownsville governing board. We disclaim any responsibility for this literature and have in every way sought to find its source and take appropriate action to stop it.

The acts of the board, however, are more important than their words. When the governing board recruited 350 new teachers last summer, more than 50 per cent of them were Jewish. Are these anti-Semitic actions?

What Is Our Board Really Doing?

The truth about our board is that it is trying to provide, against powerful opposition, the basis for a real breakthrough in the urgent problem of providing good education not only for the black and Puerto Rican children of our city but for all the children.

We all feel that education is one of the best ways to curb anti-Semitism and racism. But there is an even better way to end both anti-Semitism and anti-Negro prejudices. Black people will be turned away from anti-Semitism and white will be turned away from anti-Negro feelings only through the establishment of trust and confidence between both groups in day-to-day relationships.

We, the teachers of Ocean Hill–Brownsville, are working together with parents and administrators to teach the children of this community. We approach the children with an expectation of success, which we communicate to them and to which they are responding. In this way we are establishing relationships of mutual trust and respect, which we believe are the best ways to end prejudice now and in the future.

Why Does Mr. Shanker Persist in These False Charges?

By this time, it is evident that the city-wide strike has neither trade-union, moral, nor educational justification. Mr. Shanker's continuance of the strike now finds him in opposition to: the Board of Regents, the state commission of education, the Board of Education, the superintendent of schools, the United Parents Association, and the leaders of most major educational institutions in and around the city of New York. Not to mention more than 1 million children.

Why is this so? Because it is now clear that the strike no longer has anything to do with the return of the disputed teachers. Whatever might have been the situation earlier, the governing board on its own—recognizing its responsibility to the other children of New York, as well as to those of our district—made it clear on October 23 that the disputed teachers will be fully accepted and given actual classroom assignments:

> We recognize that each of the seventy-nine teachers returning by order of the Board of Education will be assigned actual classroom assignments with actual students, which was the fact in seven of our eight schools since the last strike of the UFT and actually achieved at JHS 271 before this last strike. Each principal will respect the aforesaid assignments.

Whom Does Mr. Shanker Trust?

Mr. Shanker's final argument is that the governing board cannot be believed because of previous experiences. Let us be clear: all the previous "experiences" arose out of agreements Mr. Shanker made with the central Board of Education, which they both tried (with incredible insensitivity) to cram down the throat of the Ocean Hill–Brownsville governing board. Now the governing board itself has accepted the return of the teachers and has agreed to "cooperate to achieve a peaceful atmosphere."

Moreover, the state Board of Regents has pledged every resource at its command to the satisfactory return of the disputed teachers, and has promised it will establish guidelines on the protection of the rights of teachers.

Mr. Shanker has now stated that the only thing he would accept is the elimination (at least for the foreseeable future) of the governing board's administrator, Rhody McCoy, and all the principals of our schools. This Mr. Shanker cannot have, and the education of 1 million children ought not to be sacrificed to his determination to wreck the first bright hope of bringing quality education to the black and Puerto Rican children in New York.

An Invitation to See for Yourselves

We, the teachers of Ocean Hill–Brownsville, invite you to visit our schools. We would like to have ministers and rabbis, educators and laymen of every color and creed come and see what we are doing. We are proud of what has been going on in our classrooms, and the children and parents are proud, too.

We would like to share with you our dream of what real community education can provide for the future of all our children.

Excerpts from the Botein Report

An appalling amount of racial prejudice—black and white—in New York City surfaced in and about the school controversy. Over and over again we found evidence of vicious anti-white attitudes on the part of some black people, and vicious anti-black attitudes on the part of some white people.

The anti-white prejudice has a dangerous component of anti-Semitism. Black leaders sincerely tend to regard this anti-Semitism as relatively unimportant in the school controversy, since in their struggle for emergence their preoccupation is with discrimination, notably in education, employment, and housing, and not with defamation, oral or written. Jews, in turn, are outraged by anti-Semitic defamation itself, fearful that such apparent indifference may spark violence and other forms of anti-Semitism well beyond defamatory expressions.

The black-white hostility also has a small measure of bigotry emanating from or directed against Puerto Ricans. Puerto Ricans found themselves split in their relationships between whites and Negroes.

Further, although it has long been known that bigotry has many shapes, it has become clear to us, at least in this controversy, that the prejudice emanating from blacks generally takes a form somewhat different from that which has emerged among whites. The countless incidents, leaflets, epithets, and the like in this school controversy reveal a bigotry from black extremists that is open, undisguised, nearly physical in its intensity—and far more obvious and identifiable than that emanating from whites.

On the other hand, anti-black bigotry tended to be expressed in more sophisticated and subtle fashion, often communicated priv-

APPOINTED BY the mayor in November, 1968, the Special Committee on Racial and Religious Prejudice was chaired by former judge Bernard Botein. It issued its report on anti-Semitism, racism, and the strike on January 17, 1969.

ately and seldom reported, but nonetheless equally evil, corrosive, damaging, and deplorable.

The Committee has decided against incorporating in this statement copies of or excerpts from any of the bigoted printed matter that has been distributed during the course of the school dispute because we see no constructive purpose served in thus adding to the circulation of such material. Similarly, the committee has decided against naming blameworthy individuals or organizations in this statement because none of them has been asked to appear before the committee to testify—under oath and protected by appropriate constitutional safeguards—in connection with their activities.

Clearly, this printed matter and the episodes of alleged bigotry require more investigation and further analysis to assess with finality their extent, depth of meaning, scope, and impact. Further study is needed, too, before gauging their permanent effect on community attitudes and the extent to which racial and religious hatred will persist after the decentralization issue has been resolved.

.   .   .

The present state of affairs, with hostility escalating on all sides, presents an intolerable situation. Of course, these tensions did not spring full blown from the current school confrontation. In a city inhabited by so many diverse groups, so many underprivileged people, it would appear that a certain amount of resentment and hatred has been simmering below the surface for many years. It is likely that similar emotions in some other cities spread and were spent, if only temporarily, in bloody riots. But in any event, there can be no doubt that the recent school conflict touched off the spate of religious and racial bigotry this city is now experiencing. It is ironic that this conflict should develop so speedily and massively between Jews and blacks—two groups who for many years have so successfully cooperated with each other in attempting to promote a higher level of human dignity, racial and religious understanding, and equality of opportunity for men of all colors and creeds. With these groups on edge, with new antagonisms fired by the school decentralization controversy, with some people using bigotry as a weapon, racial antagonism to some extent has been encouraged as an echo of the main struggle. Thus, the entire community has been riven and stirred by the spreading antagonism between these two groups of old friends.

In this controversy, some persons have distorted the issues by the injection of bigotry. These shrill voices have espoused racism, anti-Semitism, and intimidation. Hatemongers have engendered an atmosphere of fear. It is time for concerned citizens—blacks and whites—who have been too silent, to speak up for the vast majority of citizens committed to an orderly process of change in a dynamic democratic society. Their failure to do so early, clearly, and sufficiently, we found, was in itself a contributing factor to the exacerbation of hostilities; the persistent allegations of "racism" by each side against the other—ill-defined and unspecified—themselves became harmful epithets.

There is room for dissent, protest, and militancy, but anti-Semitism, racism, and violence are out of bounds in any community discussion of complex problems. If citizens do not speak out against racism and bigotry and support an orderly process, the tension between the races will intensify and tear our city apart. They must condemn and repudiate racism and anti-Semitism and all other manifestations of bigotry. We must maintain an atmosphere in which issues will be discussed without the injection of prejudice. It would be constructive for the leadership on all sides to come together in a collective statement repudiating further intrusion of bigotry in the decentralization debate.

. . .

VIEWPOINTS

"Scab" Teachers / SOL STERN

Outside their junior high school at the northern tip of Manhattan, in the middle-class Inwood area, two lines of kids stood waiting. One group was almost all black, the other was white. The

REPRINTED FROM *Ramparts*, November 17, 1968, pp. 17–25, by permission of *Ramparts* and the author.

white kids were going to be taken to a "freedom school" at a synagogue a few blocks away, which had been organized by striking teachers. The black kids were being ushered into the regular public school by teachers who were breaking the strike. One of the non-striking teachers, furious at the sight of the two lines, ran up to one of the striking teachers and said, "This is the most vicious, destructive thing that's ever happened to this school." The striking teacher screamed back, "Scab!" and some parents threatened to get the dissenter fired when the strike was over.

To the surprise of most people, New York City made it through the summer of 1968 without a major riot. Nevertheless, paranoia and race hatred seemed thicker than ever in the lingering hot, sticky summer air that smothered the city during all of September. The teachers were on strike again, and Bronx housewives sat in front of their sweltering apartment houses, muttering about the blacks "trying to take over."

After the strike at a Brooklyn school, even the youngest black children had to walk a gauntlet of police nightsticks to get into their school, and a black parent outside the line of police and picketers denounced what she termed the "Jewish Mafia," which she said was responsible for such conditions. She was referring to the UFT, 55,000 strong and probably the most powerful white-collar union in the country. The ethnic makeup of the teachers union, which is two-thirds Jewish, has led to an exaggerated perception in the black community of it's being simply a "Jewish union." And cooperating with the union during the strike was the Council of Supervisory Associations, which represents all principals and assistant principals. It is also predominantly Jewish.

In a school system where over 55 per cent of the children are nonwhite, it is little wonder that there is a sense of inequity, and that black and Puerto Rican parents and activists are trying to get a little more say about their kids' educations, in the same way that the Jews of thirty years ago had to confront the resistance of the Irish who then dominated the school system. Now the high proportion of Jewish names among the organizations in direct conflict with the black community has heated what is basically a black-white dispute into even uglier racial overtones. And to its discredit, the teachers union, particularly its president, Albert Shanker, fanned the flames by sensationalizing the issue of anti-Semitism in order to solidify and rally support from the powerful New York Jewish community.

Trouble in Brooklyn

The trouble was centered in the Ocean Hill–Brownsville section of Brooklyn, a miserable stretch of slum dwellings connecting the two large ghettos of Bedford-Stuyvesant and Brownsville. Ocean Hill–Brownsville resembles Berlin after the war: block after block of burned-out shells of houses, streets littered with decaying automobile hulks. When teachers in the area's schools ask the younger kids to draw pictures, many of them turn in drawings of burning buildings, since that has been one of their most vivid experiences.

Ocean Hill–Brownsville has no shopping facilities or movie houses, and transportation is lousy. But there is still a fairly well-developed community spirit and a plethora of block organizations, parents' groups, and poverty programs. In the spring of 1967, under the sponsorship and financing of the Ford Foundation, the parents met to elect a governing board for the school district. It was to be one of three demonstration projects in the city to experiment with the idea of decentralizing New York's mammoth, centrally directed educational system. Almost from the beginning, however, the governing board, and therefore the parents, found itself opposed by the UFT.

Almost forgotten as the crisis escalated into an ugly racial confrontation were the origins of the dispute—the nineteen teachers and supervisors dismissed (or "transferred") six weeks before the end of the last school year by the local governing board. The union says the governing board acted without cause, and went beyond its legally constituted authority; in retaliation, it pulled 400 teachers out of the district's schools, practically crippling the instructional program. Over the summer, a retired judge acting as an independent trial examiner declared that there was insufficient evidence brought by the local governing board against the teachers, and the city's central board ordered the local board to reinstate them. Not only did the board refuse, it recruited several hundred new teachers to replace the union teachers who walked out in support of the original nineteen. The refusal of the local board to accept what appeared to be impartial arbitration put the onus of unfairness on it, but the roots of the disaster lay basically in unwillingness on the part of the central Board of Education and the city of New York to define clearly the powers and legitimacy of the local board. In an unclear and confused situation, the local board believed firmly that it was hammering out its own mandate.

By the beginning of the school year the Ocean Hill–Browns-ville district had an almost entirely new staff, and its schools were open and functioning. Many of the original nineteen, as well as most of the union teachers who walked out in sympathy, have since voluntarily transferred to other school districts, but the union claims that eighty-three of the remaining teachers wish to return to their old assignments. The union called the city-wide strike to pressure the central Board of Education and the mayor to use their power to force the local board to rehire these teachers. After several abortive settlements, the teachers were finally sent back to their schools under massive police protection, but the local governing board said it would not assign the teachers to regular classroom duties.

The union says the issue is due process for teachers and the protection of hard-won rights of job security and tenure. It in-vokes the ethic of militant trade unionism, civil liberties, and pro-fessionalism against what it calls the dangers of "vigilantism" and disruption of the learning process by politically motivated black militants. Against the claims of many in the black community that the strike is racist, the union has mustered support from lib-eral intellectuals and labor leaders. The teachers, say their sup-porters, have one of the country's most progressive unions. They organized freedom schools in Prince Edward County in 1963 and in Mississippi in 1964; they sent a large contingent of teachers to join the march initiated by Martin Luther King in support of the sanitation workers of Memphis, and they were one of the only unions in the country to actively support the Poor People's March.

In any event, could a "racist strike" be supported by such people as A. Philip Randolph, Bayard Rustin, and Michael Harrington? It could and was.

"Just Take Care of the Troublemakers"

Teachers union headquarters occupies several floors of a mod-ern office building on Park Avenue South in lower Manhattan. It was there that the union teachers from Ocean Hill–Brownsville lodged their complaints whenever trouble flared in their schools. The day after the end of the strike, a dozen teachers, all white, reported frantically from IS 55: the principal had asked them to leave "for their own safety" when several student demonstrations, some led by militant black teachers, broke out in protest of the teachers' enforced presence at the school. The teachers were frightened and angry as they mingled in the hallway outside UFT President Albert Shanker's office. While waiting to see him, they let their hair down a bit.

J. O., a rugged-looking man in his fifties, who recently retired from a government job and became a shop teacher, huddled with two younger colleagues. Someone mentioned that the cops had beaten up one of the black students during the demonstration. J. O. replied, "Look, if the cops were let alone—if they roughed up a few more of those kids—all this wouldn't have happened. There's no problem teaching in those schools if we could just take care of the troublemakers."

Mrs. W., a librarian from IS 55, joined the conversation: "I've been teaching in that school for ten years. I helped start the experimental district. We wouldn't have any trouble if all those militants, the Sonny Carsons, the Fergusons, the Ralph Poynters, the Leslie Campbells, hadn't taken over. Leslie Campbell teaches his kids not to steal jackets from each other; he tells them to go get a piece, to go get ready for the war. The poverty program is paying for people like that to teach kids how to kill. How do you go about getting an investigation of the poverty program started?"

The reactions of these Brooklyn teachers are not atypical, although they don't fit the union's chosen image of itself as civil rights conscious and racially liberal. On the picket lines outside the schools during the strike, you could hear the "law and order" argument over and over again: praise of the cops, denunciation of black militants. When teachers made picket signs for a demonstration at City Hall, they spontaneously used the slogans, "End Mob Rule in the Schools" and "Stop Teaching Racism in Our Schools." Black members of the union's executive board were furious. The implication, they said, was that local black control of schools means mob rule and racism.

"Backlash" makes you think of Irish dock workers or Polish and Czech steel and auto workers. But caught in the cross fire of rising demands from the black ghettos in which they work, and confronted by the necessity of adapting to black authority, white middle-class New York teachers may quietly vote for George Wallace. How that came to be is a case study not only in middle-class liberal racism but in the degeneration of a once exciting union.

The New "Scabs"

There was a time when even the idea of a union for teachers was revolutionary. It was resisted by conservative "professionalists," who disdained trade union principles. Those who fought for the establishment of teachers unions were considered radicals and civil rights activists; they saw the union not only as a force for winning rights for teachers but as a progressive, liberalizing force within a stagnant trade union movement. In those early days it was the most adventuresome, the most socially conscious New York teachers who fought the union's battles and took the chances. The first teachers' strike in 1960 brought out only about 7,500 teachers to walk the picket lines and jeopardize their jobs. The teachers with the civil service mentalities, those most concerned about job security, were the ones who crossed the picket lines. Today the situation is reversed: the success of the union in winning collective-bargaining rights for all teachers has made it the instrument of job security, and now the conservative and the mediocre have become the union's majority. Now it is the radicals who break the picket lines. It is the conservatives, afraid of the black community, panicked about their jobs, who shout "scab" at those who oppose the strike.

One of these "scabs" is Sandra Adickes, a tall, blonde English teacher, who not only crossed the picket lines during this year's strike, but who also joined parent groups to force the reopening of closed schools on the Lower East Side. A nine-year veteran union activist, she walked the union's first picket lines and helped to organize the Mississippi freedom school. Now, like many blacks and idealistic younger white teachers, she is leaving the union. "I don't think the traditional trade union concept is any longer relevant," she says. "In six years the UFT has become middle-aged. When I started in 1960, it was relevant. We were making $4,800 a year and the union did a good job in improving conditions. But there's no pioneering trade union spirit here any more. It's all bread and butter, salaries and working conditions and job security. It used to be that young girls would teach for a few years hoping to marry a doctor or lawyer, but now they're marrying other teachers—you see them holding hands at meetings—and with two salaries they are really doing well. But their apathy is appalling.

"And now they're afraid of blacks and violence. They live in their little worlds, in middle-class enclaves. They automatically see blacks as hostile. They know blacks have suffered and they are afraid they are going to take it out on them. They know they are mediocre, that they're not doing a good job. They think someone is going to find out and get them out."

A Socialist Lobby

But despite the defection of teachers like Sandra Adickes, the union still affects a progressive image. This is partly due to a small but well organized lobby of social democrats and Socialist Party members grouped around Bayard Rustin and Michael Harrington who, in effect, act as a public relations lobby for the union.

An interlocking directorate between the teachers union and various New York social democratic organizations could easily be charted. Union President Albert Shanker was himself once a member of the Young People's Socialist League and is now a member of the board of the League for Industrial Democracy (LID), a socialist education organization. Charles Cogen, who preceded Shanker as UFT president and groomed him for the job, was once Socialist Party candidate for City Council. One of Shanker's two executive assistants, Sandra Feldman, is the wife of Paul Feldman, editor of the Socialist Party organ New America. Shanker's administrative assistant is the wife of Max Shachtman, a mentor of Harrington and Rustin and the chief ideologue of one of the more esoteric old left sects. Rustin, Harrington, Paul Feldman, and Tom Kahn, the executive director of the LID, are all personally close to Shanker and serve as a kind of "kitchen cabinet" for his union.

When you name all of the above, you have just about exhausted the active ranks of the moribund conservative socialist movement in this country. There is nothing subversive about the relationships, although they do provide an insight into the sources of intellectual support the union drew upon during its conflict with the black community. During the strike, major New York newspapers carried expensive full-page ads by two groups who supported the union's version of the dispute. One ad was signed by twenty-five white liberal intellectuals, who advertised under the rubric of an Ad Hoc Committee to Defend the Right to Teach. The address listed on that ad is the same as that of the LID and the committee's co-chairmen are Michael Harrington, chairman of the board of the LID, and Tom Kahn. The other ad was signed by black trade unionists solicited by the A. Philip Randolph Institute whose executive director is Bayard Rustin.

"The United Federation of Teachers," says Rustin's ad, "has made clear it accepts decentralization and will cooperate in its implementation." "Decentralization is *not* the issue," says the Harrington ad. "Decentralization of the city schools is under way. The United Federation of Teachers has pledged its full cooperation to make the reorganization succeed." Both ads claim that the issues are not racial—"The overwhelming majority of black teachers are supporting the UFT strike," says the Rustin ad. The issue, says the Harrington ad, "is understood by black and white teachers alike—which explains their strong solidarity."

This was all an ingenuous bit of shilling for the union—as well as a deliberate falsehood. The racial split within the union on the strike and on the union's opposition to any meaningful decentralization is a matter of public record. One week before the Harrington and Rustin ads appeared, a black caucus was organized within the UFT to oppose the strike. A press release was issued in the name of five of the six black members of the union's fifty-man executive board, plus the only two black elected officers, denouncing the strike. Most of the black teachers who stayed home during the strike did so only because of the cooperation received by the union from the supervisors' association, which ordered its members to lock the schools. Only in those areas where sufficient community and parent pressure could be brought to bear were the schools opened, and in these schools most of the black members reported for work. The ads do not even mention this unusual collusion between the union and supervisors, or the use of the lockout—traditionally an employer's weapon. And the ads conveniently ignore the history of the unions' frantic lobbying activities against an important decentralization bill at the state legislature—one of the shadiest aspects of the whole story.

Teacher Power in Albany

In Albany last May, a significant decentralization bill had been offered to the legislature by the state Board of Regents—the highest educational policy-making body in the state. Supporting the legislation were some of the most impeccable members of the establishment—the Ford Foundation, the state commissioner of education, the mayor of New York City. But in the legislature itself there was only a small handful who were in favor of the Regents' proposal—all of New York City's black assemblymen and a handful of liberal reformers. Most of the other legislators were either indifferent or afraid of backlash sentiment. A determined effort by the handful of pro-decentralization legislators, which included threats of a sit-in in the governor's office to hold up his legislative program, succeeded in convincing legislative leaders and the governor to support a compromise decentralization plan. The compromise plan was still strong enough, containing broad powers for local boards. The plan also stipulated that local boards could fire teachers only for cause and only after "due process" protection for any accused teacher.

The passion aroused by a single piece of legislation that would have reorganized the administration of education in the city of New York can only be understood against the general background of the disaster of public education there. The struggle for school integration had turned into a total fiasco because of the resistance of the white community and the impossibility of integrating ghetto children into white middle-class schools. Ghetto schools, in the meantime, were in a state of extreme deterioration. Overcrowded, full of the violence and turmoil of the ghetto, they were staffed by administrators and teachers from an alien culture who looked upon their work as combat duty. The result was that the schools were run as semi-reformatories, and learning was nil.

It was out of this bleak situation that the demand grew to give the minority communities a chance to run their own schools. New York is the first city to face this conflict, but it is clear that it is an issue of national proportions, and its rumblings will soon be heard in most American cities.

When the issue was in the balance, the teachers union came to Albany with a huge lobbying effort to kill the decentralization bill. The union spent close to half a million dollars to bring over 500 teachers and parents to Albany. They descended on the legislature like a swarm of locusts—using backlash arguments and threatening wavering legislators with political opposition at the polls. Shanker directed the whole operation from the office of Assembly Speaker Anthony J. Travia. The union president said that there was a "hoodlum element in the schools" that would be let loose if decentralization passed. Union leaflets passed out to legislators warned that with decentralization, local school districts would be operated "on the basis of local prejudices based on color, race, or religion." It was obvious that the teachers were appealing to racial fears; those who stood fast on decentralization were called "black power advocates." At a rally of the lobbying teachers in Albany, Shanker said, "If the regents' bill passes I will follow every legislator around who voted for it and kill them politically."

One of the leaders in the fight for decentralization was Jerry Kretchmer, a thirty-four-year-old quick-talking assemblyman from Manhattan's West Side. Kretchmer angrily recalls the teachers' tactics in Albany. Fifty or sixty teachers at a time would crowd into his office, berating him for his stand and warning that decentralization would lead to chaos. The confrontations grew increasingly heated as the teachers threatened to campaign against him, but Kretchmer held his ground. At one point he told a group of teachers that if "decentralization leads to a year of chaos, I am prepared for it. *There's no education in the schools anyway.*" At that, an infuriated teacher spat in the assemblyman's direction.

With this sort of overkill, the teachers easily succeeded in stampeding the legislature. A bill introduced by conservative Republican Senator John J. Marchi was passed, in effect putting the matter off for another year. During that year, all power to decentralize specific districts was delegated to the New York City central Board of Education. This was hardly a threat to the teachers, since the board, fighting for its own bureaucratic prerogatives, was totally opposed to decentralization.

Having won the legislative battle in Albany, the teachers returned home and engaged in an additional unprecedented act of piggishness. Shanker was determined that the legislators who opposed the union on decentralization should be punished in a way that would impress the legislators with the union's political power. At the union's delegate assembly, held just before the state's Democratic primary, Shanker urged that the union "undertake an intensive campaign to support those legislators who supported its position in Albany and to defeat those who did not." This resolution put the union in support of some of the state's most reactionary legislators and in opposition to most of New York's black and liberal legislators. The resolution passed easily.

Shanker then proceeded to collect a slush fund of thousands of dollars and to take off after the political scalps of the pro-decentralization legislators. A Shanker associate confides that the union made a political distinction between those legislators who voted for decentralization because they came from predominantly black constituencies and those who supported it as independents. The union patronizingly excused the former; the latter it vindictively tried to destroy. One of the latter was Assemblyman Jerry Kretchmer, whose district is 55 per cent Jewish, 12 per cent Irish, 12 per cent Italian, with the remainder white Protestant, Puerto Rican, and black. Running against Kretchmer in the primary was Thomas Daubner, an old-line Democratic Party hack, a former ally of the old Tammany chieftain, Carmine de Sapio, and a hawk on the Vietnam War. The union first threw Daubner a $1,500 cocktail party at the Park Sheraton Hotel, to which it invited all the teachers in the district. Then it sent out a letter on union stationery to all the teachers, a document which Daubner eventually used as a valuable piece of campaign literature. The letter said, "Mr. Kretchmer is the voice which, preaches chaos in the schools. He would give local school boards the right to hire and fire teachers. He would promote Ocean Hill–Brownsville throughout New York City. I urge you to vote for Daubner. He supports the UFT's decentralization plan."

The letter was signed by Albert Shanker.

Teachers also went into the district to canvass against Kretchmer, and they organized a telephone campaign to reach all the voters, telling them, "Kretchmer is for black power." Asked to comment on such tactics, Dan Sanders, the union's public relations man, said, "Well, Kretchmer *is* a black power advocate. Every organization supports and opposes people. It's perfectly legitimate for us to do that. And we're going to continue. In the future we are going to be even more active in the political arena. We can't survive otherwise."

Redefining Survival

Survival *is* the real issue at Ocean Hill–Brownsville. But given the way this socialist-led trade union has now defined "survival," it is not particularly surprising that an increasing number of black leaders have been drawn to the conclusion that for the black community's survival they must somehow break the power of the union. True, some white teachers have been treated summarily at Ocean Hill–Brownsville, but that is not an unusual occurrence in the vast reaches of the New York school bureaucracy. The union is constantly asked to intercede on behalf of teachers who have been pushed around by supervisors or summarily transferred out of their schools for political reasons; the union usually does not fight very hard.

The New Coalition, the minority anti-Shanker caucus in the union, has documented hundreds of these abuses. In one not atypical case, Michael Levien, a young radical and union member who had been teaching for two years at Junior High School (JHS) 52, an integrated school in upper Manhattan, was told after months of harassment by the principal and his department chairman not to return to the school the following year. Levien's only offense was helping the students organize an anti-Vietnam protest off school grounds. He went to the union leadership for help, but they refused to exert any pressure on the principal—let alone call a strike in order to get him reinstated. Only action by parents sympathetic to Levien, in the form of a sit-in in the district superintendent's office, succeeded in forcing the principal to change his mind.

But the union did want to dispute the action taken regarding the teachers at Ocean Hill–Brownsville, and pulled all of its 55,000 members out in a strike that crippled the entire system. The issue here was closer to its heart: the forced transfers were massive and public. (It is important to remember, however, that at no time did any of the teachers lose a day's pay. They were merely ordered to the central Board of Education for reassignment to another district.) Embattled all year in a running dispute about its powers both with the central Board of Education and with the union, the local governing board decided to flex its muscles. Instead of finessing out the undesired teachers as is normally done in districts all over the city, or waiting for the teachers to leave voluntarily (as many were doing), the local board announced their action in a press release which said that the teachers were "dismissed"—without notice. According to published reports—which the local board has not denied—the central Board of Education even offered to transfer the teachers quietly during the summer, but the local board was determined to make the matter public.

Anti-Semitism and Backlash

In terms of the over-all battle for decentralization, the seemingly crude and arbitrary action by the local board against the teachers was a blunder. It played right into Shanker's hands by making the union seem the aggrieved party. Shanker quickly seized the opportunity, stirring up the membership with scares about job security and the specter of teachers at the mercy of black extremists. Every incident of anti-Semitism was played up by the union chief. At one meeting he said, "If community control, as we see it at Ocean Hill–Brownsville, wins, there will be 'Jew Bastard' signs and swastikas in all the schools." Whenever it could, the union made sure the press understood that most of the dismissed teachers were Jewish. The president of the 26,000-member Jewish Teachers Association, Dr. Herman Mantell, jumped on the bandwagon with widely publicized charges of anti-Semitism by the local governing board. Mantell also attempted to pressure the Ford Foundation into withdrawing financial support from the local board, saying in a letter to the foundation, "I, and those to whom I have spoken, are beginning to have doubts about the anti-Semitic influence in the Ford Foundation and/or some of its officers and/or directors in their persistence in allocating funds to the Ocean Hill–Brownsville demonstration project which we have charged with anti-Semitic prejudices in its dealings with the educational personnel."

The charges of anti-Semitism and black racism spread hysteria throughout the New York Jewish community. Left unnoticed was the fact that most of the replacement teachers hired were white and Jewish. Thus obscured was the fact that the governing board's move was aimed not against white or Jewish teachers but against *union* teachers who, the board felt, used their union's power to obstruct the governing board and its appointed leadership from carrying out their policies in the district schools.

Shanker's Domino Theory

The union had very strong chapters in Ocean Hill–Brownsville when the new governing board took over in 1967, and it almost immediately tried to assert its influence. Teachers representing the board immediately came into conflict with the community members of the board over the issue of the hiring of a new unit administrator. The governing board chose Rhody McCoy, a black principal from outside the district, rather than the teachers' candidate, Jack Bloomfield, the white principal of Junior High 271, Ocean Hill–Brownsville. The board chose five new principals, three blacks, one Puerto Rican, and one Chinese. (They were, incidentally, the first Chinese and Puerto Rican principals in the school system.) But none of them was on the approved civil service list, so the teachers' representatives staged a protest walkout at the board meeting. Later, in September, 1967, when the board refused to support the city-wide teachers' strike which shut down the public schools for fourteen days, the teachers resigned from the board.

Having severed all connections with the local governing board, the union teachers came into increasing conflict with the new black administrative leadership of the district's schools. Teachers loyal to the governing board, both black and white, accused the union of using guerrilla tactics against the experiment. At JHS 271, the largest school in the district and the source of the most intense conflict, the principal, Jack Bloomfield, left in the middle of the year, taking thirty teachers, all the assistant principals and five of the six secretaries with him.

But he left behind a strong union chapter headed by Frederick Nauman. Nauman had a very special relationship with the old white principal; he only had to teach two classes per week, and spent most of his time on union business. When the new black principal, William Harris, took over in February, there was an immediate conflict about the prerogatives of the local chapter. Many of the members of the union felt more loyalty to Nauman than to the new principal. JHS 271 was in a turmoil all during the spring semester, and the governing board, rightly or wrongly, felt that the problems of discipline were being deliberately created by the white union teachers in order to prove that the experiment in community control, over which they no longer had substantial influence, was a failure. When the governing board finally acted, Nauman was one of those dismissed.

For President Shanker, however, Ocean Hill–Brownsville was one battle in a larger war. "Shanker," says UFT Vice President John O'Neill, "has a domino theory. He thinks that what happened in Ocean Hill–Brownsville will happen in thirty districts if it isn't stopped there. His basic philosophy is power. If he can destroy Ocean Hill–Brownsville, then no other district will try the same thing. They won't try to exercise their power to hire and fire for fear the union will destroy them."

The single-mindedness with which Shanker pursued his power struggle with the Ocean Hill–Brownsville board is indicated by the treatment meted out to O'Neill, the only white member of the union's top leadership who had reservations about the strike. When O'Neill publicly denounced Shanker's threat to call another strike in October and proposed instead a compromise settlement, Shanker convened the union's executive board and had O'Neill fired from his $13,000 per year staff job with the union.

One of the reasons that O'Neill had reservations about the strike is that as vice president in charge of junior high schools, he was one of the union representatives dispatched to Ocean Hill–Brownsville last May when the conflict over the teachers erupted. O'Neill was appalled at the prospect of teachers being forced upon the Ocean Hill–Brownsville community by police force. He wanted to back away from a confrontation that he felt would permanently put the union on a collision course with the community, and at JHS 271 he sounded out Rhody McCoy, the district superintendent, on the propects of reaching some compromise settlement. McCoy, also trying to avoid a direct confrontation with the union, seemed receptive to talks and even suggested the possibility of some sort of impartial hearing for the teachers. O'Neill, wishing to head off an escalation of the struggle, immediately got on the phone to Shanker, telling the union president that he saw the prospects of a settlement in what McCoy had said. Shanker replied, "Fuck you. I want those teachers in the classroom now."

Thus, from the beginning, Shanker had no intention of giving *de facto* recognition to the governing board through direct negotiations. Throughout the conflict, his strategy was to use the union's power to cripple the entire system as leverage to force the mayor and the central board to discipline and break the Ocean Hill–Brownsville board.

Community Control or Union Control?

The events at schools like JHS 271 prove that Shanker's actions do at least stem from an acute if limited sense of self-interest. Successful community control would radically affect the power of the union both at the chapter level and at the top. At the present time, when the union chapter at a school is strong, the chapter chairman is sometimes the most important person in the school, next to the principal. Union members are answerable only to the administration of the school, which in turn is caught up in a central bureaucracy and is careful not to rock the boat. Community control would mean a new explosive element that the union member has to become accountable to—parents, particularly angry poor parents, and community influences, sometimes politically threatening. "Professionalism" is the teacher's defense against the newly threatened accountability demanded of him, and the union shields him from that prospect.

Of course decentralization and community control are no panacea for the disaster of urban public education. There is not yet any piece of objective evidence that community control leads to better education, and it would be easy to be cynical about the motives of the Ford Foundation in pushing decentralization. It gets politicians such as Rockefeller and Lindsay off the hook for the failure of education, and takes the heat off the ghetto schools by turning the militants over to the black bourgeoisie to handle. A lot of middle-class blacks, those with civil service mentalities, are supporting decentralization for no other reason than the career opportunities it provides.

Yet, as one community activist said, "Ghetto schools are so bad —you could close them all now for the next year and it wouldn't have any effect on anyone." White, centrally controlled schools mean in effect not only no learning but an atmosphere of fear and alienation for teacher and child alike. Community-controlled schools, as anyone who visited Ocean Hill–Brownsville must know, at least provide an atmosphere of warmth and dignity. I asked two fifteen-year-old girls who had graduated from JHS 271 last year, and who thus had lived through that school's agonizing transition from white to black control, what the difference was between the two principals. One of them said, "Well, Mr. Bloomfield used to hide in his office all day—whenever there was trouble he would send one of his assistant principals to check it out. He was like a scared mouse. Mr. Harris we could always see. And when he took over he asked all the classes to elect a delegate to come and meet with him and tell him what our complaints were. I remember once we asked Mr. Bloomfield if we could play soul music in the cafeteria during lunch, and he said no because there would have been riots. But Mr. Harris, when he came in, let us have the music and everything was OK—there was no trouble."

The issue is power—not due process and vigilantism, or anti-Semitism. Who shall exercise power in the schools, who shall make educational policy: the community through its elected representatives, or the union hiding behind the façade of "professionalism"? Obviously there will be dangers of violations of the civil liberties of teachers. Obviously there is anti-Semitism in the ghetto, and some of it is directed at teachers. But a community can't be made sensitive to those concerns by fiat or by police power. Had the union fought for strong decentralization, with adequate legal safeguards for the rights of teachers, had they cooperated with the local governing board at Ocean Hill–Brownsville in making decentralization work, they would be in a better position today to protect their members in the ghetto. As it is, the union's behavior has undoubtedly increased anti-Semitism in the ghetto and increased the black community's contempt for the average union teacher.

A JHS 271 Teacher Tells It like He Sees It / CHARLES S. ISAACS

Landlord, landlord
My roof has sprung a leak.
Don't you 'member I told you about it
Way last week?

Landlord, landlord
These steps is broken down.
When you come up yourself
It's a wonder you don't fall down.

Ten bucks you say I owe you?
Ten bucks you say is due?
Well, that's Ten Bucks more'n I'll pay you
Till you fix this house up new.

REPRINTED FROM *The New York Times Magazine*, November 24, 1968. ©
1968 by The New York Times Company. Reprinted by permission. "The
Ballad of the Landlord" from *Montage of a Dream Deferred* by Langston
Hughes is reprinted by permission of Harold Ober Associates, Incorporated.
Copyright © 1951 by Langston Hughes.

What? You gonna get eviction orders?
You gonna cut off my heat?
You gonna take my furniture and
Throw it in the street?

Um-huh! You talking high and mighty.
Talk on — till you get through.
You ain't gonna be able to say a word
If I land my fist on you.

Police! Police!
Come and get this man!
He's trying to ruin the government
And overturn the land!

Copper's whistle!
Patrol bell!
Arrest.

Precinct station.
Iron cell.
Headlines in press:

> Man Threatens Landlord
> Tenant Held; No Bail
> Judge Gives Negro 30 Days in County Jail

1. Who is the man in the poem?
2. Why is he angry. Should he be?
3. What does he do to the landlord? Was he justified in doing so?
4. What happens to him? Does he deserve the penalty?
5. Would it happen if he were white? Why? Why not?
6. Does this poem remind you of things that happen here in Ocean Hill–Brownsville? What?
7. Why do you think Mr. Mayer has used this poem in your class?

A social-studies lesson at J.H.S. 271

The above poem is "Ballad of the Landlord," by the late Afro-American poet Langston Hughes, and it has dual relevance to the Ocean Hill–Brownsville story. Replace the landlord with the educational establishment, the tenant with the black parent, and the leaky roof with a history of inferior education—then write a sequel to the poem. The sequel will be about an educational system crumbling from its own inner decay, a bureaucracy which is afraid to enter the ghetto without police protection, and a community which will settle for no less than the freedom to rebuild for itself. The tenant decides to raze the old structure and build a new one, with a new construction company of his own choice. That is where my colleagues and I come into the story.

When Jonathan Kozol, author of *Death at an Early Age*, taught a lesson similar to the one quoted to his Boston public-school students, he was fired; no JHS 271 teacher will be dismissed for teaching that lesson. Whether we label this change "innovation," "academic freedom," or "dangerous," it illustrates the new outlook to education which the Ocean Hill–Brownsville experiment in community involvement has brought about, the type of teacher it has attracted, and the threat which produced a massive effort to destroy it before it began. Despite the concessions granted the striking teachers' union over last weekend, the sense of innovation lingers in the air.

Actually, although innovation is a major purpose of decentralization, we have a basically traditional program at JHS 271; we have few formal changes that other schools could not copy if they were so inclined. There are many reasons for this, perhaps the most prominent of which is the pressure to get more children into decent high schools. Last year, only nine out of 491 graduates went on to the "better" schools. The parents of my eighth-grade students have this very much on their minds, and many of them want community-controlled schools just so their children will be able to enter the better high schools and colleges. In discussions with these parents, it is difficult to discuss the new math, or doing away with old-fashioned grammar lessons; they want their children to learn the 3 R's. In this respect, these black and Puerto Rican parents are no different from white parents; they don't want their children to be used as guinea pigs.

The experiment has had an educational effect on many of the parents and will, in time, bring about a change in the community's basic conservatism. At one meeting, a father stood up to ask a question. He said that when he "was a boy," he wouldn't talk back to a teacher because he would get "whupped" both at home and in school if he did; he wanted to know why we didn't encourage more "whupping." He was answered by a young black college student who explained that the awe and fear of authority figures felt by children in a bygone era is counter-productive today.

The reply received considerably more applause than the question, but, sitting on the speakers' panel, I was wondering how that parent would react if his child came home and told him what he learned in "Charlie's class" that day. I had told my students that they were allowed to address me by my first name, and I had done this precisely to break down the wall of fear that usually exists between student and teacher. (It is a monument to the past that so many children have found it impossible to take advantage of this familiarity.)

Other frustrations to real innovation have been police in the schools, the uncertainty of not knowing whether school will be open or closed tomorrow, and the general tension which these have created. But there have been two more basic obstacles.

The first of these has been the presence of reporters, a presence which transforms any situation into something different from what it would otherwise be. The daily mass media understand an orderly hallway, suits and ties, but not psychodrama, or *dashikis*. As one teacher explained: "Of course we have to make the children go up the 'Up' staircase, and down the 'Down' staircase; there might be a television camera at the end of the stairs." To experiment means to accept the risk of possible failure, and no one wants to take the risk of falling flat on his face in 60 million living rooms.

An even more fundamental obstacle is built into the very nature of the project. Our experiment will be evaluated in terms of the established conventional criteria: reading scores, discipline, standardized achievement tests, etc., some of which measure what they are intended to measure, *for middle-class children*. We have a problem when these criteria fail to measure the extent to which a child has been educated, when they simply test rote memorization, stifling of initiative and training in sitting through standardized examinations. Unleashed creativity, or a critical outlook, for example, would probably lower a child's score on these exams, rather than raise them.

If the conventional criteria measure the wrong things, their effect is harmful to our students, yet they will determine to a great extent whether or not we will ever be free to develop our own yardsticks. In effect, we must miseducate the children before we will be allowed to educate them.

If we succeed where others have failed, the explanation will not lie in minor reforms of a decadent educational system. If the children learn now, it will be because they want to more than ever before. It will be because they do feel the sense of community which is developing, and because their parents now participate actively in their education. They know that their teachers have faith in them, and, most important of all, they are learning to have faith in themselves. Appeals to manhood and to pride in blackness are far better motivational and disciplinary tools in JHS 271 than threats of suspension or detention.

In order to encourage these positive factors, the faculty is trying to become truly close to the students and their families. One *Saturday*, we arranged for free buses and took 600 children on a trip to Bear Mountain. No red tape, no waiting period, and, of course, no pay for the teachers; they were having too good a time themselves even to consider it.

A large group of teachers attend all open community meetings, and the teacher-community solidarity at these gatherings strengthens all of us; at one meeting, the only speaker to receive a standing ovation was Fran Aurello, a white teacher. We have been arranging informal get-togethers with the parents at school and in their homes, and every teacher is pledged to get acquainted with the parents of all his students. All this takes time, but the possibilities for the future, as well as our successes, in this short period of time are lost on none of us.

Our assistant principals have offered an interesting comparison between the "old" supervisory personnel and those who will replace them. In September, when I began teaching, we had five assistant principals, including one Negro, who were imposed on us by the central Board of Education, and two who were hired by the local governing board. Since I had not known at first that any of our staff was of the former group, my initial experiences with them shook my faith in the experiment more than a little. One spent an entire staff meeting instructing the teachers that our major function was to discipline, regiment, and routinize the children. Another admonished the staff to wear rubber-soled shoes, as she did, so we could "sneak up on the children in the halls." Still another barged into the middle of an orderly class to exclaim: "Close those windows! If a child falls out, *we'll* really be in a fix." If this was experimentation, I thought, how much worse could things have been before?

It was not long before I found out that these people were not part of the experiment, did not want to participate in the experiment, and were, in fact, sabotaging the experiment by forcing students and teachers simply to refuse to implement such repressive policies. Finally, unable to influence their staff in any way, they were kind enough to transfer voluntarily out of the district as a group.

That left us with John Mandracchia, an experienced administrator who transferred into the district last February, and Albert Vann, an acting (uncertified) assistant principal who doubles as president of the African-American Teachers Association. Mandracchia is that rare individual who managed to survive in the so-called merit system despite substantial merit. He is white, forty years old, and lives in the suburbs; yet he has no trouble in relating to black people or young people, including pupils, and seems to understand the problems of the cities. Few teachers wake up at 4:45 each morning, as he does, and stay late every afternoon. He once slept in school overnight because he did not have time for his daily four hours of driving.

Mandracchia is an exception to the rule that a life-time of being white, combined with a career within the New York City School System, will prevent anyone from becoming a competent supervisor in a black school. Still, when I asked him what he thought our major administrative innovation was, he said: "For the first time, black kids have the opportunity to identify with black leadership in their schools."

Al Vann is one of those black leaders. Ten years in the system have taught him to hate it, and his battle against it seems to have brought wrath down upon him. One newspaper reported that he arrived at school at 9 one morning and organized and led a parent-teacher march through the community beginning at 9:02. Anyone who could have organized that march in two minutes certainly should throw a scare into the system.

It is perhaps because of fear, mixed with a generous portion of racism, that the press, the UFT, and the Board of Education credit Vann with having instigated many unfriendly actions, some of which never even took place. These allegations have led him, and three other teachers, into the Board of Education's "due process" mechanism for transfer and dismissal. Vann is a forceful, popular figure who is capable of instilling awe, respect, terror, or pride in any of the children as the situation demands. He sees his future, that of his organization, the ATA, as well as that of his people, bound up in the struggle for community control.

While most of our teachers are part of this struggle, some are apprehensive about the ATA's role in it. Just a narrow, "careerist" view of self-interest corrupted the UFT and forced it to oppose quality education in order to protect its membership, it is feared that the ATA might simply replace the unresponsive white bureaucracy with a similar black one, in order to further the career goals of its constituency. Here, Vann faces the dilemma which all black leaders must eventually come to grips with: Is he to advance himself within the existing system, and lose touch with the "grassroots" black community, or will he remain a part of that community, at whatever cost to his own career?

Les Campbell, another "black militant" facing accusations before the Board of Education, teaches Afro-American history. In a sense, both he and the course (four times a week for all students) are innovations. Both are objected to by the central system, and descriptions of both are usually distorted.

When I first met Campbell, I hardly knew what to expect: physically, vocally, and intellectually, he seemed far larger than the norm, and, supposedly, he had no use for whites. Two months of conversation and observation have discredited the latter speculation and confirmed the former. Campbell wants to see the institutions that dominate the lives of black people controlled by those people, not by white colonial masters, but he recognizes the role that can be played by white allies in the struggle.

His suspicion of the "white liberal" arises out of a history of double-cross and meaningless rhetoric, and seems to be shared by his true constituency, the black community. I expected more distrust than I actually found. I was almost disappointed.

When the UFT press releases proclaimed that "hate whitey" was being taught in Campbell's classes, I had to find out for myself. I walked into a class five minutes after it began, and took a seat in the back of the room. Campbell was showing a series of slides on the origins of African civilization. They portrayed the recent anthropological discoveries suggesting man's origin in the Olduvai Gorge in central Africa, depicted the builders of ancient Egyptian culture, including their Negroid features, and led the class into a discussion of the social institutions of some of the early, highly developed African civilizations.

The course will trace the African people from this point through the European invasion, forced emigration to the New World, slavery and slave revolt, to the present day, none of which is covered in conventional history texts or courses. According to Campbell, it is designed to answer the questions: "Who am I? Where have I been? Who and where am I today?" If the white man turns out to be the villain in this story, such is the testimony of history. If things are different today, if the children will have reason to expect anything different in the future, they must be educated by their own, and by the black faculty's every-day interaction with the white faculty. This is no insignificant part of our job.

The white teachers (70 per cent of the faculty) are an interesting, diverse group of individuals. In addition to being younger and better educated, we have less experience in working for the system, and more in working against it, than any other faculty in the city. Forty per cent of us are Jewish (some Orthodox), 30 per cent will need draft deferments in order to continue teaching, 25 per cent have never taught before; all are licensed by the central board, and nearly all are "committed" to social changes. Many sections of the country are represented, as are most major colleges and universities. Alan Kellock, a teacher of Afro-American history, is writing a doctoral dissertation for the University of Wisconsin in that field; Sandy Nystrom is a former white organizer for the Mississippi Freedom Democratic Party; Stu Russell is a returned Peace Corps volunteer; Steve Bloomfield is an organizer of the Brooklyn Heights Peace and Freedom Party.

My own background is simply this: grammar school in Brooklyn, bar mitzvah, suburban high school, Long Island University, marriage, law school at the University of Chicago. My father owns a parking lot; my mother is a working housewife. While they spend most of their time explaining me to their friends and neighbors, they actually enjoy suburban life. In another day, my twenty-third birthday would not have found me teaching in the ghetto. This generation, though, has grown up at a unique time in history. I am not alone in being a contradiction to my upbringing.

While many of us have done our best to disestablish the Establishment, no single ideology unites us, no plan of action is taken without heated debate. We do not even agree on a single analysis of the situation in which we are engaged. The school has set the stage for an interesting day-to-day drama involving the complex relationship between this group and the more united black faculty.

One observer of the opening of school noted a "checkerboard" seating pattern in the teachers' cafeteria, black teachers together at some tables, white teachers at others; this pattern, for instance, has since broken down somewhat into one of agreement on—and interest in—whatever issue is being fought out in any particular part of the room. We are integrated now, but not by pretending that black is the same as white; it is, rather, integration born out of respect for individual and group differences, and pride in, as well as recognition of, one's own heritage. We form a mixture, not a solution—a smorgasbord, not a melting pot.

The moment of truth, in this respect, came for many white teachers when we decided to organize the faculty and elect a steering committee. The black teachers demanded equal representation on the committee even though they were a numerical minority; there would be a black caucus to whom the black representatives would be responsible, and a white caucus to elect the white representatives. Some (not all) white teachers objected to this plan, maintaining that it would institutionalize race differences, and instead proposed at-large elections, based on traditional "color-blind" integration.

A long debate ensued, with Campbell calling the "at-large" plan "a step backward in the fight for black self-determination," while himself being charged with "segregationism" and "separatism." When someone suggested a vote on which plan to accept, his proposal had broad support.

At this point, Steve Mayer, a white teacher, pointed out that, in a vote on the question, the white majority would be deciding whether or not the blacks were to have self-determination. Most of us recognized this as the colonial situation we all were determined to avoid, and the vote no longer was necessary. The two caucuses met separately, elected their representatives, and the steering committee was formed. The two-caucus system has lessened racial tensions on the committee rather than having exacerbated them, and its work has been made more effective by removing the fiction on which it would otherwise have rested.

Despite whatever tension has existed among the faculty—and I think this tension has been constructive—we have been united on a few major issues and goals: we are for community control of schools; we want to educate the children; and we want the power structure (UFT, Board of Education, politicians, Selective Service) to leave our experiment alone so that we can make it work.

It was in this context that the transferred UFT teachers were put back into the school, along with a force of about 3,000 armed police bodyguards. It was absurd to think that an agreement between the UFT and the Board of Education, with community representation excluded, could have made either the community or the faculty accept those teachers back with open arms. It was more absurd to think the intimidating presence of the police would help. There had to be harassment on both sides, and there was. The harassment was petty, though, and, to the best of my knowledge, it never escalated to threats on people's lives, no matter what the newspaper stories supposedly leaked from a still-unreleased report by impartial observers may have said.

Examples sound absurd when repeated. One of the UFT teachers for instance, walked into the middle of a math class I was teaching, marched to the center of the room, and began picking papers up off the floor. I asked: "What are you doing here? You're disrupting my class." In reply, he told me that he was not disrupting the class, but I was. Then, with the students (thirteen to fifteen years old) looking at him—their eyes filled, some with amazement, some with hatred, some with confusion—I walked toward the door, opened it for him, and told him to leave. He went to the door, but rather than leave, he started rummaging in the wastebasket, for no apparent reason. Finally, he straightened up, turned to the class, belched loudly and walked out. Barely containing myself, I slammed the door shut.

Presumably he had wanted to disrupt the class and provoke either me or a student into taking a swing at him. If so, he succeeded in his first objective, and almost succeeded in the second.

After he had left the room, the students, miles from algebra by this time, released the accumulated tension by applauding and, after quieting down, they asked questions: "Why can't the kids take care of them?" "Why did they have to come back? Everything was going so good!" These questions may not display a high degree of political sophistication, but they certainly raise doubts as to whether teachers like the one who disrupted my class can ever be effective in one of our classrooms.

Sometimes, the UFT teachers did not even have to take overt action to arouse our ire. The air of arrogance with which they carried themselves was described by one nonunion teacher this way: "It's as though they're saying, 'We're back. We won. You lost. Ha! Ha! Ha!'" When the mathematics staff gathered for a departmental meeting, we found three UFT people smugly waiting in the room, their arms folded. We caucused for a few minutes, then walked out to meet some place else, leaving them alone with two of our "old" assistant principals. At the time, this seemed the only way to prevent a real incident from occurring, so high were feelings running during those days. If this was harassment, I plead guilty.

All of the abuse was verbal. We told them what we thought of them, and they reciprocated. Perhaps the UFT leadership has forgotten the distinction explained in the old "sticks and stones" rhyme. The entire issue of harassment was best summed up by the Rev. C. Herbert Oliver, the chairman of the governing board, when he said, "I wish people wouldn't interpret an exclamation of 'Drop dead!' as a threat on their lives."

. All discussions of harassment evolve into allegations of anti-Semitism. The UFT's skillful use 'of this issue exploited legitimate fears of the liberal Jewish community and turned potential supporters against us. I have spent up to eighteen hours a day in the Ocean Hill–Brownsville community, and I have never experienced any racial or religious slur against me there, nor has anyone with whom I have spoken, nor have I seen any "hate" literature besides that which is distributed by the UFT.

On the contrary, the community and the governing board have demonstrated again and again that these fears are unfounded. On the day before Rosh Hashanah, the governing board distributed to all the children in our schools a leaflet explaining the holiday, what it means to the Jewish people, and why all the city schools are closed on that day. As far as I know, no other school district has taken the trouble to do this.

The issue of black anti-Semitism is a major element in the black-Jewish confrontation which threatens to devastate New York City. Yet, here in Ocean Hill–Brownsville, in the eye of the storm, the problem seems not to exist. I read in the UFT literature and in the Jewish press about "black racism," but I have never experienced it in Ocean Hill, and, to my knowledge, neither has anyone else on the faculty. While the storm rages around Ocean Hill–Brownsville, it is not about Ocean Hill–Brownsville. But one fact of life does stand out: this issue of anti-Semitism, true or false, preys on the fears of the one ethnic group that, united behind it, could destroy us; if this happens, I expect a real problem of black anti-Semitism, and the cycle of self-fulfilling prophecy will be complete.

Unfortunately, there seems to be no effective way to discredit the UFT charges. Rumors abound in the Jewish community of armed hordes of "black Nazis." Recently, I spoke in Forest Hills to a group of Jewish parents who were understandably concerned about this issue. The meeting was organized by a veteran of concentration camps who hoped that I could relate my personal experiences to the parents, and lead a discussion of facts, rather than of wild accusations. He meant well, but the mission was pretty hopeless. These parents simply could not—or would not—believe that the charges of anti-Semitism had no basis in fact. Sometimes, they went to great lengths of logical distortion in order to continue believing what they had been told. One woman said: "You only tell us what you've seen. Shouldn't you tell us about what you haven't seen?"

This is not, however, to say that I have not been threatened. Each time my name or picture appears on television or in the newspapers, I receive a flurry of anonymous letters and, sometimes, telephone calls, all trying to put into question my job, my health, my sanity, or my continued existence. I have been called everything from "scab" to "Commie bastard" to "nigger-lover lout." One letter said: "I hope you can live with yourself. Have you been intimidated yet?" Another put a "black curse" on me; another placed the hopes of the Jewish people in not producing any more like myself. All this is sad and childish, but it does not indicate that there is an organized campaign in the white, Jewish community against me.

Black people hate the "Uncle Tom" more than any white man, and this is probably how the white racists feel about me. Depending on their particular problems, they feel that I am a traitor to my race, my religion, my neighborhood, my family, or any combination of these. It was interesting that, during our confrontations with large contingents of police and UFT pickets, the black parents spent most of their energy haranguing and lecturing the Negro cops, while the white UFT pickets harassed the white "scabs" far more than the black ones.

A year ago, I never thought that I would be crossing picket lines today. I have always supported unions, and I led a nine-day student strike at Long Island University's Brooklyn Center while I was student-body president there. Since I did not believe in the teachers' strike, I had decided not to let the pickets disturb me. Nevertheless, they did. The few pickets on the line that first day spouted more hate in two minutes than I had heard in my lifetime, and it shook me up. I knew that this could not continue long without, at the very least, making my teaching less effective.

The next day, as I approached the picket line, the UFT teachers began their catcalls. I walked to the middle of the line, turned my back, folded my arms, and simply stood there while they poured out their verbal venom. I heard a surprising number of references to my personal past, and I wanted to turn and ask where they get all this information, but I didn't. After five or ten minutes (it seemed much longer), their catharsis ended, the chanting and raving stopped—and I walked on.

It could be that my little nonviolent confrontation with the pickets made them realize how foolish they really were; they have not bothered me since. But I still don't enjoy crossing picket lines, and, after a couple of weeks, I found another route to the school.

The police, while they were at school in large numbers, were less easy to avoid. They stationed themselves on streets and roofs, in the school, in toilets, and in our meetings. During the first weeks of school, our attendance was lower than we expected, and a team of teachers canvassed the parents to find out what was keeping the children home. The answer they most frequently received was: "I don't want to send my kids into an armed camp," and no one could blame the parents for being apprehensive. The children had to squeeze through police barricades in order to reach the front door, and parents were not permitted to accompany them; more than one parent was beaten for insisting that she be allowed to bring her child into school. Even teachers were asked for identification; since none of us had any, we sometimes had to circle the block to find an entrance where there was less resistance.

The police were drawn from all over the city, from Yankee Stadium to Staten Island, they were working overtime, and they did not seem happy to be there. There was also a great deal of confusion at critical moments. At one demonstration, while we were retreating from one line of police advancing in front of us, we turned and found out we were also supposed to be retreating from those behind us. The result was blood and chaos. One quiet morning, I myself was arrested because of a similar mixup. One officer said to move on; another said to stay; whatever I did, I had to end up in jail.

I spent that entire day in the stationhouse, the paddy wagon, and the courthouse, and this afforded me an opportunity to find

out how the police themselves felt about what they were doing.
One cop I spoke to was, more than anything else, angry. It was his
fourteenth consecutive day of work, he was miles from his precinct,
and he knew there were too many police on the scene. He didn't
understand why he had to keep parents out of their schools and
take abuse from those who hated him for being there. Nevertheless, he would be back the next day and the day after that; he
wanted that pension.

And this is where we came in. The cop, the teacher, the landlord—all want to collect the rent while the roof leaks, the house
decays, and the tenant boils.

> Landlord, landlord
> My roof has sprung a leak.
> Don't you 'member I told you about it
> Way last week?

Why Teachers Strike: A Lesson for Liberals /
PATRICK HARNETT

I am not a working poet like Robert Lowell, nor a minister like
Donald Harrington, nor a journalist like James Wechsler. I am a
member of a group of 55,000 teacher employees of a school system.
I believe that this group contains the same proportion of incompetent, narrowly self-interested persons as any other group—as one
could find, for instance, among doctors, social workers, nurses, or
newspaper reporters. I believe there is no reason to expect anything
more of a mass of teachers who until very recently has been paid
the starting wage of a stenographer and has been required to submit
by way of qualifications: a college degree, the passing of a largely
ritualistic test, and proof of no police record or communicable
diseases. The people recruited in such a way have been given the
responsibility for the public education of the children of a city
with the most extensive blight and most entrenched social malaise
of any city in the Northern Hemisphere. They have had to carry

REPRINTED FROM The Village Voice, October 31, 1968, by permission of the
author.

out this responsibility while caught within the tentacles of a classic bureaucracy. In such a world, supervisors do not supervise, students do not receive books, and teachers quickly find that if they want to teach they must make a lonely, exhausting effort. Many fail to make that effort. Many more sincerely try but eventually give up. In the ghetto schools, especially, they give up early. And so today we have a system of education in which young people graduate from our high schools with a general diploma and cannot read.

Where does one place blame for this? I believe that any fair and careful attempt to answer this question must certainly take teachers to account as failures in their jobs, but it must also consider the fact that teachers are part of an institution that has failed—an institution created and maintained not by teachers but by the body politic, the "public." I submit that in the present attempt to combat the failure of an educational system, this same public, instead of eradicating the system, is attempting to eradicate teachers, confusing one thing with the other.

The thrust of the present attack on school problems is against teachers as failures and not against a school system that has failed. Never before have teachers been under such direct and heavy attack. In editorials, by-line columns, full page ads, among parents' groups, fingers are being pointed at teachers as being the chief reason for the failure of our schools.

This feeling is most widespread among the intellectual and liberal community in the city. It has given rise to a development within that community that is unique and disturbing: a tolerance for, at times even an encouragement of unquestionable violations of the professional and human rights of one group of people in the professed interest of promoting the human rights of another group. When, for instance, 250 striking teachers at one experimental school district received telegrams instructing them to report back to work in one day, or else somebody would be hired to take their job "permanently," there was not a ripple of reaction among the many liberal groups that are supporting decentralization. The typical individual reaction among liberals was something like, "Well, they *should* return to work." The New York Civil Liberties Union failed to respond. Normally one would think the CLU would rush to object to the sending of these telegrams. At least it would be interesting to see how the CLU would compare this act with similar acts carried out by the Ocean Hill–Brownsville governing board—acts which they virtually condoned in an elaborate defense of that board called "The Burden of the Blame."

There is a simple and glaring reason, of course, for this development among the liberal community. It is fervently committed to helping black children get an education. There is a prevalent feeling among liberals that if this commitment involves "stepping on the toes" of teachers' rights, that is unfortunate but necessary. It is an understandable—even commendable—feeling. It is very important, however, to examine what role this feeling has played in bringing about the present dangerous crisis in our city. It is this feeling that has been at work in the way Mayor Lindsay has conducted himself throughout the entire strike situation. There is, for example, Lindsay's remark concerning alleged abuses of teachers at Ocean Hill–Brownsville. In the fact of weighty evidence from neutral observers that teachers' lives and families were being threatened, Lindsay replied that the abuse was "99 per cent verbal." He went on to say that you cannot force people to be "affectionate," as though the teachers in question were protesting that they were not liked.

Lindsay was revealing a blind spot here, which I feel was to have a disastrous effect on his ability to judge a problem and act effectively to solve it. It was very important at this critical stage of the entire controversy that the returning "UFT" teachers be accepted in some more or less face-saving fashion, from the point of view of both sides. It was clear, however, that a relatively small group of people in one school building—the more angered members of the school staff and the community—were being allowed to "express themselves" to the returning teachers. There has been no evidence shown that either Rhody McCoy or Reverend Oliver made any active attempt to prevent this kind of expression. By neutral account, these acts went on for four consecutive days. What prevented Lindsay, one must ask, from using his considerable powers and influence to get McCoy and Oliver to call a halt to these acts —acts which threatened to put 1 million children out of school again, as Shanker kept shouting at everybody? There are two possible answers: (1) Lindsay's request to McCoy and Oliver was ignored, or, (2) McCoy's and Oliver's request to those persons doing the "harassing" was ignored. I am not aware of just what attempts of this sort were indeed made. Whatever happened, however, Lindsay did not succeed in "cooling things," something at which he is supposedly a past master.

I cannot help but feel that Lindsay was ineffectual in dealing with this matter because, in the final analysis, his real sensibilities were not affected by what was happening to the UFT teachers. In a subtle way he approved of what was happening or, at the least, he inwardly felt that the harassment was "justifiable when you consider all the circumstances," to use the current formula of many liberals in judging other incidents of the kind which have taken place during this crisis. I believe that it was this feeling that prevented Lindsay from moving directly and honestly in confronting the harassment issue, that made him vacillate and delay and, in short, force an issue that has brought on the immediate debacle in this city.

There are a few facts to keep in mind in weighing the validity of this charge: (1) The acceptance of the returning teachers in some formalistic fashion to actual "teaching duties" would not have weakened the local control principle at Ocean Hill–Brownsville in any real sense at all. The returning teachers at the most would have been an unwieldy excess in staff—but not for long, one has reason to suspect. (2) The harassment of the teachers, therefore, was not motivated by any real tactical need to keep them out of the schools. It represented by and large an emotional expression of hostility ("Do we have to sit in the same room with them?"). I believe that under these circumstances, what prevented Lindsay from stopping this kind of "gratuitous" hostility was that he basically feels the same way. Now it may be no news that Lindsay does not like UFT teachers, but what I am saying is that this dislike was directly responsible for precipitating the present dangerous situation faced by this city.

Many factors underlie Lindsay's attitude toward teachers, specifically, unionized teachers. There is, for instance, his well-known animosity, in general, toward public-service unions. Lindsay, we remember, viewed garbage collectors with four children who went on strike to make more than $7,000 a year as grasping and "unconscionable," and he was willing to call out the National Guard to combat that strike. I believe there is more to this, however, than simple opposition to public-service unions going on strike. There is in Lindsay's attitude toward teachers something more complex. I believe that people like Lindsay (and John Doar and Donald Harrington), who are products of an upper-middle-class milieu, together with intellectuals like, say, Nat Hentoff and James Wechsler, find it genuinely difficult to deal open-mindedly with a teacher group in our present society who represent, in the main, a lower-middle-class ethos. This ethos is repugnant to them for many good and just reasons, but they have let this feeling get in the way of dealing rationally—and even fairly—with the teacher class of this city. The ironic consequence is that black people are paying for it. The sympathies of white liberals and intellectuals are with the truly oppressed in our society—black people. They know that black people, in their struggle to gain the place and dignity of human beings in our society, find that their most immediate and rabid enemy is the lower and lower-middle economic class of whites. There is a reason for this, however, not always recognized for what it is. It is the white person from this economic group whose life is most immediately and actually affected by the struggle of blacks for social justice. This person's job, his home, his neighborhood—often his physical safety and well-being—are directly affected by the social waves created by an out class struggling desperately to get in. His life is affected in ways in which the white liberal minister living on Park Avenue, or the white liberal intellectual living in his Connecticut Shangri-La, can have no experience.

As one example among many, the minister and intellectual do not receive telegrams in the night telling them someone else is going to take their jobs the next day. The upper-middle-class person and the intellectual are therefore really outside the class of the conflict of black insurgency—safely removed and able to abstract the situation. What they often abstract is a group of grasping, white bigots denying the black person his basic rights for no other reason than that they are intrinsically racist. Everyone knows that the less affluent class of whites are the most "bigoted," this thinking goes. Everyone knows that the slave-owning Southern gentleman was less bigoted than the non-slave-owning white.

Now the first question is, do public school teachers really fit into this class of whites? The answer, I believe, is that they do, by and large. This is the first fact not properly understood by the most rabid of their detractors. We hear the charge that teachers today are acting like "plumbers," that they are not "dedicated." What is interesting to me about these charges is not that they are false (there is much truth in them) but that if teachers act like this it should really be surprising to anybody. The public school teachers in this city are in the main a "lower-middle-class" group of people; that is, they reflect the values, thinking, goals, and life-style of a group of people whose parents were working class. They are people who did not have "things" and now want "things," the same things that everybody in our consumer culture wants—and if they have to act like members of an electricians' union to get them, they will.

"But shouldn't teachers be different?" people ask. Yes, certainly, I would respond. Teaching calls for a special kind of person—a sensitive, flexible, humane, mentally healthy, warm, intelligent, skilled person. But is there any reason to really expect the 55,000 school teachers of this city to measure up to these qualifications? I believe that what makes people think teachers should has more to do with a certain historical image of the teacher than with any reasons. I would call this image that of the "noble slave." The teacher has historically been a kind of pathetic figure, underpaid but "dedicated." The rewards of his job lay not in the money he was paid but in the shining eyes of a child mastering his numbers. These teachers led shabby, often destitute lives; but they received an experience in the classroom which money cannot buy, so the image goes. There is much truth behind this image. Teaching young people is of itself a pleasurable, stimulating, and real activ- ity—unlike so many odious activities people must engage in to make a living. But there is a lie behind this image too. This teacher was, in many ways, an oppressed and exploited figure in our society. He did not have the same rights and prerogatives as other members of society. He was a missionary, an eccentric, some- thing of an anchorite who had renounced ordinary desires. (Only a short while ago, most female teachers were—by law—spinsters.) In short, the typical teacher was a "dropout" from society who really didn't want (and therefore deserve) a just compensation for his labor. Most of all, he did not deserve the right to organize to fight for this compensation as everyone else was doing, and—most hideous of all to contemplate—he did not have a right to strike for that compensation.

It is time that everyone recognize that this kind of teacher no longer exists (if he ever did), least of all in New York City. The New York City teacher is a member of an aspiring economic class first, and a teacher second. This may shock some people, but there is no reason it should. The present-day teacher feels that he has a basic right to strike as a last resort, and he is no longer ashamed of it. He feels that he has a right to job security and due process just as everyone else would. Most important of all, in regard to the present struggle of black and Puerto Rican people for "local control," he does not feel that he is the singular perpetrator of education crimes committed against black and Puerto Rican children, and he therefore does not feel that he should be made the scapegoat to assuage the guilt felt by much more affluent whites over their much larger role in committing these crimes.

The average New York City teacher is also by now acting out of fright. He has many years invested in his job. "Decentralization" and "local control" have become frightening words to him. He has witnessed the arbitrary dismissal of hundreds of teachers from their jobs, and he has seen that nobody really objects to it. He has been told that if he does not help join a mass effort to break the strike of his own union—a strike whose immediate issue is a "breach of contract"—then he is a "racist." He has seen teachers being terrorized and he has been told, in effect, that this is justified "when you consider the context."

Under such circumstances, many teachers who were previously open-minded have now become paranoid on the subject of decentralization. This includes Albert Shanker as well as anyone else. The mass of lower-middle-class whites in the city has also become paranoid—that is, those whites whose children are in public schools or who belong to unions, where "honoring the contract" and "job security" are holy causes. These whites have now aligned themselves 100 per cent behind the UFT and are giving full vent to an emotional fear of "black power." I do not think that Lindsay, together with editorialists, news columnists, and the liberal-intellectual establishment of the city, could have brought about a more dangerous situation of racial polarization if they had sat down and planned it that way. In fact, these people (by bringing about this polarization) have done more to scuttle chances for community control than a Shanker could ever have done.

I believe this situation was brought about by a fatal mishandling of events, based on a misunderstanding of what teachers are in our present-day society. The truth is, they are neither dedicated missionaries, nor ingrained racists, and they are no more holding a strike against black people than the Sanitation Department held a strike against black people. I am convinced that both strikes were brought about by a mayor who has catastrophically botched every labor dispute he has stepped into. The cruelest deception being manufactured now is the attempt to attribute the present botch to Lindsay's over-zealous desire to give real power to black communities in running their schools, a desire which is being "crushed" by a powerful white union. I would answer this by asking anyone to consider how Paul O'Dwyer would have handled this crisis had he been mayor. Here is a man who is more authentically in touch with both oppressed blacks and white union members than it is possible for Lindsay to be. O'Dwyer has stated repeatedly his position on the present strike: that there is nothing incompatible with granting community control in schools and maintaining union rights. Lindsay's conduct has shown unmistakably that he has quite the opposite conviction, and therein lies the present tragedy. I for one would insist that if someone like O'Dwyer had been mayor of the city, with O'Dwyer's sensibilities for the sufferings of black people, together with his objective and uncontemptuous understanding of the realities of a union, there would never have been a strike in the first place, and the "long road" toward decentralization and community control of schools would be much less long than it is now.

WASPS like Lindsay, liberals like Harrington, and "intellectuals" like Murray Kempton have failed to understand what they are dealing with in teachers. I would summarize their failure like this:

1. Teachers are no longer a missionary class who can be used in a *noblesse oblige* manner to educate our children. The way in which teachers are hired, and the subsistence wage they are offered gives no one the right to expect them to be more than a cross-section of more or less ordinary human beings from a lower economic stratum of our society.

2. These teachers must carry out their duties within a bureaucratic nightmare. Conditions in the schools in which they teach are often depressing and chaotic, which often makes otherwise normal teachers depressing and chaotic themselves.

3. The present approach to securing community control condones violations of traditional union rights, a tactic that is as unrealistic as it is unnecessary.

4. This approach is being carried out by an upper-middle-class establishment but is revealing a built-in contempt for teachers for having the normal interests, goals, and fears of any similar economic group. As such, what is being attacked is a union, not a school system. What is being served is racial polarization, not community control for black and Puerto Rican people.

Finally, I would like to say that I have found that people—all people—are not what they would like to be, but what they are made to be by the social forces working around them. If you can change conditions, you can change people. I am convinced that if you say of any one school: "Henceforth this school will be new. It will be given a meaningful curriculum, a pleasing, clean environment, abundant materials, genuinely involved supervisors, and small classes," that this kind of thing alone can change the teachers. Most of all, if you can create the *esprit* among teachers that comes simply from their feeling that they are doing something, they will be transformed. There is no question that there are "hopeless" teachers who must be dealt with, but for the most part I do not feel that it is necessary to fire teachers any more than it is to fire students, in order to make a school work.

We will have good schools and good teachers when intelligent people, black and white, begin to work toward that goal honestly, when, for instance, the conditions under which teachers are hired (and then trained and supervised) are changed, and not simply the conditions under which present teachers can be fired. We will not get this by fomenting racial divisions, nor by sacrificing the rights of a group of teachers who have been in some ways victims of the same fraudulent educational system that blacks and Puerto Ricans have been. Lindsay is not a friend of black people by being the enemy of white, unionized teachers. Nor is anyone else. No one is helping black people by telling them that the only way they can gain their legitimate right to control their schools is by firing teachers without giving them due process. The truth is that black people have been more just toward teachers than Lindsay. It is their children, not Lindsay's, who have suffered at the hands of our school system.

The very white people who are most vociferously attacking teachers today are the same people who fled with their children to the white suburbs long ago, who washed their hands of the New York City public schools ten and fifteen years ago, when the first great influx of black and Puerto Rican children took place in our schools. I think that the black and Puerto Rican people know that the wrongs they have suffered in our schools for these many years go far beyond the white teacher in the Harlem classroom. Black and Puerto Rican people will more and more insist upon having schools in this city that educate their children, but they will not be fooled by Lindsay for a minute.

I think they know that a classic fraud is being perpetrated in New York City today. Poor people—blacks, whites, *and* teachers —are at each other's throats. Hasn't it always been this way? Isn't this really what John Lindsay and *The New York Times* have accomplished?

4. Decentralization and Community Control

To many observers, the real issue in the confrontation at Ocean Hill was the future of community control and school decentralization. By the end of the strike, critics on both sides agreed that more than job security was at stake and began the serious discussion of this root issue.

Basic to any consideration of decentralization is the report of the Mayor's Advisory Panel on Decentralization of the New York City Schools, *Reconnection for Learning: A Community School System for New York City*. Released in November, 1967, and known as the Bundy Plan, the report provided the essential blueprint for school decentralization. Parent-elected local school boards were to be given final authority over budget, curriculum, and personnel; school districts were to be small enough to encourage a sense of community and allow for flexible administrative response; teachers and supervisors were to be considered qualified on the basis of state standards rather than city licensing. Perhaps no recent document relating to schools has engendered such heated reaction as the Bundy Plan.

Shortly after the release of the plan, the UFT issued its own program for reform of the city schools. In effect, its proposal called for an administrative decentralization. Almost no power over budget, curriculum, or personnel was to be transferred to local community boards; instead, such powers were to be retained in the hands of a decentralized professional educational bureaucracy.

In the spring of 1968, the UFT, still insisting that it supported decentralization, lobbied successfully against the school decentralization bill (based on the Bundy Plan) then before the state legislature; as a result of its efforts, action on the bill was postponed one year. Faced with variations on the Bundy Plan, the union refused to give endorsement; it insisted on deferring judgment until the Ocean Hill demonstration district had given clear indication of what could be expected from community control and decentralization. Many of those involved in the later clash point to this refusal as evidence of the union's intention to discredit the experiment and, thereby, the whole program of community control and decentralization.

Each of the viewpoints that follow in this chapter focuses on the issue of decentralization, though most make important points about the due process issue as well. Critic Dwight Macdonald, a signer of the original "Freedom to Teach" advertisement, challenges Michael Harrington, co-chairman of the committee that put the ad together, with obscuring the decentralization issue and misstating the due process question. In reply, Harrington attacks community control and decentralization as a cheap substitute for more needed social programs and defends the UFT's plan for administrative decentralization. The exchange ends with MacDonald's evaluation of the potential of community control.

The Harrington position on decentralization is taken up and extended by Maurice Goldbloom. A former teacher, Goldbloom questions whether community control could produce any significant educational change and concludes that the UFT's program is more meaningful. NBC-TV newsman Fred Ferretti disagrees. Observing Ocean Hill at first hand, Ferretti indicates the impact decentralization can have both on student learning potentials and on parent involvement in other community action programs.

In the final article, Jason Epstein sees the positions of the two sides—white teachers and black parents—as irreconcilable. If, then, public education cannot be salvaged by reforming the structure, the alternative, Epstein argues, may be to set up a system of private education for everyone, using public monies to fund it.

No matter what happens in the struggle for community control, the traditional New York school system can never return to its centralized structure. To that extent, the Ocean Hill–Brownsville confrontation signals the end of an era in the New York public school system.

DOCUMENTS

Excerpts from the Bundy Report

The Mayor's Advisory Panel on Decentralization of the New York City schools recommends:

1. The New York City public schools should be reorganized into a Community School System, consisting of a federation of largely autonomous school districts and a central education agency.

2. From thirty to no more than sixty community school districts should be created, ranging in size from about 12,000 to 40,000 pupils—large enough to offer a full range of educational services and yet small enough to promote administrative flexibility and proximity to community needs and diversity.

3. The community school districts should have authority for all regular elementary and secondary education within their boundaries and responsibility for adhering to state education standards.

4. A central education agency, together with a superintendent of schools and his staff, should have operating responsibility for special educational functions and city-wide educational policies. It should also provide certain centralized services to the community school districts and others on the districts' request.

5. The state commissioner of education and the city's central educational agency shall retain their responsibilities for the maintenance of educational standards in all public schools in the city.

6. The community school districts should be governed by boards of education selected in part by parents and in part by the mayor from lists of candidates maintained by the central education agency, and membership on the boards should be open to parents and nonparent residents of a district.

7. The central education agency should consist of one or the other of the following governing bodies: a commission of three full-time members appointed by the mayor, or a Board of Education that includes a majority of members nominated by the com-

---

Reconnection for Learning, released in November, 1967, was the report of the Mayor's Advisory Panel on Decentralization of the New York City Schools.

munity school districts. The mayor should select these members from a list submitted by an assembly of chairmen of community school boards. The others should be chosen by the mayor from nominations by a screening panel somewhat broader than the current panel.

8. Community school districts should receive a total annual allocation of operating funds, determined by an objective and equitable formula, which they should be permitted to use with the widest possible discretion within educational standards and goals and union contract obligations.

9. Community school districts should have broad personnel powers, including the hiring of a community superintendent on a contract basis.

10. All existing tenure rights of teachers and supervisory personnel should be preserved as the reorganized system goes into effect. Thereafter tenure of new personnel employed in a particular district should be awarded by the district.

11. The process of qualification for appointment and promotion in the system should be so revised that community school districts will be free to hire teachers and other professional staff from the widest possible sources so long as hiring is competitive and applicants meet state qualifications.

12. Community school boards should establish procedures and channels for the closest possible consultation with parents, community residents, teachers, and supervisory personnel at the individual-school level and with associations of parents, teachers, and supervisors.

13. The central education agency should have authority and responsibility for advancing racial integration by all practicable means. The state commissioner of education should have authority, himself or through delegation to the central education agency under guidelines, to overrule measures that support segregation or other practices inimical to an open society.

14. The community school system should go into effect for the school year beginning September, 1969, assuming passage of legislation in the 1968 legislature.

15. The main responsibility for supervising and monitoring the transition from the existing system to the community school system should rest with the state commissioner of education. The principal planning and operational functions should be assigned to a temporary commission on transition that should work closely

with the current Board of Education, the superintendent of schools, and his staff.

16. The transition period should include extensive programs of discussion and orientation on operations and responsibilities under the community school system and on educational goals generally. School board members should be afforded opportunities for training and provided with technical assistance on budgeting, curriculum, and other school functions.

Excerpts from the UFT Policy Statement on Decentralization

The United Federation of Teachers believes that the adoption of the Bundy proposals would irreparably harm the educational system. The Bundy model is based upon a glorification of the old-time rural school structure and is unfit for the greatest urban center in the world. The Bundy model is not decentralization; it is Balkanization. It runs counter to the current trend of enlarging school districts in order to provide both for greater efficiency and integration by narrowing school boundaries to increase administrative costs and reinforce segregation. Finally, the Bundy report ignores the new power and integrity of the professional teacher who will not continue to teach in any school or district where professional decisions are made by laymen.

UFT Proposals

Central Board of Education. The present Board of Education should be removed immediately by the legislature and a caretaker board appointed. This is not an attack on the present board or its individual members. They have tried hard. It may be that they have done as well as anyone could during these trying years. But we must recognize that they have lost public confidence and their continuation in office merely provokes increasing community hostility.

THE FULL policy statement was adopted by the UFT executive board on November 28, 1967, and by the UFT delegate assembly on December 20, 1967.

Decentralization. The New York City School System should be decentralized. The number of local school districts formed should be under fifteen in order to insure the possibility of integration within each district and to reduce administrative costs.

Local School Boards. Each local school district should have a local school board of eleven members. All should be elected by parents in the community and should serve without pay. Limitations should be placed upon expenses and reimbursement for lost salary. At least six members of the local school board shall be parents of children in the school.

District Superintendent. District superintendents who meet state qualifications shall be employed by local school boards on contract for a specified term of office.

Funding. The central Board of Education shall continue to control those parts of the budget that represent its legal and contractual obligations. Since salaries, pension costs, social security taxes, and other costs are central obligations, no service is performed by requiring local districts to act as a mere transmission belt. Funds distributed to local boards should be for their own use—administrative and educational. Local boards should be *guaranteed* funds instead of merely getting whatever remains of central funds. Thus, a fixed percentage of all new funds must be earmarked for local distribution. This proposal would make teachers and community allies rather than competitors. Under the Bundy proposal, the more money teachers receive, the less for localities. Under this proposal the greater the budget increase, the greater the sum for districts and for teachers. Whereas the Bundy Report mandates a budget based on the funds likely to be available, the Board of Education shall develop its budget request on the basis of educational needs, not the availability of funds.

New Central Board. The new central board shall be appointed by the mayor. For each vacancy, the mayor shall select from three names, these to be elected by all members of the local school boards. The board shall be unsalaried.

Teacher Licensing and Appointment. New York City should engage in a vigorous nationwide recruiting campaign. A national teacher examination and an interview by the Bureau of Personnel should be used, with a minimum exam mark established. Appointments should be made to districts from a ranked list by the central board, on the basis of vacancies. Final tenure of a teacher should depend upon successful completion of an on-the-job internship. Thus, although the Board of Examiners would be eliminated, the merit system would be maintained.

Promotion.   We oppose the continuation of the hierarchical military model of supervision. We urge a two-track system: administrators employed from nonteacher ranks on the basis of administrative competence and supervisors elected for a term of office by tenured members of their faculties.

Collective Bargaining.   All collective bargaining shall be city-wide. Present tenure provisions shall continue.

Professionalism.   Any new law must clearly recognize the right of the teacher to make educational decisions within his area of competence.

Teacher Transfer.   A permanent staff is an essential ingredient for effective schools, and the transfer plan established in the contract advances this goal. Thus, the transfer policy shall remain a contractual matter.

The UFT endorses the following innovations:
1. a two-track system for administration and education
2. increased assignments of paraprofessionals in the schools with a procedure to aid their training so that they would be encouraged to become teachers
3. the coordination of community efforts for the education of children—thus museums, hospitals, recreation centers, etc. would be utilized
4. the liaison arrangements between the community board and the UFT district chairman
5. the arrangements that might be made to educate some children for a portion of their school day in the homes of parents in the community.

VIEWPOINTS

An Open Letter to Michael Harrington /
DWIGHT MACDONALD

Dear Mike:

Thanks for asking me, along with Noam Chomsky and Jason Epstein, to join a panel discussion on "Morality and Radical Political Action." It's an important, perhaps now *the* important political topic, and I hope they will accept. But I must decline for a reason they don't share: I signed, and they didn't that September 20 ad in the *Times* you got up, as Chairman of the League for Industrial Democracy, supporting the UFT in the Ocean Hill–Brownsville dispute. Now, wearing the more splendiferous hat of National Chairman, Socialist Party, U.S.A., you want me to discuss political morality. But, after the September 20 affair, I'd prefer not to. I think you led me—and others—into a false position, and I haven't any stomach for talking about political morality, and certainly not the radical kind, under your auspices.

This letter is to tell you why I feel so strongly about it, and to provoke you to an explication of your point of view. Of the thousands of "cause" statements I've signed in my time, I've regretted more than a few, but this is the first one I've been ashamed of, also the first time I felt I'd really been "had." My own ignorance —and, more painful, my sloth in being so ignorant—was responsible, an aspect of which was my confidence in you, from which I assumed there was at least a *prima facie* validity to the statement. I soon (two weeks) discovered I was wrong and resigned from your/our Ad Hoc Committee to Defend the Right to Teach. This awakening was all the more painful because I've known, and respected, you for a long time. We first met in 1952 when you, then editor of *The Catholic Worker*, helped me find my way around while I was writing a profile of Dorothy Day—I needed no guide

THIS LETTER appeared in *The New York Review of Books*, December 5, 1968. Reprinted with permission from *The New York Review of Books*. Copyright © 1968 The New York Review.

with Dorothy, she is beautifully obvious. Then in 1963 you published your book, *The Other America*, and I wrote a review-article that was widely read, summarizing and extending your great discovery; between us, we did something to force poverty into the national consciousness. So I'm sure you won't take this letter as a personal insult—a political one, maybe—and I hope you'll correct any inaccuracies or unfairnesses and, more important, will feel stimulated to articulate the mind-set that led you to promote that ad.

Its headline was "In Defense of the Freedom to Teach." Had it appeared three weeks later—without my signature by then—it would have had to be titled: "In Defense of the Freedom Not to Teach" since Albert Shanker, supported by a big majority of the UFT, had called, over the Ocean Hill–Brownsville issue, their third strike in a year. But the original headline has now become sadly appropriate for an ad in favor of the other side, one that would support Rhody McCoy and his principals and school board (and their dedicated new corps of teachers) in their refusal to allow Brother Shanker and his equally dedicated (to another god) UFT majority to deny *them* The Freedom to Teach.

Dedicated but, I know you agree at least on this, shortsighted. How can the UFT strikers—some four-fifths of the city's public school teachers, alas—go back to teaching in ghetto schools, after abandoning their pupils for now going on two months (and on a racial issue they have largely fabricated)? How can they not expect even more recalcitrance to learning than before the strikes, if such may be conceived, and even more hostility, from black students and parents, to them as faithless teachers? There is a minority in the UFT, represented by Vice President O'Neill who was fired last month by Shanker for his opposition to the third strike and his sympathy with the Ocean Hill experiment, which has crossed the picket lines to cries of "scabs"—it will soon be "nigger lovers" after the Shanker racist demagogy hots up a bit more. But the UFT majority has actually succeeded in making the future of our ghetto schools even more hopeless than it has been for twenty years.

They have also done their best to increase the fear and hatred dividing Negro and Jew in this city, playing the game of anti-Semitic black extremists by circulating in Jewish neighborhoods and among the (mostly Jewish) rank and file of the union, reprints of nutty racist tracts issued by minuscule (and, as Jason Epstein showed in the November 21 *New York Review of Books,* in one instance nonexistent) covens of black racists. The only motive for a predominantly Jewish organization giving wide circulation to such nonsense is to imply, as the UFT does, that it represents the policy of the Ocean Hill leaders and the feelings of the parents in the community. (That the motive is not racism but trade union tactics makes it, somehow, all the more disgusting. Anyone who has heard, on television or in private meetings, Mr. McCoy, the Rev. Oliver, or some of the principals of the district, as I have, knows they are serious educators and that support from such fantasts is as welcome to them as an endorsement by the Black Panthers would be to Senator Brooke of Massachusetts. As has often been noted, although it seems not to have penetrated to the minds of Mr. Shanker and his UFT majority who keep groaning about the pogrom atmosphere in Ocean Hill—they have their little racial fantasies too—70 per cent of the new teachers hired over the summer by Mr. McCoy and his mostly black school board are white and of these, 50 per cent are Jewish. This may be a subtle plot, worthy of the Elders of Zion, to lull whitey into an illusion of security. Or, of course, it's possible that the Ocean Hill crowd is more interested in education than in race. Why do you think, Mike, that Shanker circulates that racist filth? And why does he ignore, at least publicly, those 70 per cent–50 per cent racial statistics about the Ocean Hill faculty? You're on the inside, you should know.

My complaint is not only that the Ad Hoc statement came out for the less just and the more socially retrogressive party in the Ocean Hill–UFT row, but, more specifically, that it contained two drastic misrepresentations of fact, and those on the main points at issue: (1) whether the UFT is for or against community control of schools, and (2) whether its members had been denied at Ocean Hill "due process" on job security as provided for in the union contract.

1. The ad stated "Decentralization is *not* the issue," adding that the UFT favored it and "has pledged its full cooperation to make the reorganization succeed." But I soon discovered that decentralization *is* the issue and that Shanker's UFT has been sabotaging it, while paying it lip homage, for some time. For example, last spring it bused hundreds of members to Albany for a day of intensive lobbying against a bill giving the New York City Board of Education authority to set up community-controlled dis-

tricts like Ocean Hill. The current strike aimed openly at the destruction of Ocean Hill community control, is another instance, as is Shanker's recent appeal for a special session of the state legislature, presumably in the hope it will suspend the city Board of Education (changed recently into a pro-decentralization, experimentally minded body by Mayor Lindsay's new appointees) which still hopes to institute real, as against verbal, decentralization. So we signed an untruth, my dear Mike, unless you want to take Shanker's pieties as the reality and his actions as the illusion. To anybody who had much knowledge of the school situation, it was a palpable untruth on September 20. I know why I didn't know it: as Dr. Johnson said to the lady who asked him why his dictionary defined pastern as the knee of a horse: "Ignorance, madame, mere ignorance." But you ought to have known.

2. The ad states thrice—"What I tell you three times is true!" said the Bellman—that the nineteen supervisors and teachers the Ocean Hill school board tried to get rid of last spring (out of several hundred, by the way) were "fired," but in fact, as you yourself admitted to me when I raised the point, Administrator McCoy asked for something much milder, something which is routinely done in hundreds of cases every year by the Board of Education, namely involuntary transfers, which don't mean loss of employment, or even of accumulated seniority, and so cannot be called by any verbal stretch, "firings." When a principal for whatever reason wants to get rid of a teacher, he asks Livingston Street to transfer him to another school, a request that is normally granted by headquarters. The teacher can demand a hearing but this has dangers for him, since if the principal is upheld, there is a black mark on the teacher's record and, I suppose, in extreme circumstances, he might even be fired, really fired. (Though things almost never get so awkward—Epstein's earlier piece in the NYR estimated that in the last five years, out of some 60,000 teachers in the city school system, fewer than fifty have been fired, a tribute to how effectively the system protects its own.)

In this case, the Livingston Street administrators, who viewed community control as benevolently as Mr. Shanker, recommended a hearing, with formal charges; and the Ocean Hill people—whose power to transfer teachers and choose their own faculty had never been clarified by the central administration—made the tactical mistake of agreeing to participate on the central administration's terms, without insisting that their ambiguous rights as an experimental district first be defined. The trial examiner—a retired Negro judge—found for the defendants (now reduced to ten, the other nine having been transferred out at their own request). Then the Ocean Hill leadership made its second tactical error. When the Persistent Ten came back in the fall, they were not exactly welcomed: they—and some eighty UFT strikers who returned at the same time—were made to feel unwanted, as they were; Mr. McCoy and his principals seem to have made little effort to produce a more agreeable atmosphere. This was wrong, though understandable (which doesn't mean it wasn't wrong), but (a) nobody was threatened with being "fired" so the voltage of the "due process" charge in our ad is considerably stepped down, and (b) to decapitate the Ocean Hill experiment and to hold the whole city school system up for ransom if one district isn't punished seems to me Vietnam overkill and I'm ashamed of having lent my name to a statement that may have encouraged the UFT in its rule-or-ruin course.

If they do succeed in ruling, for a time, like the Bourbons returning after Waterloo, it won't be for long, and meanwhile there will be more ruin than rule in our public schools. But aside from these grand historical analogies—"perspectives" we used to call them in my Trotskyist days, as I dare say you did in yours—there is the specific little fact that our ad three times spoke of teachers being "fired" when actually they were threatened only with being "transferred," not at all the same thing either practically or in emotional connotation. If you didn't know this, you should have. And if you did, the use of the stronger term was demagogic at best, and, at worst, a lie. The New York Civil Liberties Union's report of October 9 last, "The Burden of Blame: A Report on the Ocean Hill–Brownsville Controversy," seems to me to withdraw, stone by stone, in laborious historical detail, the underpinnings of Shanker's "due process" charge against Ocean Hill. I'd be interested to have your reaction to it, as well as your present feelings about the semantics of "firing" v. "transferring."

One of the problems in this problematic tangle is that while I've found no lack of arguments and data supporting the Ocean Hill side, there seems to be, in print or verbally, a paucity of discourse on the Shanker-UFT side—the one I joined, with visions of due process dancing in my head, for an uneasy fortnight. You haven't been of much help, I'm afraid. On October 8, I sent you a note of resignation from your committee, enclosing a carbon of a two-page letter I'd written to the other Harrington, Donald, explaining why I had decided to join his group, The Emergency Committee to Save School Decentralization and Community Control—neither side can be accused of catchy nomenclature. No response. I called you several times, before and after my change of mind, leaving messages at your office and home. No reply. Finally, early in November, stimulated by a letter from a nonstriking teacher who had just received from UFT pickets a reprint of the September 20 ad with my name still attached—and who chanced to have seen in Hentoff's column in *The Village Voice* that I had long since joined the opposition—I called you again to ask you to take my name off and, at last, had the pleasure of a talk with you. You admitted you weren't happy about the third strike, and you agreed that to paralyze indefinitely the whole school system to a win a contractual dispute in one district was not justifiable trade union practice. You said you had been meeting privately with Shanker and had tried to persuade him to moderate his demands for the extirpation of Ocean Hill and to settle the strike. You regretted your efforts had, so far, been unsuccessful, but you had hopes. You granted that Brother Shanker had certainly gone "too far."

"Then why not say so publicly?" I asked. "It seems to me immoral, in your position, to keep quiet if you're against this strike." To which you, patiently reasonable as always: "But I've told you I've been telling Shanker for weeks now he should compromise. He doesn't see it that way yet, but he's not entirely unreasonable, Dwight, you have to understand his fears as a trade unionist. There'll be real problems for him if the school system is split up into thirty or forty or sixty autonomous districts." "How many would you say was the maximum, from the union's point of view?" "Well . . . even thirty seems too many . . . fragmentation . . . chaos . . . and those white racists on Staten Island could fire all the liberal and colored teachers. . . ." But the issue right now isn't the future of the UFT or the possible Birchite control of future school districts but the survival of Ocean Hill. Shouldn't you speak out now against Shanker's use of a city-wide strike to destroy it?" "But if I did, I'd lose my influence with the union, can't you see that? And I resent your bringing morality into it, really. It's not that I'm afraid to criticize the union. It's just that I know I can be more effective if I don't get in a position of public opposition."

We also discussed the September 20 statement. You told me

that Ned Polsky and Arthur Schlesinger, Jr., had also withdrawn their names, which I knew, but that you still stood by it in general —you seemed surprised I'd asked the question. (You may recall our conversation differently, I didn't take notes, but the above is my recollection of what was said.)

I also told you I'd just spent a day poking around in four of the Ocean Hill schools and had been impressed by the friendly, serious, relaxed atmosphere in the dozen or so classes I sat in on; by the easy way the young, mostly white teachers related to their pupils, talking to them without condescension; by the order, if not exactly quiet, in the halls between classes—I saw no fighting and only three or four instances of rowdy behavior (which were dealt with promptly by passing teachers who didn't threaten or shout—I don't remember hearing a teacher raise his, or her, voice the whole day). "Discipline," the Calvary of "normal" ghetto schools, was rarely apparent. The teachers generally seemed to like their pupils and find them interesting and vice versa, so that a mildly disorderly hum of cooperative effort was the usual classroom atmosphere. I'm told it used to be rather different in the ghetto schools when the UFT veterans ran them in professional style. Ocean Hill reinforced the prejudice I've always had in favor of amateurs who don't know how to do it but, as the etymology suggests, love doing it. I was allowed, by the way, to wander anywhere I liked, sometimes without a guide, which, I'm also told, would be unthinkable in the normal, or professional, ghetto school. It was a moving and satisfying experience, that day at Ocean Hill. I hope you'll try it yourself, before you reply to this letter. It might make a difference. I suppose it wouldn't be practical to take Mr. Shanker along too?

Best regards, as always,
Dwight

An Open Letter to Men of Good Will (with an Aside to Dwight Macdonald) /
MICHAEL HARRINGTON

The New York City school crisis has the aspect of an Antigone-like tragedy. On one side, there are those who justly denounce miseducation in the ghetto which, in this technological society, effectively programs innocent children for a life of adult poverty. On the other side, the members of one of the most progressive labor organizations in America—on issues stretching from civil rights to Vietnam—assert principles of academic freedom and due process when a professional is dismissed from his or her post.

So there is not a simple conflict of right and wrong but an antagonism of two rights. As a result, you are torn no matter what position you take.

I was sensitive to these complexities and ambiguities when I helped initiate the Right to Teach statement which supported the union on the basic issue in dispute: whether or not there had been a violation of due process at Ocean Hill–Brownsville. I resolved my conflicting loyalties in this fashion for two reasons. I was convinced—and I most emphatically still am—that substantial procedural rights had been denied the teachers and therefore, on the specific issue in contention, the union was right. Secondly, and even more fundamentally, I felt that the local board's tactics would not advance the goal of genuine, effective decentralization which I also advocate. I thought that the version of community control being urged in Ocean Hill–Brownsville gave unwitting support to a conservative, and even reactionary, position. And I believed that any decentralization plan which abrogated union rights was politically doomed to failure.

As the conflict escalated, no decent person on either side could be happy. New York was racially polarized as never before; hundreds of thousands of public school children were not being taught; and the parent-teacher relationship in the slums was transformed

---

THIS LETTER appeared in *The New York Review of Books*, January 2, 1969. Reprinted with permission from *The New York Review of Books*. Copyright © 1969 The New York Review.

from alliance (which it had been only a few years ago, when, for instance, the UFT supported the first school boycott) to bitter antagonism. Clearly, then, this was not a traditional labor dispute pitting worker against boss, nor a traditional freedom struggle of black against racist. So without changing my basic view of the issue, I favored the quickest possible just resolution of the strike.

Now the dispute may be over (though as I write on December 4, there are persistent reports of violence and breakdown of the agreement). Nothing constructive will be accomplished by rehearsing the old issues at this point, for what is needed is reconciliation between the black parents and the union teachers, difficult as that may seem. If such a *rapprochement* does not take place, all the indicators point to a worsening of the *status quo ante*. The legislature, responding to backlash sentiments, will end the entire decentralization experiment; the ghetto will be stuck with the same utterly inadequate schools, and the fact will be all the more intolerable because it will be more widely known by the victims; and the hostility of black and white, parent and teacher, will be institutionalized with disastrous consequences for all progressive causes.

So the main, substantive point of this Open Letter is to try to clarify the decentralization question itself as part of a dialogue among the men of good will on both sides who favor real, effective community involvement in the educational process. Unfortunately, I must preface this serious point with an aside about Dwight Macdonald's comments to me (*New York Review*, December 5).

Macdonald tells how our personal relationship dates back to 1952. He accurately states what I have often acknowledged publicly: that his *New Yorker* review of *The Other America* helped transform the fate of that book, the issue which it raised, and its author. For that I have been, and still am, grateful. Macdonald then honors these sixteen years of friendship by betraying a confidence which he explicitly states he knew I did not want made public. He does so through serious misquotation which makes me look treacherous to my friends and hypocritical to my opponents. He prefaces this flagrant violation of the most elementary code of friendship by implying that my ethics are so suspect that a man as principled as Dwight Macdonald cannot ever discuss morality under the same roof with me. In the process, Macdonald proves

himself more reprehensible than a wiretapper, for he uses inti-
macy, rather than electronics, to do his dirty work.

Macdonald says that through sloth, ignorance, and misplaced
trust in me, he signed a statement which did not even have *prima
facie* validity. Having thus established his expertise, he is now
so infallibly certain of the facts in Ocean Hill–Brownsville that
anyone who disagrees with him is either ignorant and slothful,
as he himself was only yesterday, or deceitful. For my part I am
willing to grant the sincerity of the majority of intelligent, decent
people on both sides—and even to entertain the possibility that I
am wrong. Indeed, when Macdonald first discovered how stupid
he had been, and how right he had become, I helped supply him
with the names and addresses of all his fellow signatories so that
he could invite them to a meeting where spokesmen of the Ocean
Hill–Brownsville board would try to persuade them to remove
their names from the "Right to Teach" ad.

I was out of town and could not attend the session, but I sent
Macdonald a friendly wire telling him that I hoped that concerned people on both sides could carry on a dialogue. My reward
for this essay in fraternity was Macdonald's semi-fictional, garbled version of our private conversation.

On the issues which Macdonald raises in this duplicitous way,
I will be brief for the reasons I stated earlier. I am convinced
that the UFT was genuinely for decentralization, in part because
the first advocate of this kind of a plan to whom I talked was
Al Shanker. In 1966, he asked me to write an article on the
union's advocacy of such an approach and particularly insisted
that the local boards would have to have independent funds of
their own. (I referred briefly to Shanker's position on page 130 of
Toward a Democratic Left, which was completed in October,
1967, almost one year before the strike.) Moreover, through the
League for Industrial Democracy I helped organize, and attended,
off-the-record conferences which brought together union leaders,
black advocates of community control, and people from City
Hall and the Ford Foundation. We tried to discuss and resolve
the differences within the group, and though we obviously failed
spectacularly, the experience convinced me that the union was
indeed for decentralization even though it differed with some of
the black leaders present. (Not being a licensed moralist like
Dwight Macdonald, I am not at liberty to report on these closed
meetings in any detail.)

Secondly, I remain convinced that a due process issue was very much at stake, and that the ad was right on this basic count. But since I don't want to stir up old animosities I would simply refer Macdonald, or anyone else who is interested, to Maurice Goldbloom's excellent critique of the New York Civil Liberties Union Report. (It can be obtained from the Ad Hoc Committee to Defend the Right to Teach, Room 1105, 112 East 19th Street, New York City.) It contains documentation for my position which I find persuasive.

I should also note that Macdonald did not simply publicize a friendly, explicitly private conversation, but he did so in such a distorted way—I will assume unwittingly—as to suit his own purposes. I did indeed have tactical differences with the union leadership at certain points in the strike, and I spoke to Al Shanker about them in a private meeting which will remain private. Macdonald's secondhand and remembered transcription of this conversation—heard, so to speak, through the keyhole—is erroneous in significant sections. It also publishes details which one might even think malicious: I have not used the term "colored," which Macdonald attributes to me, since I was a boy in St. Louis. When he put the word in my mouth, did he know it suggested genteel, middle-class racism?

I have long thought Dwight Macdonald charming and decent. His lack of diplomacy seemed a mark of integrity, his constant changing of positions a sign of restless honesty. He was our own Pierre Bezuhov. But there is no holy obtuseness, no saintly stupidity, which justifies the betrayal of a friend. In *The Root Is Man*, Macdonald rightly identified the notion that one sacrifices the present, living generation in the name of a distant future as a source of Stalinism. And now that the preacher has used a personal relationship as an expendable means for his political ends, he lectures me on morality.

But let me turn to the real issue: how to develop effective decentralization of the New York school system.

When the union, and others like myself, objected to the original Bundy proposals on the grounds that they would create too many school districts, some took this as an evasion on the part of the enemies of community participation. I simply do not think that is true. Even more to the point, I believe that some of the militants and radicals who have embraced an extreme version of local control (small, neighborhood, or near-neighborhood units of administration) are the unwitting agents of a reactionary scheme which could do much harm to black and Spanish-speaking children. Therefore it is precisely because I want decentralization to work that I am opposed to the proposal in this form. And I think there is some mighty fancy manipulating going on among some of the corporate liberals who have made an alliance with some black powerites.

Cutting up the city into a multiplicity of districts has many dangerous consequences which are so obvious that I will only list them. It institutionalizes segregation (and I am for integration on moral, economic, social, and educational grounds). It opens up the possibility of political, and even witch-hunting, job criteria in units which are so small that they can be dominated by a minority of activists, whether of the Ultra Right or Ultra Left. It could lead to a fantastic reduplication of effort in contiguous districts and a resultant waste of resources which would injure every school in the city. It would allow middle- and upper-class city dwellers to imitate the worst example of their suburban cousins by effectively establishing lily-white public prep schools in order to maintain the unfair advantages which their children have.

These are just a few of the objections to the notion of the neighborhood school unit of administration. But there is an even more pertinent point which a recent ad of the New York Urban Coalition illustrates perfectly and outrageously. Entitled "If it works for Scarsdale, it can work for Ocean Hill," this statement is either unbelievably incompetent or else the most obscene act of Machiavellianism on the part of white corporate wealth in recent years.

"Scarsdale," we are told, "has one of the finest school systems in the United States."

It has 5,122 students. And a school board consisting of seven members. Which makes one board member for every 732 students.

New York City has much the same system.

It has 1,100,000 students. And a Board of Education consisting of thirteen members. Which makes one board member for every 84,615 boys and girls.

The arithmetic alone shows us why our school system is in trouble . . .

Doesn't anybody give a damn that less than 25 per cent of our high school graduates go on to college?

And that figure for Scarsdale is 99 per cent . . .

Doesn't anybody give a damn that 55 per cent of the children in our public schools are behind in reading? . . .

If you give a damn about our children, we see only one answer.

Community control of the schools. [Emphasis added. I have skipped about half the ad but not changed its essential meaning.]

Now this is, of course, the most preposterous sociology and economics one can imagine. You take a white, upper-class suburban community in which the overwhelming majority of the parents are college graduates, and where practically everyone enjoys the benefits of affluence. You then use the zoning power, and other techniques, to wall off this island of prosperity from the sea of urban troubles in New York City. And, if that is not enough discriminatory advantage for such a community, just to be sure that the kids will stay way ahead of the blacks and the poor, you spend much more money on their schooling than impoverished communities can afford. So it was in 1966, the White House Conference on Civil Rights noted that those seven board members in Scarsdale accomplished their prodigies in part because they spent $1,211 per capita on each child while rural Georgia was paying out $265 a year and Cleveland $447.

You then compare this suburb, with its princely federal and state subsidies, with the most victimized, disadvantaged black ghetto areas of New York. And ignoring the whole institutionalized, corporatized system of economic and social racism, you argue that the difference in educational achievement in the two areas is a function of the structure of the school board. And therefore, the clear implication goes, if only there is community control in Ocean Hill–Brownsville, then there will be a rapid progress toward a 99 per cent figure for college entrance. The slums are left to rot; no new appropriations are mentioned for school buildings, teachers, or equipment; and there is painless, costless, and fundamental change.

It can be justly argued that this is an extreme statement of the case and that the more intelligent supporters of a great number of small districts do not buy this propagandistic thesis. There are two important comments which have to be made to such a response.

First of all, as the battle lines hardened during the strike, the partisans of the Ocean Hill–Brownsville board tended to make centralization *the* problem, community control *the* solution, and to regard even the most sincere statement of the case for a limited decentralization within larger, integrated, and economically functional units as treason to the cause. Now that the day-to-day escalation may have come to an end, isn't it possible to discuss the complex causes of ghetto miseducation in a more serious way?

Moreover the fact that some of the Ocean Hill–Brownsville supporters, even those on the Left, adopted Goldwaterite economic arguments in defense of their position shows how reactionary the logic of this panacea can be. I expect a Milton Friedman to believe that if, in a class-stratified and institutionally racist society, one gives each family unit a voucher and allows them to bid for education on the "free" market, that will result in justice. That has been the conservative argument for some centuries now. But people on the Left should certainly understand that the exercise of such equal rights to education within a profoundly unequal economic and social structure will shore up privilege and intensify discrimination. That is not theoretical speculation; it is historical fact.

Indeed, I would argue that a certain measure of financial centralization is necessary in the New York school system precisely in order to allow for greater per capita funds to go to areas with higher per capita disadvantages of housing, health, income, and the like. If, however, there is going to be an "equal" competition among a multiplicity of community boards, then the districts with the greatest economic, social, and political power will prevail. (Ironically, *The New York Times* reports that the Urban Coalition is supporting my position in a Detroit lawsuit. Why, then, does the New York Coalition take a full-page ad which rebuts the parent body's attitude in Detroit?)

I am ready to assume quite sincerely that most of the black community control enthusiasts and their white supporters are led to a potentially dangerous and conservative position by an understandable outrage against the indignities of the *status quo* and a determination to try something, almost anything, new. I do not feel so kindly about the Urban Coalition.

The great impetus for the decentralization controversy in New York came from two Republicans, John Lindsay and McGeorge

Bundy. If the notion of corporate liberalism has any relevance—and, as I pointed out in *Toward a Democratic Left*, I think it does—Mr. Bundy is eminently qualified to be included in, and Mr. Lindsay only a little less so. Now they are joined by the Urban Coalition in backing a scheme which is the very essence of Let Them Eat Cake! In order to get the children of Harlem up to the educational level of those in Scarsdale, it is not necessary to invest in decent housing, build new towns, create genuine full employment, or even make a modest little contribution to improving the quality of segregated education in the slums right now. It can all be done by that magic change in the structure of the Board of Education which is going to abolish the three centuries of racism which are so incarnated in our basic economic institutions.

What becomes almost obscene about such a reactionary shell game—with all those pious "give a damns"—is that these very same corporate chiefs are right now planning an increase in unemployment in order to protect the stability of prices and the worth of the dollar in Scarsdale at the expense of the poor in Ocean Hill–Brownsville. At its October meeting the Business Council—which is about as close to an executive committee of the American *haute bourgeoisie* as one can get, and contains some of the most socially conscious Give-a-Damners in the country—discussed hiking the jobless rate to 5½ per cent or 6 per cent. And although there has not been much candid talk about the scheme since, there have been enough hints that the Nixon Administration will fight inflation in this cruel manner.

The most monstrous part of this situation is that it allows Urban Coalition executives to parade as the allies of militant black power even as they, or their allies, are preparing to increase black unemployment. And that is a particularly insidious form of corporate liberalism since the only concessions it makes to the poor in order to strengthen the *status quo* are psychological. For though a community board might have the appearance of control, effective power will be exercised by the major economic and social forces manipulated by the corporate leaders. Under such circumstances, it is small wonder that people like Barry Goldwater and William F. Buckley, Jr., have had kind words to say about black control of black misery and white control of the nation's wealth. What is surprising is that people on the Left should join in the chorus.

All of us became, I am sure, somewhat polemical and sloganistic under the pressure of the strike. But now it should be possible to have serious discussions of the complex causes of mis-education in the other America and the need for massive, democratically planned social investments, as well as functionally structured decentralization, in order to do something about the intolerable situation. I understand perfectly well that a Nixon Administration is not exactly likely to adopt the necessary policies and that, in the immediate future, there may be no choice except to settle for a slice of bread rather than a loaf. But the reality must be accurately described so that, when the political possibility of effective action once more emerges, the partisans of social change and genuine black freedom will know what to do. And that cannot happen if all criticism of the community control version of a decentralist panacea advocated by both militants and the corporations is seen as treason.

The growth of race consciousness and pride in the black slums of America is one of the most momentous and positive developments of the decade. But that new spirit must now inspire economic and social programs capable of dealing with the enormous, interconnected outrages suffered by the black masses. There are militants who say there must be a transfer of resources and power from the white rich to the poor, both black and white. Precisely! But that is not done simply by changing the structure of the school board, as the New York Urban Coalition would have one believe. It requires, among other things, a new majority including both blacks and trade unionists joining in a common struggle. And it would be a sad day if the Left were to buy the sophisticated, reactionary argument of big business for inaction and the intensification of the economic and social bondage of black Americans.

If the strike is over, as I fervently hope, it is time for the most earnest discussion, not for recrimination. Either those of us who were on different sides of the immediate issue, but who share common values and concerns, will once more come together or else the only victors in the tragedy will be backlash and poverty.

Reply to a Non-Reply / DWIGHT MACDONALD

The editors headed Michael Harrington's piece last issue a "Reply," but they should have pondered his own title: "An Open Letter to Men of Good Will (with an Aside to Dwight Macdonald)." Or they could have used their rulers. Out of a total eighty-two inches of type—he's even more long-winded than me, by two feet—the "Aside," which is the only direct reply to my letter, takes up twenty-three inches. And two-thirds of them are devoted not to the question but to complaints about an alleged impropriety I committed by quoting a private phone talk (leaving seven inches of specific response to my own fifty inches of specific argumentation). The allegation is true but his indignation seemed to me excessive.

Since the "duplicity," "dirty work," "flagrant violation of the most elementary code of friendship," "betrayal," etc. in one-sixth of my letter preoccupy Harrington more than the arguments advanced in the other five-sixths, I'll begin with this embarrassing question. If only I'd been clever and just asked him in print, innocently, whether he approved of Shanker's third strike! But I suppose he would have thought that, too, a bit duplicitous. And I suppose it wouldn't have made it any more respectable even if I'd known, as I found out after my letter appeared, that Harrington had expressed to two other journalists of our acquaintance the same distaste for Shanker's Third as he did to me? Yes, I feared as much. Also I'll point out, before he does, that neither of them put it into print. But neither of them was writing him an Open Letter, into which it did fit beautifully. But as the context makes clear, he didn't want his position publicized, and it was wrong of me to do it and I'm very sorry and will try to be more decent in the future. I suspected Harrington might be peeved but had I dreamed he'd be so upset I wouldn't have done it.

There's one complaint I have, if a man who has lost his character may venture it: Harrington claims my report of the phone talk is inaccurate: "garbled," "semi-fictional," "serious misquotation," and climactically (he doesn't spare the horses): "Macdonald's secondhand and remembered transcription of this conversation—heard, so to speak, through the keyhole—is erroneous in significant sections." I don't understand, by the way, what he can mean by "secondhand"—does he imply somebody else, masquerading as me, was talking to him for half an hour and that I got my information from him as to what was said? But what I find strange is that after all this abuse Harrington produces only one misquotation: my quoting him as referring to "colored teachers," on which, after observing "one might even think it malicious," he comments: "I have not used the term 'colored' since I was a boy in St. Louis. When Macdonald puts the word in my mouth did he know it suggested genteel, middle-class racism?" He might have asked me that question before he used "malicious"—but he's not on speaking terms with me any more except for one call from him to bawl me out, which he did, loudly, until his moral indignation overcame him, as I was trying to get in a word, and he hung up on me. Since nobody can not be on writing terms with anybody, I'll tell him the answer is No, I didn't know "colored" was a genteel-racist term. Myself, I've always used "Negro"—with a capital N, please—until lately when I've adopted the ungenteel, unracist term, "black," which they seem to prefer—it used to be considered vulgar-racist, these things change in time. And in place: perhaps "colored" doesn't seem pejorative to me because I was brought up in New York and not in St. Louis. In any case, I can't see how this sole example he gives to support his repeated charges of misquotation can reasonably be called either "serious" or "significant."

But let's get down to business. My letter was devoted mostly to demonstrating, or trying to, that two crucial statements of fact in the "Freedom to Teach" ad Harrington and I signed (for a while) were in fact not facts. (1) The Ocean Hill board did not fire the UFT teachers last May, as the ad stated three times; they had no power to deprive them of employment, which is what "firing" means except in UFT dialectics; they had tried to "transfer" them, involuntarily, out of the district for reassignment to some other district by the Board of Education, something they thought they might have the authority to do—their powers in this as in other crucial respects were not well defined by either the Marchi bill or the board, whether from inadvertence or calculation. (2) Decentralization *was* the issue, the real one not the formal one of "due process" the UFT insisted on for tactical reasons. And the UFT was not for it—unless "decentralization" be defined in the Pickwickian sense Shanker and Harrington use —as was shown by its massive lobbying in Albany last spring which helped to defeat the stronger, more specific Regents bill— and its attempt, unsuccessfully, to defeat such liberal assemblymen as Jerry Kretschmer and Al Blumenthal who defied the UFT on the Regents bill—see Sol Stern's detailed account in *Ramparts*. Also, of course, by its three city-wide strikes last fall, each of which had for its chief aim the removal of Rhody McCoy and his principals and the local board at Ocean Hill.

On (1): Harrington doesn't defend using the emotive "fired" as against the accurate but unexciting "transferred" in his/our ad, indeed he doesn't mention that word, of which, I imagine, he and Shanker are by now heartily sick. His total comment on (1) is: "I remain convinced that a due process issue was very much at stake and that the ad was right on that basic count. But since I don't want to stir up old animosities, I would simply refer Macdonald, or anyone else who is interested, to Maurice Goldbloom's excellent critique of the New York Civil Liberties Union Report." I have read Goldbloom's paper, twice; it is objective in style and specific in documentation. The first reading, I was impressed, even a little worried, would I have to change my mind again, and so soon? A second and more analytic reading—without benefit of the NYCLU's rebuttal which came later, I might add—reduced its impact considerably. It has the virtues, and the defects, of a competent but not imaginative lawyer whose aim is to score points rather than to tease out the truth in the style of Learned Hand or Jerome Frank or Clarence Darrow.

Goldbloom's points often seem solid enough, until one puts them in the broader, sloppier context of the reality (which of course one has to know something about). Then one finds, or I did, that his scrupulous documentation and clear argumentation mostly support irrelevancies (as the pages devoted to the activities of "Sonny" Carson and other black racists with hardly a perfunctory stab at connecting them with Ocean Hill). Or quibbles: he cites the UFT's support of the Marchi bill as evidence of its being for decentralization without mentioning it did so in order to kill the stronger Regents bill. Or *non sequiturs:* "Unilateral removal from a completely decentralized district would be dismissal, as this [the Ocean Hill transfers] was intended to be." But there isn't complete decentralization yet and so Ocean Hill's intentions, which were not good, granted, were only daydreams and Goldbloom has merely invented a novel kind of anachronism that might be called "futuristic" or "projective."

He does have two real points. The appointment by the Ocean Hill board, and Mr. McCoy, of Herman Ferguson as one of their new principals shortly after he had been indicted for conspiring to murder Roy Wilkins of the NAACP and Whitney Young of the Urban League—he has since been convicted and sentenced—was disgraceful, irresponsible, inexcusable, and, as Goldbloom puts it in his low-keyed style—what a relief after Harrington's—"it hardly contributed to an atmosphere of confidence." I'd add that anybody who even in fantasy—for the affair seems not to have gotten beyond that level—could think that eliminating Mr. Wilkins and Mr. Young would change anything is not mentally qualified to conduct a nursery school. That the Ocean Hill board shouldn't have realized this is also shocking.

Goldbloom's other point is semi-solid—a half point, let's say. He claims and backs it with a press quote from Dr. John Niemeyer, of the Bank Street College of Education, who wrote an important report on the controversy last spring that both sides cite, that the Ocean Hill board rejected an offer from Superintendent of Schools Donovan to make the transfers in a routine way without publicity and insisted on making an issue of them as a way of asserting—and testing—their power. This is denied by McCoy, who says he wanted to do it quietly but was forced by Shanker and the board to bring charges and thus get into a public showdown with the teachers. His version is backed by knowledgeable observers not connected with Ocean Hill. It's a complicated story and I'm not sure which version is right, something of both maybe. So—a half point to Goldbloom.

On (2), the question of decentralization: Harrington says he is "convinced that the UFT was genuinely for decentralization" because in 1966 Shanker asked him to write an article advocating it. Also because later (date unspecified) he, Harrington, as chairman of the League for Industrial Democracy, helped organize several conferences "which brought together union leaders, black advocates of community control and people from City Hall and the Ford Foundation. . . . The experience convinced me that the union was indeed for decentralization even though it differed with some of the black leaders present. . . . Not being a licensed moralist like Dwight Macdonald [he doesn't let go of an advantage, a real pro] I am not at liberty to report on these closed meetings in any detail." Okay, who am I to judge, my license has expired. But, without going into scabrous detail, might he not have given us just a teeny hint as to *why* "the experience convinced me the union was indeed for decentralization"? Just enough to give the reader some way of deciding whether Harrington was intelligent as well as convinced. I'd also be curious to know, hope I'm not being prurient, on what issues the union "differed with some of the black leaders present." I suppose we'll have to wait until The Revolution opens the Harrington Archives like the Bolsheviks in 1918 or the Columbia strikers with Dr. Kirk's (rather dull) correspondence files last spring. Until then, if he must be so discreetly uninformative, he would be better advised not to bring up such delicate subjects. The striptease has its charms, but not in serious discussion.

Even if we grant that Shanker was for decentralization in 1966, I don't see what this shows about his stand today. Two years ago decentralization may have been for the liberal leader of the liberal UFT—I intend no irony by the adjectives, alas—a beautiful ideal. But it has become an ugly reality now that the Ford Foundation has funded and the Lindsay Administration has created, responding to recent pressures from the black ghettos, three functioning experimental districts, with a good chance of the experiment soon becoming standard throughout the whole school system. This new order of things, which may or, if the UFT prevails, may not be enacted into law this spring by the state legislature, is doubly threatening to a white union like the UFT. Technically, bargaining will be more difficult, since agreements must be reached not with one central Board of Education but with many—thirty is the Board's own recent proposal—autonomous local boards. And racially, while the Board of Education, and its bureaucracy, are practically all white, many of the new districts—half of them if their composition reflects that of the city's public school population—will have predominantly nonwhite governing boards. Shanker's rule-or-ruin strategy in his three anti–Ocean Hill strikes will not ease future relations between the UFT and such nonwhite decentralized districts as may be created. His injection of racism by circulating among his mostly

Jewish rank and file as examples of "the kind of thing" that goes on in ghettos (like, say, Ocean Hill?) anti-Semitic black racist tracts was, likewise, not calculated to make things easier when and if the school system is decentralized. The latter was one of many criticisms of the UFT in my Letter that Harrington didn't take up; maybe he's working quietly on the inside.[1]

Of the three-quarters of Harrington's Open Letter which is addressed to those "men of good will" the most striking characteristics are antique political narrowness and (perhaps therefore?) often slight relevance to the educational topics he thinks he is discussing. "The great impetus for the decentralization controversy in New York came from two Republicans, John Lindsay and McGeorge Bundy," he begins one paragraph, later throwing in a sneer at "corporate liberalism." Why Republicans should still be automatic villains even to the Chairman of the Socialist Party after four years of a Democratic administration in Vietnam, I don't see; nor what's so bad about "corporate liberalism"— would he prefer "corporate conservatism"? Republicans or not, Bundy and Lindsay have given our black communities new hope for at last maybe getting their kids educated, and new pride by proposing to hand over to them the control of their local schools —up to now they have had as much say as the patient does in running the hospital. In either socialist or Socialist terms this would seem to be a good thing. Chairman Harrington isn't impressed, however, he's after bigger game.

.   .   .

Where to begin? The long passage about the Let Them Eat Cake scheme is a heavily ironical paraphrase of a silly ad put out by the Urban Coalition entitled "If It Works for Scarsdale, It Can Work for Ocean Hill." . . . Some truth here, namely, there are too many students under the central control of one Board of Education and its Livingston Street bureaucracy and

[1] Henry Addis of Bayside High School objects, among many other items, to my reference to the "mostly Jewish rank and file" of the UFT. "It is a long time since a union has been identified as a 'predominantly Jewish organization,'" he writes, adding ironically: "Perhaps Jews should now keep quiet?" I described the UFT as mostly Jewish because (a) it is and (b) that fact, as the above passage indicates, is as relevant to the UFT–Ocean Hill conflict as the fact that most of those involved in Ocean Hill (except for the teachers!) are black. Why doesn't Mr. Addis object to my saying *that*?

breaking the monolith up into thirty-three autonomous districts would be a big improvement. But it's on the whole one of those brainstorming gimmicks that make copy writers think they're creative. It has no connection with Bundy, Lindsay, Rhody Mc-Coy, Kenneth Clark, Jason Epstein, or any other serious proponents of decentralization, including John Lotz and his colleagues on the Board of Education who have just produced a realistic, sober, and workable plan for decentralization that will be voted on in Albany this spring.

The ad has no connection with anything, indeed, except Harrington's polemical convenience, and if I may speak as one with some experience, breaking a butterfly on the wheel goes down only with the most unreflective type of reader. The thoughtful kind may wonder why he wasted so much space—twice as much actually, as he found it convenient to devote refuting my arguments in an Open Letter that was addressed to him—on demolishing a statement which, at most, proved the publicity department of the Urban Coalition is not bright. And Harrington then offers us this statistical clincher: "Those seven board members in Scarsdale accomplished their prodigies in part because they spent $1,211 per capita on each child while rural Georgia was paying out $265 a year and Cleveland $447." What's wrong is that Harrington has simply left out the figure for New York City, which is what he and the ad are comparing Scarsdale with. I'm sure it was an oversight due to simple ignorance and in no way connected with the fact that the New York City figure squashes flat his argument that Scarsdale "accomplished prodigies," as against rural Georgia and Cleveland, because it spent so much more per capital on its schools. For New York is now spending per capita on its public schools not much less than what Scarsdale does: $1,000 as against $1,200.

Finally . . . Harrington has concocted what we Trotskyists used to call "an amalgam." And of the crudest kind of linkage—the late Senator McCarthy's trick of "guilt by association."[2] First

___

[2] I wonder why Harrington's friend and elder counselor, Max Schachtman, didn't warn him, or at least smooth down some of the rough edges. Max was very good on amalgams in the old days. The Stalinists were always trying to amalgamate us with the Nazis or the Liberty League or the Dies Committee because we detested Stalin and so did they, but Max was always on the job "exposing the amalgam."

Lindsay and Bundy appear, penitentially garbed as Republicans.
Then "they are joined by the Urban Coalition in backing a scheme
which is the very essence of Let Them Eat Cake." They didn't
join the Urban Coalition, which would be normal behavior for
individuals—the UC "joined" them, which is abnormal, in fact
impossible behavior for an organization. Anyway they are "joined"
and they and the UC are next glimpsed "backing" a Let Them
Eat Cake "scheme." However it's not a scheme but, as Harrington describes it, a foolish one-shot ad which doesn't commit its
sponsor, the UC, to anything and has no connection with the
original pair, Lindsay and Bundy, except that the ad, the UC,
and they all agree about decentralization (just as the Trotskyists,
the Nazis, etc. all agreed about Stalinist Russia). Next we learn
that "these very same corporate chiefs" (no names given and back
reference unclear, are Bundy and Lindsay still implicated or only
that UC which joined them?) are planning to force unemployment up for the benefit of Scarsdale and ruin Ocean Hill. Then it
seems these chiefs have joined some other chiefs in the Business
Council, which is really sinister—*haute bourgeoisie* no less—and
not just hypocritical and absurd like the UC (though it includes
some of the UC) and the BC has "discussed" hiking the jobless
rate "to 5 per cent or 6 per cent" and there are "enough hints"—
how many are enough, I wonder—that the Nixon Administration
will join, or possibly be joined by, "these very same corporate
chiefs" plus the UC, the BC and, now let's see, what's become of
those two Republican decentralizers?

Harrington's leitmotif is reconciliation: Forgive and Forget, or
in General Grant's unmemorable words, Let There Be Peace.
"Nothing constructive will be accomplished by rehearsing the old
issues at this point, for what is needed is reconciliation between
the black parents and the union teachers, difficult as that may
seem. . . . If the strike is over, as I fervently hope, it is time for
the most earnest discussion, not for recrimination." (I should have
thought an even more appropriate time would have been before
the strike was over but let it pass, let it pass.) A full-page pro-
UFT ad in the *Times* of November 24 got up by Harrington's
colleague at the LID, Tom Kahn, sounds the same note: "There
must be reconciliation. . . . Parents, teachers, and community
groups will have to forge a strong alliance. They will have to or-

ganize and stand together, black and white, overcoming the bitterness and frustration that now separate them."[3]

I hope it's not too cynical to detect beneath these pieties a
change of tactics rather than of heart. Neither document makes
any specific concessions to the opposition, as against heartwarm-
ing generalities addressed to men of good will. Furthermore, both
Harrington's letter and Kahn's ad were composed while Shanker
was still rejecting all settlements of his third strike which, for all
they knew, might continue for a second five weeks, yet they venture no criticism of Shanker's intransigence nor express any concern for the survival of the Ocean Hill experiment, the symbol of
decentralization against which it was directed. "So," writes Harrington, "there is not a simple conflict of right and wrong but an
antagonism of two rights." Whenever he argues concretely, however, there seems to be only one right. So, conclude I, tactics.
Now that direct attack has failed to wreck community control in
Ocean Hill, an armistice is proposed, to be followed by negotiations.

As a man of peace, if not good will, I'm for armistices and for
sitting down amicably at any "negotiating table" in sight. But I
wonder if they realize the complexities of "decentralization" and
"community control"; certainly Harrington's letter doesn't seem
to. But I've run out of space and must postpone till another issue
some notes on what these emotion-laden generalities mean in
specific terms of educational and social practice.

---

[3] Although this was a lineal successor to the September 20 ad of the Ad
Hoc Committee to Defend the Right to Teach of which Harrington and Kahn
were co-chairmen, the intervening two months, which included Shanker's
third strike, seem to have put some strain on the original Ad Hoc group that
supported him. Tom Kahn was now the sole chairman, the name was changed
to "the Ad Hoc Committee for Justice in the Schools," and although I
gather it was circulated to the signers of the September 20 ad, only nine of
them signed this one, not including such recognizable "names" as Daniel Bell,
Robert Heilbroner, Sidney Hook, Irving Howe, Leon Keyserling, Reinhold
Niebuhr, Harold Rosenberg, and Arthur Schlesinger, Jr. Also not including
Michael Harrington. There were about three times as many signatures as to
the September 20 ad, beginning with Elliott Abrams ("Student, Harvard
University") and ending with Norman Zukowsky ("President, International
Leather Goods, Plastic and Novelty Workers Union") with in between a thick
sandwich of equally familiar names—though my eye did pick up three
"names," two not unexpected, Louis Hacker and Seymour Lipset, but the
third a bit of shock: Meyer Schapiro. *Que diable allait-il faire dans cette
galère?*

The New York School Crisis /
MAURICE J. GOLDBLOOM

"The axe," Sir Walter Raleigh told his executioner, "is a sharp medicine but a cure for all ills." A good many people seem ready to resort to Sir Walter's prescription to remedy the ills of New York's schools. One may admit that the schools are sick and still doubt the wisdom of this particular treatment.

And there can be no question that the schools *are* sick, or that they have failed to give a satisfactory education to a large part of the Negro and Puerto Rican population. Contrary to a widespread belief, however, the disease from which they suffer is neither new, nor peculiar to New York, nor the result of a sudden and catastrophic deterioration of the system. In the words of one school official: "We never really did succeed in educating the other side of the tracks." Neither the Irish, nor the Italians, nor the Slavs found the road to education an easy one; in the periods of major immigration they remained to a large extent functional illiterates. In the absence of compulsory education and child labor laws, few of them completed elementary school, but the failure to teach them was masked by their early leaving of the schools.

A basic reason for this problem is that the immigrant groups in question came—as many of today's Negro and Puerto Rican migrants also come—primarily from rural areas organized on a semi-feudal pattern. For such groups adjustment to the disciplines of urban society has often been a matter of decades. The difficulties of that adjustment are reflected not only in the schools but in the crime statistics and the welfare (in the nineteenth century, charity) rolls.

Not all immigrants have shared these problems; the two exceptions most frequently cited are the Jews and the Chinese. Both groups adjusted with relative, but only relative, ease to the conditions of American city life, largely because they had centuries of urbanization behind them. As to the independent yeomen who

THIS ARTICLE appeared in *Commentary*, January, 1969. Reprinted from *Commentary*, by permission; copyright © 1969 by the American Jewish Committee. Used with permission of the author.

left the farms of the Northeast and Midwest to flock to the cities, they had only minor problems of acculturation; they were already highly literate.

To say that the problem is not a new one, and that it has not been solved in the past, is not to say that it is unimportant or that we are not bound to seek solutions today. Both in terms of the accepted goals of society and the realities of the economy, the problem has a degree of urgency which it did not possess a century or even a generation ago. Not only is society today unwilling to accept as the natural order of things a situation in which a large section of the population is debarred from the opportunity to fit itself for anything except unskilled labor, but the opportunity for unskilled employment is itself rapidly vanishing. If we fail to give at least a basic education to our entire population, the victims of our failure will to an increasing extent be doomed to remain outside the economic process except as subsidized consumers—a condition, moreover, they will no longer passively accept.

Yet to recognize that a problem must be solved is not automatically to solve it. Whatever enthusiasts for the idea of community control may think, the failure of the New York school system—which is, by the way, less abysmal than that of most other school systems throughout the country—is more to be blamed on a lack of skill than on a lack of will. It is also, and perhaps mostly, to be blamed on a lack of money. There have always been techniques for increasing the effectiveness of education, which have been neglected because they required more money than the city was able to pay. Nor has it been merely the teachers and supervisors who were deficient in skill; nobody, least of all the teachers' colleges, has offered definitive answers to the question of how children from "the other side of the tracks" can be adequately educated.

The teachers' colleges have nevertheless insisted that anyone who wants to teach must spend at least a year absorbing the non-answers available in education courses. This is certainly one of the factors that has made it increasingly difficult to recruit good teachers, although it is not of course the only one. Teaching often involves a degree of nervous strain that many people simply cannot face. Its material rewards are also limited; despite the substantial salary increases the United Federation of Teachers has won in recent years, New York City still starts its teachers at a considerably lower wage than its police and firemen.

But even if the school system were suddenly overwhelmed with highly qualified applicants, as it was in the early 1930's, its main problems would persist. Indeed, despite the real difficulty in getting good teachers—or any teachers—the New York schools are today substantially better in terms of most indexes than they were three decades ago. Average class size, for example, has fallen in the high schools by about a fourth since the 1930's, and a similar decline has taken place in junior high and elementary schools. Average class size now ranges from 21.6 in kindergarten to 28.4 in "special service" junior high and intermediate schools—those in disadvantaged areas—and 30.1 in schools on that level elsewhere in the city.

The decline in class size, however, does not seem to have significantly improved the educational record of the elementary and junior high schools. In the Negro and Puerto Rican ghettos, the typical student is below the national reading norm from the first grade on; the median reading score in ghetto schools at the end of the ninth grade is two to three years behind the national average. Critics of the schools note that the scores fall further behind the norm as the student progresses through the grades. This is misleading: the *rate* of retardation is fairly constant. It should also be noted that the degree of retardation is lower in New York than for the same groups elsewhere in the country, especially in the South. Thus at every grade level there is a new infusion of children with even poorer educational backgrounds than those of the pupils already there (about a fourth of all junior high school graduates have migrated to the city at some time during their school career). Apart from the almost inevitably deleterious effects this has on the educational process itself, it pulls down the median score.

If the record is not quite as bad as it seems at first glance, it is still bad enough to show that drastic improvement is needed. And the variations that exist among schools indicate that such improvement is in fact possible by the use of techniques already available within the school system. Sometimes, to be sure, the differences can only be attributed to intangibles such as the enthusiasm that exceptional principals and teachers are able to inspire. But in many instances they are directly correlated with specific programs.

The intangible factors of enthusiasm and talent afford a basis for hope but not a technique for realizing it. The recruitment of better teachers and supervisors is obviously desirable, but it scarcely offers a panacea at a time when the nationwide shortage of teachers has everywhere forced a sharp downgrading of standards. The New York school system, like most others throughout the country, is so desperately in need of teachers that it is ready to accept almost anyone who has taken the required education courses without fatal consequences. This does not mean that the quality of the teaching staff cannot be improved; I believe it can, and substantially. But doing so will require a drastic reduction—perhaps even the elimination—of the present education course requirements for teaching positions and the substitution of in-service teacher training.

The obstacles in the way of such a revision are enormous. Some of them are within the school system; the natural resistance of any bureaucracy to radical innovation is reinforced by the tendency of those who have invested years in the taking of education courses to protect the value of their investment. Even more formidable, however, is the opposition of the schools of education, whose domination of the educational scene would be undermined and whose very existence might in some cases be threatened by the sort of change that is needed. Under their influence the trend in recent years has, in fact, been toward making completion of the required courses the sole basis of appointment, to the exclusion of any actual test of knowledge or ability. (This is the meaning of the oft-repeated emphasis on "state certification," which is in New York a purely formal process based on the courses one has taken, and the demands for abolition of the Board of Examiners.) The course requirements have narrowed the field of available candidates for teaching positions to such an extent that examinations must be so framed as to minimize the possibility that any of the applicants will fail. This contrasts sharply with the situation in the 1930's. Then, the excess of applicants over jobs was so great that examinations were used less to test the qualifications of applicants than simply to eliminate enough of them to produce eligible lists of manageable proportions. Those who passed were usually well-qualified; so were many of those who failed.

Techniques are something else again. There are new and old procedures that help at least some pupils to learn reading and arithmetic. These can be extended with comparative ease; they threaten no entrenched interests. Few work equally well with all pupils, and many require specially trained personnel. Some also are questionable on other grounds; the authoritarian use of rote-learning procedures, for example, may produce improved reading and arithmetic scores in some cases, but at the cost of damage to the child.

Two techniques have, however, scored outstanding results. The first of these is the More Effective Schools program (MES), sponsored by the UFT and a major issue in its 1967 strike. This program is based on the use of a whole battery of remedial services in particular schools in ghetto areas; the ratio of pupils to staff is approximately 12 to 1 as compared to a city-wide ratio of about 16 to 1. MES has not been uniformly successful; there are great variations among the test scores achieved by different MES schools. Nevertheless, when school-by-school reading test scores were made public two years ago, for the second and fifth grades, 30 per cent of the groups tested in MES schools scored at or above the norm; another 10 per cent showed a retardation of only one month.[1] Almost no other ghetto schools achieved comparable results, and the average retardation for the MES groups was well under half that for ghetto schools as a whole. But it is also true that about two-fifths of the MES groups showed no significant gain. In the opinion of some teachers in the program this reflected the fact that they had received no training in the methods it required. Even here, however, there were intangible benefits; the children enjoyed school even if they learned no more.

Another technical experiment that has produced really spectacular results is the Responsive Environment, better known as the "talking typewriter." This is a computerized typewriter equipped with a loudspeaker and viewing screen. Initially, a letter appears on the screen and is pronounced by the loudspeaker when the appropriate key is hit. Later, it can be programed for words and even sentences. Under a grant from the U.S. Office of Economic Opportunity a center with twenty talking typewriters was established in the Brownsville area of Brooklyn under the direction of Dr. Benjamin L. Israel. In the first year, staying open until 9 P.M., the center was able to serve some 650 persons, ranging

[1] Since this was written, the 1968 reading scores have been published, showing more than half the MES at or above grade levels.

from pre-kindergarten children to functionally illiterate adults. Notable progress was made on all levels. Pre-kindergarten and kindergarten children learned enough in approximately ten minutes a day to surpass by far normal first-grade reading levels; first-graders reached the second-grade norm. Eighth-grade pupils with severe reading problems improved their scores by an average of 1.4 years in about the same amount of time, divided into fewer but longer sessions.

Full utilization of the present twenty machines—six days and evenings a week—would permit them to serve about a thousand persons. But because the OEO, which had allotted $440,000 for the operation of the center in the first year, sharply cut its grant this year, the center is now operating only during the school day, and only about half as many persons as last year can make use of it.

MES and the "talking typewriter" have a number of things in common. Both demonstrably work, in terms of specific results as well as in terms of an improved educational atmosphere. Neither represents any threat to anybody. But both are expensive. MES costs about 50 per cent more per child than the present average expenditure, or $400 to $500 more a year. To extend the program to all the schools that need it would increase the school budget by about a fourth, or $300,000,000 a year. Since smaller class sizes and more services require more room, there would also be substantial capital costs. Similarly with the Responsive Environment Program; to make it available to all the half-million students in the New York school system who are currently reading behind grade would require an operating budget which might reach $300,000,000, in addition to the expenditure of up to $400,000,-000 for the purchase of ten thousand machines.

Now, programs requiring large expenditures are not politically popular, unless they offer opportunities for patronage of one sort or another. The New York City Board of Education has no taxing power of its own: it depends on city appropriations and state aid. Each year the mayor and the governor seek to maneuver each other into supplying the bulk of the new money that the school system requires and shouldering the blame for the inadequacy of the amount eventually doled out. It is a game the school system seldom wins. The result is that there is seldom enough money to finance any really major innovation; what is available is dribbled away in small-scale experiments that cannot be followed up even if they succeed.

The presence of major and pressing problems and the lack of adequate funds to deal with them produces a situation made to order for gimmickry. The basic requirement is that whatever is proposed should be, or should appear to be, cheap. It should also offer sufficient novelty to divert from the heads of those in power the wrath of groups who have reason to resent the *status quo*.

One such gimmick, a few years back, was the legislative removal of the entire Board of Education and the establishment of a selection panel to nominate members of a new board. In one sense it worked beautifully; the new board appointed by Mayor Robert Wagner from among those suggested by the panel was as good a Board of Education as New York City has ever had. Unfortunately, it was given neither the means nor the authority to change very much. And some of the problems it faced could not really be solved within the framework of the school system—the problem of integration, for example.

New York's school system had never, of course, been legally segregated. But there had long been many schools with completely black student bodies, and the number was increasing rapidly as Negro immigration into the city skyrocketed while whites left for the suburbs or sent their children to private and parochial schools. (There was a corresponding decline in the number of all-white schools as the ghetto burst its boundaries.) This *de facto* segregation was the result of residential patterns. To fight it effectively would have required the scattering of public housing throughout the city and suburbs, as well as the rehabilitation of existing ghetto areas. It would have required the cooperation of federal, city, state, and perhaps neighboring local governments. It would have been expensive, and it would have infringed on important vested interests. It did not happen.

Instead, there were gimmicks. Some were obviously bound to fail. Thus in most cases one could almost guarantee that the "instant integration" resulting from the building of a new school on the boundary between black and white areas would quickly evaporate as the ethnic frontier shifted. Other gimmicks offered more chance of real integration in specific, if limited, situations. There were a number of places where pairing seemed capable of working for a while. But in most of these, local opposition arose and the plans were dropped. Educational parks offered some promise in a few localities, although there were relatively few suitable sites in the city. One which did exist was in Canarsie; it could have served large sections of Brownsville and East New York. But the business-oriented Lindsay administration preferred to use the site for an industrial park, and the opportunity for school integration in that area was lost.

Another gimmick, originating with the Board of Education, provided for replacement of the existing pattern of six-year elementary schools followed by three years of junior high school and three of senior high school. In its stead there were to be four years each of elementary, intermediate, and high schools. But since the existing junior high school buildings were inadequate for four grades, there was to be an interim 5-3-4 pattern. The theory was that students would be attending high schools, which had the greatest degree of integration of any section of the school system, a year earlier. At the same time it would be possible to develop feeder patterns for the new intermediate schools which would increase the degree of integration on that level.

It was a plan that had one great advantage: it was cheap. It did not, however, provide any significant integration on the intermediate school level. The new intermediate schools continued to draw the same students as the old junior highs, but a year earlier. Or rather, they would have done so if the change had actually taken place. For in fact only 3 four-year and 42 three-year intermediate schools have come into being, while there are still 96 junior high schools.

Since the new system had been heralded as a royal road to integration, its failure to provide any integration naturally produced a good deal of frustration and resentment. One place where these feelings erupted was the new Intermediate School 201 in Harlem. In the face of protests from many elements of the community, the school had been built at Madison Avenue and 126th Street, on the border between Harlem proper and predominantly Puerto Rican East Harlem, but too far north to attract any significant number of non-Puerto Rican whites. (Integration has never been a major Puerto Rican concern, since most Puerto Ricans see their problems of adjustment as more linguistic and cultural than ethnic.)

A small group, not all of whom lived in Harlem and a number of whom were on the staff of the anti-poverty agency MEND, endeavored to channel the discontent over the choice of a site for IS 201 into a demand for a black principal. A boycott sponsored by these groups led to the setting up of a Planning Board —dominated by some of the same people who had instituted the boycott—to work out a proposal for a more or less autonomous district consisting of IS 201 and its feeder schools. While the group did not to begin with have the support of many sections of the community, overt opposition later died down. According to some parents and teachers, this was the result partly of outright intimidation and partly of the use of patronage.

The major source of this patronage was a grant from the Ford Foundation in July 1967, which was announced together with similar grants to planning boards for two other proposed demonstration districts, Ocean Hill–Brownsville in Brooklyn and Two Bridges on the Lower East Side of Manhattan. In none of these three areas had there been advance consultation with the local parents associations of the schools to be included. In Ocean Hill–Brownsville a planning board had emerged from the local supporters of the "Peoples' Board of Education" established by the Rev. Milton Galamison (later appointed to the central Board of Education by Mayor Lindsay). In Two Bridges, the initiative came from staff members of a local anti-poverty group who had approached the Ford Foundation for a different grant, and then asked for a grant to assist in the establishment of a demonstration school district when they learned that the Foundation was now interested in education rather than the sort of project they had originally had in mind. Although the formation of the Two Bridges district was—and still is—opposed by the parents associations of the schools included in it, the anti-poverty group received the grant and recognition from the city.

Despite, or perhaps because of, the sharp differences within the Two Bridges local governing board itself and the widespread opposition to the board within the community, the district's history has not been marked by the spectacular clashes which have characterized the IS 201 and Ocean Hill–Brownsville districts. Two Bridges is the most ethnically varied of the three districts; the two largest groups are Chinese and Puerto Rican, and there are smaller numbers of Negroes as well as remnants of the various groups of European origin who were formerly predominant in the area. In contrast, both of the other demonstration districts have Negro majorities, Puerto Rican minorities, and only scattered members of other ethnic groups.

Although the Ocean Hill–Brownsville district eventually became the focus of a struggle that has disrupted not only the school system but the city itself, it initially seemed to have the best prospects for success. The original planning board had the support of the UFT, and teacher representatives helped to draw up the original proposals for the demonstration district. JHS 271, the key school in the district, had an unusually able principal, Dr. Jack Bloomfield. In the three years he had headed it, the school had established close ties with the community and had made substantial academic progress. Students' reading scores had improved by 3 years and 2 months and their vocabulary scores by 3 years and 7 months in a period of 2 years and 10 months. Whereas only 5 per cent had passed the algebra regents in 1965, 62 per cent passed it in 1967— 10 per cent better than the city-wide average. The school's magazine and newspapers had received Columbia University scholastic press awards. The school also won first prize in the mayor's Salute to Youth for its internship program, under which students were trained for leadership in adult organizations.

The cooperative relationship which had hitherto existed between 271 and the community, however, rapidly evaporated after the Ford Foundation grant to the district. The grant was made to Father John Powis, a white Roman Catholic priest. It was Father Powis who took the lead in setting up the planning board, but he seems not to have waited for it to be fully constituted before taking action on its behalf. When the newly elected teacher representatives joined the planning board on June 29, they were told by Father Powis that Rhody McCoy had been selected as unit administrator.

There were other signs of rapid change as well. In June, Mrs. Elaine Rooke, as president of the Parents Association, had written in the 271 school magazine: "The teachers of the school have certainly shown you how much they too feel that you are special. . . . We have worked closely and harmoniously toward keeping Coleman Junior High School [271] among the top schools that New York City has ever had." In July, as a member of the planning board, the same Mrs. Rooke was denouncing the school in a television interview. (Although she had moved out of the district a year earlier and no longer had any children in 271 after June 1967, Mrs. Rooke served as its "parent representative" on the planning board and is still serving in that capacity on the local governing board.)

Meanwhile, the planning board appears to have called meetings without notifying its teacher members; at one of these it was decided to hold a community-wide election to choose "parent representatives" from each school to serve on the governing board of the experimental district. This was contrary to the understanding the teachers thought they had with Father Powis, under which the parents and teachers of the individual schools would be permitted to vote in September as to whether they wished to participate in the project; only after that had they expected a community-wide election to be held.

The election was as much a surprise to the Board of Education as it was to the teachers. The Board of Education's Advisory Committee on Decentralization, headed by President John Niemeyer of the Bank Street College of Education, reported:

Movement was pushed as rapidly as possible toward local election of project boards, loosely defined both as to composition and function, for local special school districts equally vaguely conceived. *In the case of the Ocean Hill–Brownsville demonstration project the administration and the Board of Education suddenly were confronted early in August 1967 with the fact that an election was in full swing* [emphasis mine—M.J.G.]. No guidelines or stipulations concerning legitimacy of procedure had been laid down by the Board of Education and none were expected by the local planning council. The Board of Education expected that ensuing action would await the full approval of the board of a plan for each local project; the local representatives had no intention of waiting for such a procedure to occur, but moved to establish themselves in power.

This contrasts sharply with the account given by Richard Karp, in an article in *Interplay* (August–September 1968). Karp writes as though the planning board had made a long and unsuccessful effort to secure Board of Education cooperation in holding an election, was unable to collect the addresses of students, and then "got sympathetic teachers to canvass students for their addresses. Then by going from door to door, they finally got 2,000 parents registered by August." One wonders how during the summer, *when there were no students in school,* "sympathetic teachers" could "canvass students for their addresses." Did they perhaps visit them at their homes and *then* ask them where they lived? As it happens, we know in at least one case how the planning board really got the addresses; those of the two thousand children at 271 were given them by the principal, Dr. Bloomfield, with the approval of the Board of Education!

The ensuing election itself was conducted by a staff that was paid by the planning board with Ford Foundation funds. To get out the vote they made use of canvassing and sound trucks. Nevertheless, only about 22 per cent of those eligible voted. Some supporters of the governing board have made the demonstrably false assertion that this was higher than the number who had ever voted in local elections; the usual turnout in local elections is over 70 per cent. Interestingly, those paid to get out the vote were also candidates for the governing board. Not surprisingly, they turned out to be the successful candidates. No formal procedures for the election or qualifications for candidates were set by the planning board, which also took charge of counting the vote. One result was that the "parent representatives" elected to the governing board from two of the schools in the district neither had children in them nor lived in the district. This did not prevent them from participating with the other "parent representatives" in the choice of "community representatives" to sit on the board.

One wonders what theory of democratic representation, if any, can lie behind the assertion later made by Jason Epstein in the *New York Review* that a board so elected and constituted not only represents the community "but in a curious way embodies it." The election itself was subsequently challenged in court, and approximately twice as many parents as had voted in the original election petitioned for a new one. Perhaps "in a curious way" they felt disembodied. (A public opinion poll taken in the district in the spring of 1968 showed that 29 per cent of the parents supported the governing board and that 24 per cent supported the teachers, while the rest were not sure where they stood. A third of those polled felt that they would get into trouble by taking a stand against the board.) In any event, no new election was ever held; the board's term of office is undefined.

In addition to choosing the "community representatives," the "parent representatives" also tried to induce the teachers who had been elected to the original planning board to consider themselves as "teacher representatives" on the governing board. The teachers, on the other hand, claimed that they had no mandate and therefore could not vote on the governing board. They nevertheless attended meetings—or, to be more exact, those meetings to which they were invited. Although they were placed under great pressure to vote when they were present and sometimes yielded, their participation in discussions was discouraged by denunciations and charges of sabotage when they offered criticisms or raised questions. (The UFT later adopted a general position opposed to teacher membership on local governing boards on the ground that it could involve a conflict of interest.)

After the election, the governing board hastened to ratify the nomination of Rhody McCoy as unit administrator; this was accepted by the Board of Education. It also proposed the names of five principals to fill vacancies at four existing schools and one, Intermediate School 55, which was still under construction. None of those proposed was on the existing civil service list for principals, a fact which subsequently gave rise to a court challenge to their appointment.[2] The five did meet state certification standards; this simply means that they had some teaching experience and had taken certain courses.

No personal objections were raised against four of them; they were unknown. One—the first to be named—was very well known, however. Herman Ferguson, proposed as principal of the new IS 55, had been suspended from his job as an assistant principal after being indicted on a charge of conspiring to murder Roy Wilkins of the NAACP, Whitney Young of the National Urban League, and others. (He has subsequently been convicted and is now appealing the conviction.) He had distinguished himself by charging that the school at which he had previously been employed —an MES school whose students had reading scores substantially above the normal grade level—with "educational genocide." Ferguson was not only nominated as a principal but worked with McCoy in drawing up plans for the district and interviewing possible appointees.

The Board of Education accepted the other principals nominated, but never approved Ferguson. He was nevertheless kept by the local board as "principal of record" for some months. (During the same period he also served as a paid consultant to the IS 201 local governing board, which dropped him only when it

---

[2] On March 4, 1968, Justice Rinaldi of the New York Supreme Court ruled that the appointments were illegal. His decision was upheld by the Appellate Division on November 15, 1968.

became clear that the board would get neither official recognition nor further Ford Foundation money as long as Ferguson remained.) Ferguson's role certainly did not contribute to the development of a climate of confidence, nor can Mr. McCoy and the Ocean Hill–Brownsville governing board have expected that it would.

The 1967–68 school year opened with a teachers' strike. For months the UFT had made it clear that in the absence of a satisfactory offer on salaries and, more important, on the extension of the MES program, it would have to go out. (A good deal of nonsense has been written about this strike by anti-union propagandists. For example, a pamphlet published by the New York Civil Liberties Union and purporting to be a factual account of the controversy[3] asserts that "the local governing board perceived the strike as a show of power aimed against Ocean Hill–Brownsville and specifically in relation to its hiring of the 5 principals." If the local governing board *had* perceived the strike that way, it would have been a clear sign either of ignorance or hopeless paranoia. In fairness to the governing board, I have seen no statement from anyone connected with it which would justify the NYCLU's assertion.) A settlement on economic issues was quickly arrived at, but the strike continued for some days because of the union's demand for improvements in the quality of ghetto schools.

The strike was thus essentially one *for* the interests of the black and Puerto Rican communities, and the teachers hoped for their support. But it was presented by the mayor, with the unstinting aid of the news media, as a strike *against* those communities, since theirs were a majority of the children unable to attend school. (In a number of areas, especially underprivileged ones, union teachers working without pay conducted emergency schools in settlement houses, churches, etc. This was also done in the 1968 strike. The number of students attending these emergency schools was only a fraction of the normal school enrolment, although it appears to have been substantially above the attendance at those public schools which were nominally "open.") The

[3] This pamphlet manages to compress an astounding number of misstatements and misrepresentations into a relatively short compass. I have analyzed some, though by no means all, of these in some detail in "A Critique of the New York Civil Liberties Union Report on the Ocean Hill–Brownsville School Controversy," available from the Ad Hoc Committee to Defend the Right to Teach.

same anti-union point of view was also pushed by various "militant" and "black power" organizations, as well as by the city anti-poverty machinery, in which leaders of such groups had important positions.

The teacher members of the Ocean Hill–Brownsville planning board asked the new governing board to support the 1967 strike on the ground that it was primarily aimed at securing improvements in ghetto schools. The governing board not only refused but attempted, with little success, to recruit parent help in an effort to break it. In this it had the cooperation of Robert "Sonny" Carson, head of Brooklyn CORE (who later left national CORE after its convention had refused to adopt various resolutions he was backing, including one for all-black schools in the ghettos and another for the establishment of a separate black nation in certain parts of the United States). Carson and his friends tried to intimidate striking teachers; he warned them against attempting to return to the district after the strike ended. Under the circumstances, it was only the efforts of the UFT to persuade its members to return after the strike that made it possible to staff the district's schools.

Tensions never disappeared in the district, but for a while they seemed to die down. In some schools excellent working relationships developed between the teachers and the acting principals nominated by the governing board and approved by the Board of Education. Meanwhile, negotiations on the setting up of the demonstration district were going on between the local governing board, which as yet had no recognized legal status, and the Board of Education.

The original proposal agreed on by the planning board had been modified during the summer without the participation of the board's teacher members and was submitted to the Board of Education on August 29. One major change was the elimination of a section providing that the elementary schools in the district be brought under the MES program. It is not certain who was responsible for the change, but it did bring the proposal into line with the position of Superintendent of Schools Bernard Donovan that the experimental districts should receive no better financial treatment than other comparable areas. Donovan argued that if they received favored treatment the results achieved would not be a test of the value of decentralization. (In fact, however, Ocean Hill–Brownsville has received a considerably higher per capita allowance than other comparable areas, though it has no MES program.)

The Ocean Hill–Brownsville governing board and its defenders have maintained that it was unable to function because the Board of Education refused to clarify its powers. The implication in such accounts as the NYCLU report and Richard Karp's article in *Interplay* (as well as in the articles of those like Murray Kempton and Jason Epstein who have been content with the governing board's version of the facts at every point) is that the Ocean Hill board was desperately attempting to get the Board of Education to define what it might and might not do, while the latter refused to give it a hint. According to this version, all the subsequent troubles originated from a confusion which the central board had deliberately created and could have dispelled at any time.

What actually happened was rather different. The Ocean Hill board submitted its proposal on August 29—*after* it had installed Rhody McCoy as unit administrator, conducted elections without consulting the central board, and nominated Herman Ferguson and four others as principals. The proposal was received by the Board of Education on September 1, and *on the same day* representatives of the central board conferred with Mr. McCoy on the questions involved. This was the first of some twenty such conferences that took place before the Board of Education finally, in February, 1968, issued guidelines (drawn up by the Niemeyer Committee) for the decentralized districts.

These meetings were held in an effort to reach agreement between the Board of Education and the local governing board. The problem was not that the Board of Education was unwilling to clarify the powers of the governing board; it was that the latter was unwilling to accept the clarification. It continued to demand that the Board of Education transfer powers to it which the latter had no legal right to transfer and in certain cases did not even possess. (For instance, one of the things the local board wanted was the right to maintain its own bank accounts and draw its own checks; all Board of Education funds are in city bank accounts administered by the Comptroller, who pays out money against Board of Education vouchers.) It is worth noting, however, that one of the things the governing board did *not* ask for, and which was therefore never an issue, was the right unilaterally to transfer teachers out of the district or to dismiss them without a hearing.[4] The attempt to attribute the governing board's subsequent actions in this respect to any confusion over the extent of its powers is obviously fraudulent.

The guidelines finally issued gave the local boards all the powers the central board felt it was legally entitled to delegate. These did not satisfy the local boards, and have been violently attacked by their apologists. Thus the NYCLU pamphlet charges that the Board of Education "scuttled the experiment" with guidelines that "completely emasculated the experiment by stripping the local governing board of virtually all of its substantive powers." The Niemeyer Report is rather closer to the truth:

> The suggested guidelines prepared by this Committee attempted to formulate the actual authority to be delegated to the project boards. In March 1968, however, the three demonstration projects agreed upon a consensus document *which demanded full authority although the Board of Education could not go beyond the legal limits placed upon it by the State Education Law. . . . in some local communities militant groups may be expected to continue to demand powers for which no one yet has proposed legislation. That is, in order for those who want to control all aspects of their local schools to accomplish their objectives, legislative changes would be required that would seriously affect many legal and contractual relationships affecting conditions of employment, such as tenure, that go far beyond the power presently held by the Board of Education* [emphasis mine—M.J.G.].[5]

In the meantime, the Ocean Hill board was consolidating its control of the district's schools, where personnel changes were

[4] Professor Lockwood of Brooklyn College is a consultant to the local governing board. According to President Harold C. Syrett of Brooklyn College: "Professor Lockwood has shown me a copy of the governing board's bylaws that call for, in the case of transfer or dismissal of teachers, a procedure whereby a principal may bring such matters to the unit administrator, who then refers them to the local board, which after hearings may request the superintendent of schools to act in the matter. In other words, the controversial actions taken by the Ocean Hill–Brownsville board and its unit administrator are contrary to the organization's own bylaws. Professor Lockwood informed me that he opposed this action."

[5] Many such changes, affecting contractual rights, would probably be barred by the clause in the U.S. Constitution banning state laws impairing the obligation of contracts.

occurring at a rapid pace. Only one of the seven principals who had been serving in the district in the previous school year was still there at the opening of the spring semester. Largely because of the efforts of the UFT to persuade teachers to remain, changes on the classroom level had been relatively few. At the time, Mr. McCoy seemed anxious to retain the experienced teachers then in the district.

But the problems of Ocean Hill and the other demonstration districts might have been gradually worked out, or they might have developed to a point where the experiment would have been recognized as a failure, without involving the entire city, if it had not been for the simultaneous controversy over proposals for decentralizing the entire school system. Suddenly the demonstration districts were seen by supporters and critics of the various decentralization plans—and by themselves—as a microcosm of the entire city's problems. It was not a situation conducive to quiet and orderly compromise.

Although there had in the past been many proposals to shift authority in the school system from central headquarters to the districts, and the Board of Education had taken some steps in this direction in 1965, the idea of drastic decentralization had originally been brought forward less for educational than for fiscal reasons. The formula for the distribution of state aid to schools was such that breaking up the New York school system, at least formally, could increase the amount of aid to which the city schools were entitled. A proposal to establish five borough school systems for this purpose was advanced by Dr. Marilyn Gittell in 1966 in a report prepared, significantly, for the Temporary Commission on City Finances.

It seems likely that Dr. Gittell's suggestion was the origin of Mayor Lindsay's request to the state legislature, in March, 1967, that it divide the city school system into five borough systems, *but only for the calculation of state aid*. The idea was not too kindly received in Albany, since any additional aid received by the city would decrease the amount available for other parts of the state. But, apparently through the intervention of the governor, a compromise was reached under which the division would be made provided that the mayor submit a plan for *actual* decentralization by December 1.

One effect of this that the legislators may not have taken into consideration—though one may suspect that Mr. Lindsay was fully aware of it—was that it suddenly catapulted the mayor into a central role in regard to the operation of an educational system over which he had no direct legal authority. The insulation of the schools from the power of the mayor was the result of a long struggle to free them from the grip of political hacks. To Mr. Lindsay, who had been multiplying high-salaried patronage posts at a rate unequaled by any other administration in recent years, the independence of the school system appears to have been a source of considerable frustration. Although the Board of Education (with State Commissioner Allen's backing) objected that planning the school system was its function rather than the mayor's, and The New York Times charged that the bill constituted political interference with education, the mayor said that it was too late to make any changes. While the bill was still before the legislature, the Board of Education offered its own plan of administrative decentralization, designed to give more autonomy to district superintendents and principals and a greater voice to local school boards. The Times urged the mayor to accept it.

The mayor, instead, appointed a committee headed by Mc-George Bundy of the Ford Foundation to draw up a plan. Of the committee's members only Alfred Giardino, then president of the Board of Education, had any personal experience with the New York school system. On November 9, the committee, with Mr. Giardino dissenting, presented a proposal for the establishment of thirty to sixty largely autonomous school districts controlled by community school boards; each of these was to have eleven members, of whom five would be appointed by the mayor and six chosen by local selection panels who would in turn be chosen by parent assemblies in the various schools. There would still be a central board that would conduct collective-bargaining negotiations, set some standards, administer special and vocational high schools, make lump sum allocations to the districts from a central budget, and perform any other services for districts that these desired to obtain from it. Local boards would be entitled to recruit personnel subject only to state standards, to use their budgets for whatever purposes seemed to them desirable (e.g., shifting funds between instruction and building maintenance), to determine such matters as curriculum (subject to minimum state and perhaps city requirements) and class size, and to incur financial obligations. Central purchasing services would be available, but the local boards would not be required to use them; it was not clear what this would do to existing requirements for competitive bidding.

In view of the Ocean Hill controversy it is worth mentioning that, although the Bundy committee wanted prime responsibility for recruitment and sole responsibility for the granting of tenure (except to those employed in centrally administered services) to rest with the community boards, this did not apply to dismissals and transfers. The committee proposed that while charges might be brought by local boards, all hearings on the charges were to be conducted under the auspices of the central board. And the plan provided that "No person presently holding a tenured appointment as a teacher may be transferred out of a district without his own consent; he may be transferred by the community board between schools within the district, but must be placed in a similar position."

The Bundy Plan, as it was generally called, quickly became the center of a storm of controversy. One of its sharpest critics was Borough President Herman Badillo of the Bronx, a leading spokesman for the Puerto Rican community. He declared:

I can't think of anything that would be more conducive to civil strife. The election of local neighborhood boards would create strife because in many areas candidates would be running on ethnic lines. It makes no sense at all. . . . It assumes a civil stability that doesn't exist. It's an incredible proposal. It shows a lack of understanding of New York City today. There are many groups that don't get along. In many parts of the city busing would be abolished and extremists would be running for office.

Badillo added that the Bundy Plan would introduce the same sort of disruption in the educational system that had prevented the anti-poverty program from functioning properly anywhere in the city.

The Board of Education asserted that "Hiring by thirty to sixty different school districts of teachers and others could increase political, racial, and religious interference in the selection process." One board member, John A. Lotz (who has since become one of the more extreme advocates of community control and chairman of the board's committee on decentralization), warned that giving local boards the power to hire and fire would let teachers shop around and the experienced ones would wind up concentrated in middle-class neighborhoods. The Bundy Report had argued against the likelihood of this danger by postulating that decentralized districts in disadvantaged neighborhoods would possess an attractiveness for which there was then no objective evidence and which subsequent experience contradicts.

President Albert Shanker of the UFT, while crediting the plan with good features that would help to loosen the existing bureaucratic rigidity of the Board of Education, warned that other aspects could promote "years of chaos and eventual destruction of the city's school system." Pointing out that the proposals would give the mayor effective control of all positions in the school system without any restrictions from the merit system, he called the plan "the greatest piece of political patronage ever perpetrated." And he expressed the fear that "Negro teachers would be hired in Negro areas and white teachers in white areas," while in many districts "extremists would have veto power." Editorially, the *Times* wrote:

> The major worry, expressed independently by board and union, appears to be the protection of school administrators and teachers against improper interference by political or racist-extremist pressure groups. This is an entirely legitimate area of concern. It would be indefensible indeed to exchange the present unsatisfactory system of staffing with an equally unsatisfactory system that would place racial considerations about educational effectiveness.

To some, such a system seemed not "equally unsatisfactory" but a great deal more so.

The executive committee of the UFT met with Mr. Bundy and offered a decentralization plan of its own. This provided that there should be not more than fifteen districts "to insure the possibility of integration within each district and to reduce administrative costs." Each local board would be fully elected by the parents of the district and would have the authority to choose its superintendent. Teachers would be selected on the basis of the National Teachers Examination, and appointments to the districts would be made by the central board from a ranked list on the basis of vacancies.

Rejecting this proposal, Mayor Lindsay submitted to the legislature a decentralization plan that differed only slightly from the Bundy Plan. A few months later, the Board of Regents offered yet another modification of the same basic plan, extending the number of contemplated local districts to as many as a hundred. The mayor then threw his support to the Regents Plan instead of his own; this was not surprising, since it gave him even more power than the previous proposals. Giardino, the UFT, and the United Parents Associations expressed their opposition to the Regents Plan, with the union urging passage instead of a bill introduced by State Senator John Marchi authorizing the Board of Education to transfer certain powers to the existing local school boards of the city's thirty districts, and directing it to prepare a definitive plan of decentralization for submission to the next legislature.

In the midst of the controversy over decentralization, relatively little attention was paid to an event with somewhat more immediate impact on the schools, the city budget director's announcement—made appropriately on April 1—that funds for education would be cut by 10 per cent. All funds for educational improvements were eliminated, and the appropriation for mandatory expenses was sharply cut—which meant that the money to meet them had to be found by reducing expenditures for existing programs. The city administration obviously found decentralization a pleasanter subject to discuss than money. (Yet the Bundy Report had stressed that "Decentralization is no substitute for other deeply needed changes—and in particular it is no substitute for the massive infusion of funds the school system now needs. . . .") The next day the three demonstration project boards threatened a school boycott—*not as a protest against the gutting of the school budget* but to enforce the demand that the powers they sought be transferred to them at once, despite the fact that no one had the legal authority to do so. Some days later, the Ocean Hill board actually called such a boycott; it was successful at JHS 271 and IS 55, although a majority of the children in the district's elementary schools went in.

This was the background against which the Ocean Hill–Brownsville governing board suddenly notified nineteen teachers and supervisors—by letters sent to their classrooms on May 9 without prior discussion of any sort—that their services in the district were terminated forthwith and that they were to report to the headquarters of the Board of Education for "reassignment." The Board of Education, which had received no more notice of this directive than had the teachers, immediately declared the action of the governing board illegal and directed the teachers to report to work as usual.

Since this incident triggered the conflict that led to the UFT strikes at the beginning of the 1968–69 school year, it is worth examining in detail. As has been pointed out by both the Appellate Division of the New York State Supreme Court and Federal District Judge Anthony Travia, the local governing board at the period in question still had no legal status and had been granted no authority. It was in *de facto* control of the district's schools only because those with legal authority—the Board of Education and the superintendent of schools—were carrying out its decisions.

The governing board was quite conscious of its lack of legal authority, but was still determined to assert its power. In her memorandum recommending the "removal" of the nineteen, the governing board's personnel chairman, Mrs. Clara Marshall, wrote: "We were constantly told that our demands 'were opposed to state laws' but we found that the people in the street considered these laws written to protect the monied white power structure of this city." And she added: "So we will have to make our own rules for our own schools. Enforcement of these rules will have to be carried out by the people of the community."

The question was not even one of actual, as opposed to theoretical, control over staffing. For, as Dr. John Niemeyer stated in the press conference in which he made his report public, the Board of Education had offered to arrange quiet transfers for any teachers the local board did not want. According to *The New York Times* of September 14, 1968:

He said the offer was made last spring before any controversy had developed over the governing board's power to make such transfers. *But [he] asserted that the governing board was determined to prove it had control of the schools by circumventing normal procedure* and announcing that nineteen teachers and supervisors must be reassigned elsewhere.

Mr. Niemeyer . . . said the United Federation of Teachers would not have objected to the transfers if they had been made routinely. "It would have been worked out; it's done all the time," he added.

The Rev. C. Herbert Oliver, chairman of the governing board, declined to comment last night on Mr. Niemeyer's assertion. "I don't recall any promise," he said, "but I won't deny it." (emphasis mine—M.J.G.)

The procedure followed was not only without legal warrant; it was also a violation of Mr. McCoy's public pledge that if teachers were not desired in the district, he would "see to it that they are transferred out only after due process." One may also note that the Bundy Plan provided that "No person presently holding a tenured appointment as a teacher may be transferred out of a district without his consent." And, as we have already seen, the dismissal of the teachers was a violation of the governing board's own bylaw.

Yet granted that the local board wished to assert its power by defying the law and the central board, why did it choose this particular time and mode? Several answers suggest themselves. One is Richard Karp's idea, in his article in *Interplay*, that the governing board was probably encouraged to act as it did by the mayor and other sympathetic members of the establishment. On most questions Mr. Karp is not a very reliable authority. But since all his information appears to come from Ocean Hill officials, his statement may indicate that the latter at least *thought* they had the mayor's support in their action. It is hard to believe that the mayor could have wished to encourage the governing board in a course with such an explosive potential, although the Ocean Hill situation certainly diverted attention from his maiming of the education budget. There has been speculation, however, to the effect that without Mr. Lindsay's authorization a member of his staff might have appeared to have committed him to support of the governing board. At any rate, it is an interesting coincidence that David Seeley departed from his post as the mayor's chief educational adviser before the beginning of the new school term.

But there is an additional explanation of the course of action that the governing board took in dismissing the teachers. On the day after the assassination of Martin Luther King, the principal of 271, Mr. William Harris, called an assembly. In his opening remarks he said that the white teachers might leave if they wished; they remained. Mrs. Elaine Rooke, president of the Parents Association and a member of the local governing board, and Walter Lynch, its community liaison officer, spoke. So did Leslie Campbell, vice president of the African-American Teachers Association. Among other things, Campbell told the children:

Brothers and sisters, you have to stop fighting among yourselves. You save your money and finally get enough for a leather jacket and your brother steals it. You've got to get your minds together. You know who to steal from. If you steal, steal from those who have it —stop fighting among yourselves.

He was also reported to have made a number of other statements, some of them highly inflammatory, but in regard to these his version differs from that of others who were present. Following the assembly, there were a number of incidents of violence. A young woman teacher was attacked by students who punched her, tore out her hair, and ripped her dress. (She had reportedly been taking down signs that read: "Martin Luther King was killed by a vicious white man—Prepare yourselves.") A male teacher was knocked unconscious and had to be taken to the hospital. Another, attempting to go to another school, was pelted with beer cans, punched, and chased back into the school building.

The union chapter at 271 protested to Unit Administrator McCoy and asked that Campbell be removed from the school, that inflammatory signs be banned, and that community leaders explain to students in an assembly that white teachers were not the enemy. Mr. McCoy said that he would have to discuss the requests with the governing board. The termination notices to the teachers may have been the governing board's answer. As to Mr. Campbell, his reply was perhaps given in a statement he issued together with Albert Vann, president of the African-American Teachers Association, on April 15:

What courses of action are open to the parents and community leaders of the demonstration school project? We see only one. Disregard the New York City Board of Education and assume whatever powers you can in running your schools. Hire and fire the teachers and administrators of your schools. Revise your curriculum to fit the needs of your community. . . . While you are legally fighting for other powers assume those that you can *legitimately assume*. (Emphasis in original.)

When the teachers returned to their schools in accordance with the instructions of the Board of Education, they were faced at 271 and two other schools by mobs assembled by the governing board with the assistance of Brooklyn CORE and others, reportedly including officials of the anti-poverty program. A series of confrontations followed. At first neither the police nor the Board of Education acted. Then the teachers were temporarily escorted in by police, but as rioting continued the affected schools were closed down by the city. Mr. McCoy and the local governing board responded by closing down the entire district. A boycott of seven other schools in support of the Ocean Hill board was called by the Rev. Milton Galamison, whose organization SCOPE had received $160,000 from the Ford Foundation to develop community action on the schools. The Galamison boycott fizzled.

In view of the stress later placed by the New York Civil Liberties Union and other partisans of the Ocean Hill board on the contention that the teachers were merely being "transferred," it is worth noting that Mr. McCoy was quoted by *The New York Times* of May 16 as declaring: "*Not one of these teachers will be allowed to teach anywhere in this city. The black community will see to that.*" (Emphasis mine—M.J.G.) He had already accused the teachers of "insubordination" when they reported to their schools in accordance with the instructions of the Board of Education, and had demanded that they be placed on departmental trial.

Mr. McCoy was very reluctant to file formal charges against the teachers, however, asserting that he did not wish to "smear" them. This commendable wish did not prevent him from listing new charges—but never with specifications or evidence—for each interviewer. The original accusation that the teachers had tried to "sabotage" the demonstration district was supplemented by such charges as discriminating between Negro and Puerto Rican students, disregarding the safety of the students, and letting them run wild in order to discredit the experiment.

The role of Superintendent of Schools Bernard Donovan, whose responsibility it was to see that the Board of Education's policies were carried out, can only be called an ambiguous one. Repeatedly he announced decisions and then withdrew them, made threats and then failed to carry them out. Thus on May 20 he suddenly ordered the teachers to hearings before the state mediation board; the UFT demanded that he follow normal procedure, under which the teachers would be given three days notice of charges before hearings. The next day some 350 other teachers from the district accompanied the thirteen to the Board of Education. Donovan canceled the proposed hearings and directed the teachers to return to their schools on the ground that Mr. McCoy had failed to submit charges. Mr. McCoy, for his part, denied that he had ever promised to submit written charges. He claimed that the governing board was willing to give the teachers fair hearings, but was adamant about not taking them back.

When the thirteen teachers returned once again to 271, they found Mrs. Rooke and others telling the pupils to leave; several hundred of the children did. Soon after, Principal William Harris dismissed the school. No trouble developed at other schools. The next morning, May 22, the 350 teachers who had supported the thirteen found letters in their mailboxes from Mr. McCoy. He wrote: "We are offering fair hearings to all teachers *if the teachers and the union are willing to support total community control.*" (Emphasis mine—M.J.G.) And he directed all 350 to report to his office—which could not have held a tenth of them—at 9 A.M., "to sit with the governing board to clarify their working with this board in recognition of community control."

The teachers went home, and UFT President Shanker announced on May 23 that they would not return until they were guaranteed that they could teach their classes. On the same day Superintendent Donovan directed the principals of all the schools in the district to let the teachers return to class or face charges of insubordination; on that day, too, Mr. McCoy denied that any teachers had been prevented from entering the schools. But on May 24 he again declared that he would not let the teachers return under any circumstances, adding that he realized he was disobeying orders and faced charges of insubordination.

In response to Superintendent Donovan's pledge to act against any administrator interfering with the return of any teacher, the UFT asked the teachers to resume work on May 26. But the next day, after Mr. McCoy had announced that he was "suspending" seven of the original thirteen teachers and Superintendent Donovan had said that this meant nothing, the UFT charged the superintendent with bad faith. (It was at this time that Mr. McCoy finally presented formal charges against the seven teachers in question.)

On June 14, Judge Francis E. Rivers, whom the board had chosen as a hearing officer to try the charges against the teachers, recommended that seven of the remaining eleven—two had meanwhile dropped out—be permitted to return to their classes because the charges against them were not serious; the others, he said, should be assigned to the Board of Education pending the disposition of their cases. But the governing board still refused to take any of the teachers back, and Superintendent Donovan, who had threatened to close the schools of the district in case of continued defiance, said that he would not do so because he did not wish to penalize the children who were still attending them.

Not surprisingly, the developments in Ocean Hill had by this time made many legislators in Albany skeptical of the whole idea of decentralization. The UFT has been charged with trying to sabotage decentralization while paying lip service to it. What the union in fact opposed, and lobbied against, was the Regents Plan, and it made no secret of its reasons.

Breaking the school system up into 20 to 100 districts is a segregationist move. It leads to ethnic and racial domination of particular districts. This is apartheid education for living in an apartheid world. This is the kind of education that leads to Watts and Newark, to hate and violence, to crime and chaos. . . .

Such districts would compete for public and private funds, employing Madison Avenue techniques and educational gimmickry to gain an edge. There would be competition for good teachers too—on an ethnic or racial or political basis. Make no mistake about it: the result will be a more vicious inequality in the distribution of teaching talent. Many teachers will leave the school system altogether. Who will suffer most? Minority groups and the poor. . . .

No reform can be abstracted from the circumstances of its proposed implementation. The tendencies to polarization and extremism in our society would, under the proposed decentralization, be virulently concentrated in our schools. Racial animosity, petty factionalism, and grasping ambition would dominate the atmosphere. Our schools would be transformed from centers of learning into maelstroms of ideological and emotional conflict. This is already the scene at IS 201 and elsewhere. . . .

Decentralization is both necessary and inevitable. But it should not mean destructive fragmentation of the city. The number of local school districts should be kept under fifteen in order to reduce administrative costs and to insure the possibility of *integration*. This cannot be achieved, overnight but much can be done. The Coleman Report and the Civil Rights Commission Report show that what children learn from each other and their social interaction in the classroom setting is a more important variable in academic success than textbooks (or teachers). . . .

Money is no more a panacea than decentralization. It does not answer complex questions about the learning process itself. But it is the precondition, the *sine qua non*, of improving educational quality —no matter who controls the schools.

The Regents Plan, whatever chance it might have had before the Ocean Hill events because of its massive backing from the city administration and certain big business groups, was now effectively dead. (A small group of legislators from upper-income districts threatened to stage a sit-in in the governor's office to force its passage; they got as far as the headlines and no further.) But it is important to recognize that decentralization itself would probably, at least for the time being, have died along with the Regents bill if the UFT had not continued to support the Marchi bill, which had been modified to permit the mayor to appoint four additional members to the existing Board of Education and to authorize the continuation of the demonstration projects. In the form in which it was finally adopted, it also authorized the Board of Education to delegate a wide range of powers to existing local boards and the three demonstration districts for the 1968–69 school year. Meanwhile the board was to draw up a definitive plan of decentralization for submission to the 1969 legislature.

The summer was devoted largely to preparations for future warfare; little effort was made to reach a settlement of either the Ocean Hill dispute or of differences on the broader issues. Mayor Lindsay appointed his four new members and a fifth to fill the vacancy resulting from the expiration of the term of former board president Alfred Giardino. Later he was able to make three more new appointments, which finally gave him control of the board.

Of all the new appointments, by far the most important was that of Mr. Galamison. He was the ablest and most experienced of the new members, he knew what he wanted, and he had a large staff—which he moved into Board of Education headquarters— paid for by SCOPE with its Ford Foundation grant. He also could, and did, mobilize the forces of Brooklyn CORE and similar groups to give him extra-legal support when he felt that would be useful. And through such former lieutenants as Thelma Johnson and Major Owens, who held key posts in the anti-poverty machinery, he was also able to bring that machinery into play to bolster his hand.

Just before the schools were opened for the 1968–69 year, the

UFT voted to strike. The extension of the strike from the Ocean Hill district to the entire city was partly the result of the UFT's desire to have clauses protecting the rights of teachers inserted into the decentralization plan, and partly of the fact that the resources of the central board had been used to help Ocean Hill replace the striking teachers. While Mr. McCoy had repeatedly stated that he had more than enough applicants for posts to fill the jobs of the 350 teachers in the district who had walked out in support of those he had sought to dismiss, this turned out not to be the case. When special examinations were held, in which the candidates were to apply directly to Mr. McCoy, only nineteen showed up. But with the aid of the recruiting facilities of the central board, he was subsequently able to obtain replacements for all 350, although almost all of them were substitutes and most had obtained their licenses through emergency examinations. (Of the teachers in Ocean Hill at the opening of the current term, roughly four-fifths were substitutes as compared to about 30 per cent the previous year. Many of them seemed unlikely to stay in teaching for very long; they were young men trained for professions that did not carry draft deferment, while teaching in underprivileged areas did.)

On August 26, Judge Rivers presented his final verdict, which was accepted by Superintendent Donovan on September 5. Of the eleven teachers whose cases were referred to Judge Rivers, one did not appear for the hearings. The charges against three teachers— Cliff Rosenthal, Barry Goodman, and UFT district chairman Frederick Nauman—were dismissed when the counsel for the Ocean Hill board stated that he had no evidence to offer against them; in all three cases the charges were essentially that they had expressed opposition to the project and had contributed to the growing hostility between Negro and white teachers. In the other seven cases, Judge Rivers ruled either that the charges were inadequate to justify disciplinary action even if proved, or that the evidence that was presented did not support the charges.

After two days, the initial strike ended with an agreement that appeared to cover all the points in dispute. The Board of Education stated its belief that

the governing board will act in good faith and that their public assurance to the mayor at City Hall on Sunday will be honored. To the Board of Education this means that each teacher who wants to return to his former school and to his professional assignment will not be prevented from doing so, and that these actions will be carried out in good faith and without reprisal.

Everything was apparently settled, and Mr. McCoy declared that the teachers could return. But when they showed up at their schools, they were met by mobs organized by the governing board and including members of that body as well as numerous individuals brought in from outside by "Sonny" Carson and others.

Teachers had to be escorted into 271 by the police because Carson and others had blocked the door. They were then all sent to one room where a group including Carson denounced and threatened them. Then they were summoned to meet Mr. McCoy in the auditorium of IS 55; they found there a group of "community" people who shouted such things as: "If you try to enter the schools we'll throw lye in your face." "Wait until we get the lights out—you'll be very visible." (The lights in the auditorium were turned out several times while the teachers were there.) "Some of you will be going out in pine boxes." Some teachers were hit or shoved.

When the teachers returned to 271, they were again blocked by a mob, again including members of the governing board, among them Mrs. Marshall and Mrs. Rooke; again the police had to escort them in. After school they were told the new teachers wished to meet them; when they went to join these teachers, the latter subjected them to the same kind of abuse as before. None of the returning teachers was given his normal teaching duties.

Mr. McCoy announced he could not guarantee the safety of the returning teachers. And governing board chairman Oliver asserted that he could not control the community's opposition to the teachers, *and that he hoped the community would again block the entry of the teachers on the following day.* He also denied that he had ever promised the mayor that the teachers would be allowed to return to actual classroom duties. Meanwhile the Board of Education, by a vote of 7–2, approved the agreement with the UFT.

But the agreement remained on paper. Because it was sabotaged by the governing board and because the Board of Education and the city administration failed to take any effective steps to enforce it, the union went back out on strike after two days. Again there were intensive negotiations, and a new agreement was reached on September 29. The teachers were to be returned to the district, and observers from the Board of Education and the UFT, as well as from the mayor's office, were to be present in all the schools. The governing board did not even pretend to accept this agreement; when the teachers returned, they were again met with mob action, threats, and violence in which members of the governing board took an active part, as did certain individual teachers. The governing board even announced that it was sending its own observers into the schools—and gave credentials to "Sonny" Carson and persons associated with him. A flying squadron of pupils and teachers from 271, led by Albert Vann, marched to other schools to intimidate the teachers there.

But this time the Board of Education and the mayor did try, initially, to enforce the agreement. First Mr. McCoy and then the principals were suspended for sabotaging it. This was followed, however, by more rioting at 271. Outsiders permitted by the police to enter the school after having been "identified" as "parents" by Walter Lynch, the governing board's community liaison officer, harassed teachers and observers. One Board of Education observer was threatened with death. The office of Mrs. Evelyn Farrar, a Negro assistant principal who had been designated as acting principal by the Board of Education, was invaded in relays throughout the day by groups of outsiders and "militants" among the McCoy-appointed teachers. They denounced and threatened her; the threats had special meaning for her because on one previous occasion she had been hit by a board—it narrowly missed her head—dropped twenty feet from a projection booth which was supposed to be unoccupied at the time but in which one of the "militant" teachers and a student belonging to the same group were actually present. At the end of the day, Mrs. Farrar had had enough; she requested a transfer out of the district. Following this incident, the Board of Education closed down 271. For the rest of the week, education proceeded in the other schools of the district.

But on Friday evening Superintendent Donovan suddenly announced his intention of reopening 271 and restoring the suspended principals on Monday, despite the absence of any pledge on their part to honor the agreement. This decision was taken without any advance consultation with the UFT—and without notifying the then president of the Board of Education, Mrs. Rose Shapiro. It apparently reflected the fact that during the week a majority of the board had agreed to replace Mrs. Shapiro with one of the new appointees, John Doar, and to make Milton Galamison vice president. Whether the new board officers gave the superintendent instructions without waiting until they had actually been elected, or whether Dr. Donovan simply anticipated what he believed to be their wishes, is not clear. In any case the UFT's reaction was that it had been double-crossed once again, this time by the Board of Education and the mayor. By Sunday night the UFT's executive board, its delegate assembly, and its membership had all voted overwhelmingly in favor of going out on strike Monday morning for the third time. The union now said that it would not go back unless the governing board, Mr. McCoy, and the principals were kept suspended at least until peace was established in the district; it also demanded the suspension and trial of four teachers at 271 accused of harassing and threatening others.

A new factor now entered the situation. Mayor Lindsay, although he had no love for the union—or indeed for public service unions in general—seems to have been considerably more interested in arriving at a settlement than his appointees to the Board of Education were. On more than one occasion he suggested compromise formulas only to have his own appointees on the board vote them down. Board meetings reportedly were devoted almost entirely to discussion of ways to break the strike; ways of settling it did not concern the new members. Indeed, in the negotiations that preceded the first strike, an old member who sided with the new appointees, John Lotz, threatened in so many words to break the union. He had been regarded as the mayor's candidate for the board presidency; his frankness may have caused the mayor to change his mind.

State Commissioner Allen was also brought into the discussions on a number of occasions. He proposed the institution of a trusteeship for the Ocean Hill district under which Mr. McCoy and the principals would be in charge but would be supervised by a representative of the commissioner's office. This did not satisfy the union for two reasons; it did not believe that the presence of a trustee would bring Mr. McCoy and the principals into line, and it did not trust the commissioner, who had never liked unions and had taken an extreme position in favor of local hiring and firing without regard to civil service regulations. There was increasing public pressure for a special session of the state legislature to end the impasse by repealing the decentralization law and wiping out the demonstration districts. The UFT itself, which had hesitated to support a special session precisely because it feared that decen-

tralization of any sort would be killed, finally decided that there
was no other recourse in the face of the intransigence of Ocean
Hill and the crescendo of attacks to which the union was being
subjected by the city administration, the Board of Education, and
the "corporate" establishment, as well as its intellectual hangers-
on, in general. (It has been suggested that the union feared that a
special session would have resulted in more drastic anti-strike legislation. That could only have happened if the call had included
amendment of the Taylor law; it is most unlikely that Governor
Rockefeller would have subjected his alliance with labor to that
strain.) But the governor, who had the power to call a special session, was not eager to do so; he preferred to let his rival in city
hall struggle to extricate himself from the mess. After all, when
the governor had imposed a settlement in the sanitation workers
strike, the mayor had made political capital out of a demagogic
attack on his rescuer. So Mr. Rockefeller simply said that the
mayor had all the powers he needed to settle the strike, and let
the possibility of a special session continue to hang over his head.

Even in the absence of a special session, however, the potential
role of the legislature was still an important factor. For the regular
session would begin in January, and it was becoming increasingly
clear that, in the absence of significant concessions to the UFT,
the strike would still be on at that time. The union membership
was in no mood for surrender, nor was there any sign of a crack
in its solidarity. The almost frantic efforts of some Board of Education members, and various groups of "concerned parents," produced a nominal 7–9,000 teachers in the theoretically open schools
(as compared with an average of 18,000 during the 1967 strike
when the issues were economic and educational; this time the
teachers felt that they were fighting for their lives, professionally
and perhaps even literally). Of these, according to reliable sources
at the Board of Eduaction, fewer than 3,000 were regularly appointed teachers. Some of the others were day-by-day substitutes,
while some were people with long-dormant substitute licenses or
suddenly acquired emergency ones who had entered the schools
for political reasons and were unlikely to maintain any future connection with them.

In any case, whatever satisfaction having a school "open" might
give someone whose main priority was breaking the teachers'
union, the educational results were slim. This did not, of course,
apply to those few areas like Ocean Hill–Brownsville itself, where

a fairly full complement of teachers was actually present. The children in Ocean Hill–Brownsville probably learned no less than usual during the strike; as the world was informed by an endless parade of instant experts, most of whom had probably never set foot in a school since childhood and some of whom had never set foot in a public school at all, the children may even have learned more, since the absence of at least half of the student body resulted in a ratio of pupils to staff which ranged between 6½ to 1 and 7½ to 1. With *that* sort of ratio (not exactly testimony to actual community support of the governing board), it would take a very special skill to avoid imparting some knowledge.

The event that finally broke the log jam was one that had long been foreshadowed, the action of the Appellate Division of the State Supreme Court in upholding the earlier decision by Judge Rinaldi that the appointment of the Ocean Hill "demonstration principals" was illegal. This enabled the city to make a major concession to the union without loss of face, while the union on its side was now willing to have Rhody McCoy remain as unit administrator in return for his pledge to cooperate with a state-appointed trustee. The UFT also received guarantees against harassment elsewhere in the city. To enforce them, Commissioner Allen—who may have been rather more conscious of the meaning of the coming legislative session than those less wise in the ways of Albany—appointed a committee of three persons whom the union trusted and who superseded the Board of Education in some respects.

The strike was, of course, important enough in itself. The New York school system is the largest in the country. The UFT is the largest local union in the country.

But it was more important for the issues it involved and the forces that were mobilized around them. These issues remain and will be fought out for a long time, whether in the political field or in future strikes. They will recur in other areas and other occupations. One of these issues is the status of public employees. An American superstition has it that there is something sacrosanct about public employment that makes strikes against the government equivalent to sinning against the Holy Ghost. In a time in which government employment is a rapidly and inevitably increasing sector of the economy, such a doctrine has totalitarian implications. (The Thirteenth Amendment bans involuntary servitude except as a punishment for crime. So far as I know, working

for the government is not yet officially regarded as a crime anywhere in the United States—though it may well be a blunder.) It
was for this reason that the labor movement as a whole regarded
the issue as a crucial one.

Another issue that received constant stress in the news media
was the Jewish-Negro confrontation. The union was constantly
referred to as Jewish, and the Ocean Hill district was always called
a Negro ghetto. There were charges and counter-charges of racism
and anti-Semitism. On a more fundamental plane, the charge was
made that the merit system, which the union claimed to be defending against a patronage grab by the mayor in collusion with local
power seekers, was actually a device for protecting the ethnic *status
quo*—Jewish predominance in the schools, Irish in the police,
Italian in the sanitation department—and an obstacle to Negro
advancement. In fact, the reverse has been historically true. The
merit system has served one minority after another in its struggles
to circumvent the barriers of discrimination. Negroes, too, are
finding the civil service a relatively smooth road to advancement;
they are already proportionately more numerous in the post office
and many other federal departments than in the population as a
whole.

But perhaps the most complicated issue that emerged out of the
conflict was that of the orientation of society to the problems of its
least privileged sectors. There is a widespread movement now afoot
to ally the bottom and top layers of American society against those
in the middle—and especially against the organized workers. This
strategy has its implicit assumptions; it stems from the belief on
the one side that the first enemy of the man at the bottom is the
man one step up, and on the other that the discontents of the
most wretched can effectively be appeased without any expense to
those at the top.

It also has its political implications. Such an alliance cannot,
for instance, challenge those facets of the economy from which its
corporate sponsors benefit. It cannot aim at the elimination of
exploitation; at best—and a rare best—it can be directed against
the most flagrant forms of exploitation. (I have yet to see an advertisement of the Urban Coalition urging people not to buy grapes, yet
a victory in the California grape strike would be of more direct
benefit to American minority groups than any number of ads suggesting that we "Give a Damn" for the Ocean Hill governing
board.)

The natural enemies of this new alliance are those groups that are troublesome to its upper, rather than to its nether, millstone; in an alliance between the elite and the sub-proletariat, it does not take a course in Marxism to know who is going to use whom. The specific idea of community control of the schools, in the form in which it has been advanced in New York is one that can offer quite tangible benefits to certain sections of the economic elite. For example, it affords an excuse for not increasing expenditures and taxes; we have seen the relationship in the genesis of the issue in New York. But to the people of the community, the *actual* community, it offers only the simulacrum of power—for they have no command over the economic resources that real power requires —in place of the reality of improved, and more expensive, education.

Who's to Blame in the School Strike /
FRED FERRETTI

It was 5:30 in the evening of October 8, in the tiny, paper-strewn office of Rhody McCoy, for fifteen months unit administrator of the eight-school Ocean Hill–Brownsville demonstration school district in Brooklyn.

One hour before, McCoy had been relieved officially of his job by New York City's superintendent of schools Bernard Donovan. He was annoyed: not because he had been relieved ("He's got to do what he's got to do and so do I") but because Donovan had delayed one hour and a half past the scheduled announcement time of three o'clock. And McCoy was hungry.

"Hey, Bill," he called to an assistant, "how about calling Chicken Delight and getting a basket of. . . ." He surveyed the two other people in his office. ". . . 12 pieces. Four pieces of chicken should be enough for any one man." While the order for dinner was phoned and McCoy waited for the members of his school district's local governing board to assemble, he was asked what he intended

THIS ARTICLE appeared in *New York Magazine*, November 18, 1968, pp. 22–35. © 1968 New York Magazine Co.

to do the next morning. The Board of Education, through Donovan, had ordered him and the principals of his eight schools out.

"We'll be at our desks tomorrow," he said. "Words don't mean too much."

Wasn't he saying, in effect, that he was defying Donovan's order?

"I'm not saying anything *in effect*. I *am* defying Donovan's order. I was elected by the people of this community and I'm here until *they* tell me they don't want me. That's the crunch."

Donovan had reported earlier that he would be out in the district the next morning to see that the principals were removed and to personally take over McCoy's duties.

"He may come out. I expect he *will* come out. But *I* got the keys to the office." McCoy grinned.

It was pure McCoy, spoken softly, without rancor. While his unique experiment in public education was being torn apart with a powerful thrust of power-hungry unionism; while the attack was being abetted publicly by a supine and ineffectual Board of Education; while the experiment was at best uncertainly supported by the mayor of New York, Rhody McCoy had stood firm.

He had stood firm because he felt he was right, that the school district experiment was right, that the principle of decentralized and community-controlled schools was the only right course for public education today. After twenty years as a teacher—a black teacher and "a product of the best education black schools can offer"—Rhody McCoy became, in the setting of Ocean Hill–Brownsville, a symbol of radical change in education.

McCoy is 45 years old; lives in a Roosevelt, Long Island, split-level; has seven children, four large boxer dogs, two not-so-new cars, one swimming pool in need of slight repairs, a collection of odorous, well-used pipes, and is addicted to Saturday morning tennis.

He is also a revolutionary. On the surface an implausible one, but a revolutionary nevertheless.

As unit administrator for the Ford Foundation-funded Ocean Hill–Brownsville demonstration project, he has wrought, in slightly over a year, deep organic change in the eight schools of the district. With this change has come a sense of community pride, confidence, and purpose, for which McCoy could, but does not, claim much of the credit.

"I'll tell you something," McCoy said to columnist Murray Kempton, "partly because I'm proud of it and partly because it's what we've been trying to do: We've kind of gotten those youngsters to understand that these are *schools*."

Or as he said another day: "Me a revolutionary? Revolution implies change, great change. I've seen no great changes yet. We've only had cars since 1901, and I see more changes in them than in the way teachers teach. But we *have* changed a few things. We're trying to get teachers to teach, get involved with the kids in a one-to-one relationship, not simply stand up in front of a class and dispense facts.

"Out here we tell them jump in. Go beyond the printed page and the blackboard. We want them to think of themselves as coordinators of resources. The bastards have been losing sight of what the kids need. What's relevant. What they relate to. We've got to motivate kids. And teachers."

It is revolutionary in this white- and blue-collar city today to believe that children in an almost totally black neighborhood might possibly be taught to read as well as kids in "better" all-white schools. McCoy believes it and the kids in Ocean Hill–Brownsville *are* reading better, despite the pamphlets of the United Federation of Teachers. It is a revolutionary thought to most whites that black and Spanish-speaking kids might actually *like* to go to school. They appear to like it in Ocean Hill. It is revolutionary to believe that teachers might *want* to teach in schools of what is considered a neighborhood completely "changed" from white to nonwhite. Many teachers will say that although they really want to teach "minority group" children, those children just don't seem to have the capacity to learn. But after a mass walkout of teachers in Ocean Hill–Brownsville, young teachers of varying grades of experience flocked to the district. Despite UFT propaganda, Ocean Hill–Brownsville has not become an anti-Semitic haven for black teachers wearing African *dashikis* and scourging white teachers from the district. More than 70 per cent of the 250 teachers hired by McCoy are white; more than 50 per cent are Jews.

McCoy would like to hire more black teachers. He has hopes of assimilating them into the district with training programs. "The problem with most black teachers," he says, "is the same rotten system of education. They can't fill the bill yet. They've been put down by the rigid Board of Education exam system. They've been suppressed by unionism. You take black supervisors.

We have the only black principals in the whole damn school system. Why? The guys qualified just sat back. The system kept them down so long they just never went out and fought. But we tell them go back to school. Learn some more. Learn so you can compete with whites, instead of among yourselves, for advancement on the basis of color. Let's have a change. Let's have quality. And," McCoy says, "we're starting to see areas where they're able to peep through."

"Seniority for one. Seniority doesn't mean a goddamned thing anymore. It's simply not relevant any longer," he said, emphasizing that black teachers, like their white counterparts, have been mired in the system of job tenure and security (many times to the exclusion of teaching itself) for too long. But where tenure has worked for the white teacher, it has held back the black teacher. "The union has made teachers more union than professional. This is a problem. We have to give these teachers—black and white—the degree of professionalism they need."

McCoy wants black teachers. But he wants good black teachers. So he'll hire the best teachers he can get, and he has new training programs for blacks. "The pool right now we can draw from is mostly white, a consequence of the system."

Ocean Hill–Brownsville has four black principals: Percy Jenkins of IS 55; William Harris of JHS 271; Ralph Rogers of PS 144; and Mrs. Eileen James of PS 137. It has the city's first Puerto Rican principal, Louis Fuentes of PS 155; and the city's first Chinese principal, David Lee of PS 178. The other two principals are Ralph Grandenetti of PS 73 and Irving Gerber of PS 87. Three of the four black administrators, however, are still rated only acting principals. Ironically Mrs. James received confirmation of her status as a full principal on the same day she was formally relieved of her school.

But while McCoy and the nineteen-member local governing board of Ocean Hill–Brownsville believe in the workability of decentralization and community control of local schools, the UFT doesn't believe in it—despite its public utterances. Last November, after McGeorge Bundy reported to Mayor Lindsay a proposal for decentralization, the UFT's executive board adopted a position which criticized the Bundy proposals and said the panel headed by Bundy "ignores the new power and integrity of the professional teacher who will not continue to teach in any school or district where professional decisions are made by laymen."

It was further stated that

tenure is a precious teacher right. Tenure gives teachers the security they need to teach honestly, free from community pressures. Under the tenure concept, a teacher can be dismissed only for cause after a hearing on the basis of charges brought against him *by other professionals who are competent to evaluate professional performance. Under the Bundy Report, charges could be brought against a tenured faculty member by a community board of laymen with no professional expertise.* This proposal is anti-professional. It would encourage local vigilantes to constantly harass teachers. No teacher with professional integrity could teach in such a district. UFT urges that this proposal be rejected." (Italics UFT's).

It is this issue, specifically, whether local communities within the city shall have or shall not have the right to control their school and to hire, transfer, or fire staff teachers; and generally, whether the table of organization of the school system shall or shall not undergo a revolutionary recasting, which led to the onslaught on Ocean Hill. Ironically in the current dispute (and assuredly in the future) it has been the UFT teachers and the union leadership who have resisted any change. Historically it has been the educator and the trade unionist who have been for, and have helped bring about, change. In the case of school decentralization, it has been the teachers' union, fearing local participation, particularly local black participation in teachers' affairs, that has been the instrument of reaction. Teacher opposition to community control translates into phrases such as "job security" and "the right of due process."

The teachers' union is largely white, almost totally middle class, made up of people who have inched along for years building up tenure and civil service security. The prospect of radical change for them is terrifying, even more so if it appears to be black change.

It was against this background that, last May 8, nineteen teachers received registered letters notifying them they were being transferred out of the Ocean Hill–Brownsville district. Among the group were one principal and five assistant principals. All, it should be stated, were union people—the administrators were members of the Council of Supervisory Associations, and the teachers were dues payers to the UFT. Some were union officials.

The letters were simple and direct. They were also, it developed, more than slightly naive.

The governing board of the Ocean Hill–Brownsville demonstration school district has voted to end your employment in the schools of this district. This action was taken on the recommendation of the Personnel Committee. This termination of employment is to take effect immediately.

In the event you wish to question this action, the governing board will receive you, Friday, May 10, 1968, at 6 p.m. at Intermediate School 55, 2021 Bergen Street, Brooklyn.

You will report Friday morning to Personnel, 110 Livingston Street, Brooklyn, for reassignment.

The letter was signed by the Reverend C. Herbert Oliver, chairman of the district's governing board, and by McCoy. Copies were sent to school superintendent Donovan and to his deputy for personnel, Theodore Lang.

The recipients made no effort to appear for reassignment as they were directed by their superior. Nor did they appear before the district governing board to ask why they were being transferred, or to protest the transfers. Instead, they yelled like hell. UFT president Albert Shanker denounced the transfers as "illegal firings," and as violations of the teachers' contractual rights of tenure and due process. Shanker knew that the tenure and due process concepts related to dismissals, so to make the argument stand up he repeatedly protested that the teachers had been "fired" without benefit of due process. As president of the UFT, Shanker certainly had to be aware that administrative transfers are legal; that there is nothing in the bylaws of the Board of Education forbidding them.

Soon the transfers became "firings" in the newspapers and on radio and television, with little effort made in any medium to be accurate. Small attempts to differentiate between "transfer" and "fire" or "dismiss" were put down as semantic exercises. Shanker rode the public wave. The immediate consequence of the transfers was a walkout of 350 teachers from the Ocean Hill–Brownsville district in support of their fellows. This represented almost two-thirds of the district's 556-teacher complement. Subsequently there was confusion and a series of contradictory decisions by Superintendent Donovan; wide-ranging resentment in the Brownsville community; chaos in the schools; and a severe amputation of decentralization by the state legislature.

This September there were three city-wide strikes by teachers, interrupted by eleven school days. And more significant there were (and continue to be) increased demands to see that school decentralization and community controls of schools be killed legislatively in the city and state.

Why? Because of nineteen transferred teachers? Because nineteen people were allegedly denied due process in violation of a trade union agreement? Because the UFT does not want nonprofessionals judging professional performance? These would appear to be localized issues. Why should the city and the state be exercised? What are the real issues? And what are the circumstances behind the Ocean Hill–Brownsville community confrontation with the power structure? What happened, I believe the facts show, is that a major change began out in Brooklyn, which frightened the school system, its overseers, most of its members and the mayor of New York, who was supposed to be in favor of broad sweeping change in the city's education, who had fathered the decentralized experiment, then left it abandoned. A history is in order.

The Ocean Hill–Brownsville demonstration school district was established in July of 1967 with $44,000 of Ford Foundation seed money. It has since received more than $128,000 for development of its programs. It grew, according to a March, 1968, report on decentralization by the New York City Commission on Human Rights, "out of events demonstrating great community interest in the schools." But it grew without roots. According to the Human Rights Commission report, the district faced "many early troubles, most of them resulting from the Board of Education's delays in allocating it funds and office space for its operation."

At the end of July, the local board in the district submitted a written set of proposals to the Board of Education defining specific powers, responsibilities, and functions of the board. It suggested that the local board would be directly responsible to the superintendent of schools and to the state education commissioner. The local group clearly asked for community control of its educational affairs but by no means asked complete independence. It also proposed that, although it would review teacher performance, any evaluations made would be governed by existing Board of Education procedures.

Nevertheless, the board refused to act on the local proposals. A study by the New York Civil Liberties Union reported recently that "once the Board of Education understood that what Ocean Hill–Brownsville really wanted was an experiment in genuine community control, it backed off even before it had begun."

Planning for the new district began in the spring of 1967, and, according to the report, "early notification permitted some teachers to participate in the planning during the summer, *but did not induce meaningful participation by supervisors.*" (Italics mine.)

Elections for the governing board were held on August 3, 1967. Seven parent members were elected. They had been nominated in a canvass of families living in the district, who filled out forms distributed by election teams. There were no fewer than four candidates in each of seven local school areas within the district, and in one section there were thirteen candidates. The seven elected parents are Mrs. Clara Marshall, vice chairman of the governing board; Mrs. Blanche Pile; Mrs. Haddie Bishop; Mrs. Elaine Rooke; Mrs. Agnes Hanson; Mrs. Lillian Davis, and Mrs. Wilda Henderson. The day-long balloting was proctored by the Bank Street College of Education, the city's Human Resources Administration, and by the Police Department. Of about 4,000 parents eligible to vote, 1,049 cast ballots. This represents slightly more than 25 per cent and has led critics to say that the board was elected by, and represents, "only a minority" of the community. Quite the contrary. The large vote is a testimony to the concern over education by the Ocean Hill district, when compared to the 400-voter turnout when a state assemblyman was elected last year.

The seven elected parents then chose five community leaders for inclusion in the board. These are Reverend Oliver, pastor of the Bethany United Presbyterian Church, later elected chairman; Walter Lynch; the Reverend John Powis, a Catholic worker priest; State Assemblyman Samuel Wright; and Mrs. Dolores Torres. In addition, two supervisors and four teachers were chosen by their colleagues in the eight district schools. These are Percy Jenkins, principal of IS 55 and Louis Fuentes, principal of PS 155; Ronald McFadden, a teacher at JHS 271; Colene Blenman of PS 87; Theodore Fletcher of IS 55, and Mrs. Albertha Loften of PS 137. The nineteenth member is Stephen Lockwood, a professor of education at Brooklyn College, who acted as a consultant to the board before his election to it.

Despite the election and the content of the board, the impression persisted in the newspapers, on radio and television, that the nineteen people were some sort of rump vigilante group that was riding roughshod over the rest of the Brownsville community as well as the teachers in the schools. One television commentator delivered himself of an "analysis" which called the board a "small minority" which was "conspiring" to keep UFT teachers out of the schools. Albert Shanker continued to give the impression that the board was composed of nonprofessionals who knew nothing of teaching and who were not representative of the community.

The local board, as its first function, was permitted by the Board of Education to recommend appointments for unit administrator and for principal. In addition to its four black principals, the local board selected Fuentes and Lee, the first Puerto Rican and Chinese principals, respectively, in New York.

But these appointments required a special ruling from State Commissioner of Education James Allen, authorizing selection of principals who had state certification but were not on the city's examination lists. This ruling and the appointments made under it have been challenged in court by the Council of Supervisory Associations. The CSA suit contested the appointments because the people selected had not come off civil service principal lists. McCoy, acting principal of PS 148 in Manhattan, was hired on July 5, while the planning for the district was going on. He functioned as an interim administrator. Subsequently he was one of a number of candidates nominated for unit administrator, which is akin to district superintendent in other city school districts. His chief rival for the permanent appointment was the then principal of JHS 271, Jack Bloomfield.

It was this contest which signalled bitterness in Ocean Hill. Bloomfield was the selection of a group of assistant principals and teachers, many of them UFT functionaries in the schools, and they let it be known, according to local board member Walter Lynch, that "if Jack got to unit administrator they'd stay and work in the program here. If not, they'd leave." Bloomfield was interviewed. So was McCoy.

Says McCoy, "I personally thought I blew it. Usually you go for a job interview, you're careful, very conservative and you try to come up with the right answers. I didn't. I disagreed with some of the people who were going to hire me." But the governing board voted the job to McCoy. Subsequently eighteen assistant principals in the district asked for and received transfers, as did five of the district's principals.

That summer of 1967, the job was to get the community and its new governing board and its new administrator to "swing together," said McCoy. "I remember the first time I got with my new board. I could see them thinking, 'Look at this fair-complexioned guy trying to tell us what to do.' [McCoy *is* fair, with sandy hair and light blue eyes.] So I decided we better settle that real quick. We went into a room in one of the schools. We locked the door and had a family fight. We gave up proper language and went at each other pretty good. Since then it's really been like a family. I'm locked in with them. When their hearts beat, mine beats.

"With this governing board, I find now that I don't have to listen to what's going on when we talk. I just watch the faces and I know. I feel." Just feeling made McCoy takes his Board of Education salary check that summer and deposit it in the school district account when the Ford Foundation grant was delayed. It was with McCoy's money that Ocean Hill–Brownsville began to "get moving."

It was his idea to sell the education experiment to that part of the community which was either on the fence or unaware of its existence. Teams of volunteers circulated through the area with what he called "data books" and compiled daily logs of complaints about housing, employment, medical ailments, "and then we pooled the information and tried to do what we could outside of the educational field to help. We called city departments. We told the people whom to call. It was something to pull the community together.

"The attitude here was interesting. It had been as it is with churches. They weren't involved. They'd *gone* to school, as they'd *go* to church. On Sundays to pray. They'd send the kids to school. They didn't know the philosophy of and the history of religion, nor that of schools, of education. With the schools they felt the teachers should do everything. We tried our damnedest to change all that." It was a long indoctrination process that produced its greatest results in the current crisis when community support became the rock base for McCoy and the local governing board.

In the meantime, while Louis Fuentes, principal of PS 155, was speaking to Puerto Rican parents and students in their own language, Herman Ferguson was selected as principal of IS 55. Ferguson had been arrested for (and recently was convicted of) conspiracy in Queens. He was alleged to be a member of the black Revolutionary Action Movement (RAM) and was found guilty of conspiring to kill NAACP executive director Roy Wilkins and Urban League director Whitney Young. According to McCoy, the board approved Ferguson, the community reacted favorably to his appointment, but the teachers did not. He said teachers within the district refused assignments to IS 55, "despite the fact that Donovan told me I had the right to deploy teachers within the district. Cooperation declined and there was further polarization."

This continued, McCoy said, with the community becoming impatient and with his attempting to mollify them, while at the same time attempting to "keep the lid on" for a year as Donovan had asked him to do. There was an extraordinary number of teachers who simply, and in violation of Board of Education policy, refused transfers within the district. But, said McCoy, "I didn't press it. Many times I called Donovan but I was just told to ride out." Teachers refused to report to IS 55 because of Ferguson, or to PS 155 because of Fuentes. The UFT wage strike that September of 1967, which kept schools closed for two weeks, didn't help ease tensions.

Then there were what McCoy calls "those unreal sessions" with the Board of Education. "See, here was this new group of people who got together, got themselves a school district, wanted nothing but good schools, didn't want to play politics. They didn't know anything about Board of Education policy. Well, we'd go down to the board to make presentations for things we wanted. And I'd coach one person to be our spokesman. We'd drill it into him or her. You know, now here's what you'll say. And the rest of us were supposed to sit still. Be cool.

"So down we'd go. And we'd go inside and there'd be Jerry Kovalchik (assistant superintendent of schools) and he'd say, 'Well, hi, How are you today? And what can we do for you?' Our spokeswoman would get up and make her presentation and we're sitting, congratulating ourselves. Kovalchik's looking interested. Then he says, 'Excuse me a moment,' and leaves. Then in would come Nate Brown (Dr. Nathan Brown, executive deputy superintendent of schools).

"He'd shake everybody's hand and look interested and say, 'Now, what seems to be the problem?' And up would get our spokeswoman and she'd go through it all again. Some of the gang is getting teed off at this point. And Brown is looking interested and he says, 'I see, excuse me,' and off he goes.

"Next, enter the Great White Father (Superintendent Donovan). 'Well, hello!' he'd say. 'What seems to be the trouble?' That did it! Our spokeswoman gets up. She's confused. Donovan's sitting there like a fat cat. The rest of us get angry. And we start yelling. Oh did we blow it! Those board cats are beautiful. Especially Donovan. Don't let anybody tell you anything about Donovan. He's *very, very* good at what he does. A tough cat."

Also that November a committee headed by Ford Foundation president McGeorge Bundy, appointed by Mayor Lindsay to study decentralization, came up with a series of recommendations in a report entitled "Reconnection for Learning." It suggested that local school boards have the right to hire, fire, and assign teachers within their districts; have the right to develop educational programs and to manage the educational affairs, including the budgets of their districts. Ocean Hill–Brownsville, already operating under the Ford Foundation grant, was four months old then. The UFT disputed virtually every major recommendation contending that it was merely a "glorification of the old-time rural school structure and is unfit for the greatest urban center in the world."

The demonstration project however had reason for hope because Mayor Lindsay had publicly and vocally committed himself to decentralization through the Bundy panel.

Backed by growing community support McCoy fleshed out the school district. The district's new school, IS 55, was opened. Class sizes were reduced drastically—the average in Ocean Hill–Brownsville is 1,100 students per each of its eight schools, 70 teachers per school, or about one teacher for each 16 pupils. The September UFT strike had hurt not only the beginnings of the new school programs but had increased community resentment against the UFT. When the eighteen assistant principals and one-fifth of the district's 550 teachers transferred out after the school year had started, the community's anger grew. The people of Ocean Hill believed, according to McCoy, that it was simply a teacher tactic to "torpedo the district." On the basis of subsequent actions, their reasoning could be correct.

There was a period of surface stability through the winter. Substitute teachers filled the vacated classrooms. New assistant principals took over jobs left by their predecessors. The personnel turnover forced McCoy to introduce experimental, unorthodox educational programs into the curriculum at a slower rate than he had wanted. Some early efforts were shot down.

Staff additions came hard for McCoy, and the Board of Education apparently gave little help. "I'd call and ask. They'd say we'll see. And then I'd get a shipment of new directives. Now what in hell do I need a sheaf of directives for. I want teachers. I want books. I want equipment. Most of all, I want good teachers. Not the subs they kept sending by the carload. But I got directives." He concedes that most times, "I'd just tear them up 'cause my office is too damn small to hold them all and when Nate Brown called to ask if I'd gotten them, I'd say, 'Directives? No, can't say that I have.' So I'd get another pack." But as for what he really needed, says McCoy, "They weren't answering."

Despite this apparent lack of interest from the Board of Education, McCoy introduced into Ocean Hill–Brownsville "Project Read," a system of vari-colored reader-workbooks through which children learn to read by sound, letter identification, color, repetition. They test themselves and proceed at their own speeds. The course, devised by the Behavioral Research Laboratories of Palo Alto, California, has succeeded in raising the reading levels of many children in the district in a remarkably short time. There are the already mentioned bi-lingual Spanish-English classes, open to all children on a voluntary basis. There is a Montessori class in one school, an experiment McCoy hopes to expand. There are courses in black culture and African history, and there'll be more. McCoy is a student of multi-media presentations in class—"projection, closed circuit TV, tape recorders, radio, imitation TV-record players, anything, any way other than just the teacher standing and talking. Any way to get information across to the kids. After all this bullcrap is solved, if it ever is, I'm going to look at it all. Is it worth it? It could be. Obviously the kids respond. If the board gives us enough money to really and truly do these things, and if the parents can be made to think on a massive scale." He'd like a district-wide tennis program and a community band.

"Behind it all is this: if something's happening in the classrooms, the kids won't roam the damn halls."

The response he received from the teachers, McCoy said, was minimal. Instead, open opposition increased, and there were instances, he said, of UFT teachers publicly announcing their intentions to sabotage Ocean Hill-Brownsville. SCOPE reported "during the months of March and April (1968), particularly at JHS 271, the majority of UFT teachers stopped teaching and even supervising. Twenty fires occurred at JHS 271 in April. Some teachers told Puerto Rican students that the school was now only for blacks. Many of the teachers and assistant principals refused to respect the authority of McCoy or the principals." McCoy says he repeatedly asked Donovan for help, but received none.

The local governing board chairman, Reverend Oliver, said there were twenty-eight fires in JHS 271, and "oddly no teacher was ever able to catch anybody. The children were doing what they wanted. The teachers were unable to control the classes. I was told by one teacher that the children were nothing but 'little savages.' It is apparent to me that the UFT was shafting us every chance it had." There were many instances of excessive lateness and absences, said Reverend Oliver, "in short, there was complete and utter chaos."

Late in April a pamphlet was distributed anonymously throughout the community. It was called a "No Man's Land School Report Card," and it contained a number of charges against the district's personnel in the form of questions, such as: "Is there an assistant principal at PS 144 who is trying to divide the community against our new principal?" "Are there a lot of teachers who are missing days at the price of our children's education; were there twenty-eight teachers out 'sick' on Friday, Feb. 23, the day after the holiday, at JHS 271? On Monday March 4, were there fourteen teachers 'absent' at IS 55 and eighteen teachers 'absent' at JHS 271?" and "Has the unit administrator agreed to leave some of these uncooperative people in the school system?"

Among specifics cited by McCoy against some of the teachers in the district are "an instance of one teacher sent to us who had been transferred four times, all with satisfactory ratings: there must have been some reason for his transfers. Another fellow was conducting his moonlighting business on school phones. Another fellow couldn't control his art class. So he took away the paint. Another fellow let a kid who had been in an accident sit around and bleed for a couple of hours. You just had to beg these bastards to react."

While disruptions in Ocean Hill grew last spring, UFT president Shanker lobbied arduously in Albany and successfully forced the state legislature to vote down significant moves toward decentralization, including the dissolution of the New York City Board of Education and its replacement by a smaller board with fewer centralized powers. The proposals had been made by Com-

missioner Allen. Instead, the legislature passed a resolution com-
pelling Mayor Lindsay to come up with a formula for decentralization by this December 15 for submission to the next session of the
legislature. This effectively left those districts already established—
the IS 201 complex in Harlem; the Two Bridges district on the
Lower East Side; and Ocean Hill-Brownsville—still in limbo. Authorized, but not really. With duly elected governing boards that
could be suspended at will. With powers implied, but never
spelled out.

McCoy said he spent a good deal of his time trying to negotiate
for what he called allowable controls, and that the Board of Education could have granted them if it had so wanted. "I suggest
that if for no more than a token of good will, there were many
areas in which they could have granted a great deal more authority
than they were willing to. The board did not give us the powers
they claimed they could give."

McCoy said he asked Donovan "any number of times" to transfer out those teachers that he and the community felt were undermining the work of the district. Said Reverend Oliver, "We attempted to get the board to do something. We needed to start
somewhere. They would do nothing. If we did nothing we felt
our project was doomed for that year and we'd have to fight
another whole year to get some meaningful progress. We were
unwilling to do that."

So the letters of transfer, signed by McCoy and Oliver, went
out "amidst total chaos, particularly at JHS 271 and a refusal on
the part of a number of licensed assistant principals to recognize
the principals" of the district, according to SCOPE. Said Reverend
Oliver, "Our governing board did not fire anyone at all; we simply
transferred certain personnel out of our district.

"Filing of charges is not necessary when only transfers are to be
effected. Letters from principals, the unit administrator (McCoy),
and a recommendation from the Personnel Committee formed
the background of the action of the governing board to transfer.
This more than meets the requirements. Then the governing board,
by a majority vote, approved the recommendation to transfer. Not
all were pleased but it was a majority vote of a duly elected
board."

It should be stressed further that McCoy, acting under orders
from his governing board, did nothing more than do district superintendents in any of the city's thirty-two other school districts.

If a principal is unhappy with a teacher, or with an assistant, he is administratively transferred, and usually the teacher accepts the transfer in lieu of an unsatisfactory rating.

Those transfers became Shanker's weapon. Stressing that he was fighting for the right of due process for his union members, Shanker said that before a teacher could be discharged or dismissed, charges had to be filed against him formally and he had the right to an administrative hearing.

It has subsequently been disclosed in a report by Dr. John H. Niemeyer, president of the Bank Street College of Education, that in March and April, at the time of greatest chaos in the Ocean Hill–Brownsville schools, the Board of Education told the local governing board that teachers considered unacceptable could be transferred out of the district so long as no great publicity was attached to such transfers.

Also, the NYCLU Report disclosed, the UFT had won in Ocean Hill–Brownsville the right for unlimited numbers of teachers to transfer out at will for the duration of the experiment, "to abandon the experiment for as long as it continued and then to be free to return, presumably when 'normal' conditions had been reinstated." The Board of Education's present policy provides that teachers must serve five years on regular appointment before being eligible for transfer. It also limits transfers to no more than 5 per cent of the teachers at any one school in any school year. Except in Ocean Hill–Brownsville. The UFT had the right of unlimited transfer, but it wanted the experimental district to have not even half a loaf.

Prior to the Niemeyer Report, there are the findings of a Board of Education consultant, retired Civil Court judge Francis Rivers, who, although he recommended that the transferred teachers be readmitted to the Ocean Hill–Brownsville complex, nevertheless wrote ". . . perhaps if the unit administrator had sent to the superintendent of schools a simple request to transfer the teachers, without assigning any supporting charges, he, the superintendent, may have been able to do so without a hearing. . . ."

The Niemeyer Report was commissioned by the Board of Education. Judge Rivers is a Board of Education consultant. The board refused to listen to either of its experts or to honor its agreement with the local board. It refused the transfers, and it demanded, through Donovan, formal charges against the teachers when none should have been required.

There existed no guidelines as to the powers granted to demonstration school districts. There was informal agreement between the central board and the local governing board that undesirable teachers would be transferred quietly. There is an opinion that a request for transfer might have made Donovan exert his power as superintendent of schools. The governing board honored its charter, even though so loosely drawn. It acted within the legal limits then existing with the Board of Education.

Yet the transfers became first "firings" then later "*illegal* transfers." How? By simple repetition by Shanker, by Donovan, and most recently by the mayor of New York.

Only Donovan and Shanker can say why they acted, but others can speculate. If true decentralization and community control of schools becomes a reality, then there exists no real need for a central Board of Education or a powerful superintendent of schools. With decentralization, the UFT would be forced to bargain collectively, not with a single adversary but with 33, or 25, or 15 or 5, or however many decentralized districts might emerge.

Shanker had a union election coming up. There was opposition to his re-election from a group within the union calling itself the New Coalition of the UFT. There was further opposition, which became public only later, from one of Shanker's own vice presidents, John O'Neill. Ocean Hill–Brownsville provided a ready-to-order cause, something behind which all UFTers could solidify when their president went out to do battle.

Also it was a perfect time to show the state legislature that decentralization couldn't work, because it abused teachers, denied them simple justice and encouraged "vigilante" attacks.

Donovan refused to back up McCoy as he should have as a duly elected and approved district superintendent. He ordered McCoy to take back the nineteen transferred teachers. McCoy refused and, following a series of administrative ploys by McCoy, Shanker and Donovan, the teachers were ordered back and promised police protection.

The community reacted. On May 10 and May 13, the teachers attempted to enter the schools. Members of the local board, the community, and supporters from other parts of the city set up stair-blocks. There were scuffles with police, some minor fighting, some arrests, and vast amounts of tension and venom.

Each day the transferred teachers would appear before the schools. Each day there would be members of the community standing on the steps and in the entrances, blocking any attempt at entry. Other teachers, members of the UFT, stayed away from their classes in sympathy. First there were a few, then came a mass exodus. Three hundred fifty of the district's 556 teachers stayed. For a time the schools were closed in Ocean Hill–Brownsville. "Fear of violence," said the UFT.

From the latter part of May through the end of June, there were only 200 teachers deployed around the schools caring for 9,000 students. Conditions in the schools were chaotic, but many parents gave their time to come to school as monitors, as hallway and lunchroom assistants. When the schools were declared closed for a time, liberation classes were set up in churches and public halls around the district. Again the parents joined with the teachers who had stayed.

In mid-June, McCoy invoked another right he had, or thought he had, as a district superintendent. He formally notified all 350 teachers who had walked off their jobs that unless they reported to their classrooms he would order those who were substitute teachers dismissed and recommend Donovan take disciplinary action against those who were regular teachers. The justification: extended absence from class, and under Board of Education bylaws and the state Taylor law which penalizes municipal employes who strike, his action was legal. The teachers failed to come to school and McCoy made formal notification to Donovan.

But again he was ignored by Donovan. No action was taken against 350 teachers who simply walked away from their classrooms for six weeks. Instead Donovan insisted further that McCoy file charges against the nineteen teachers he wanted transferred. The cases against them were presented by McCoy in hearings at the Board of Education before board consultant Rivers. McCoy and the local board stated that they believed the hearing process irrelevant since they had not sought dismissal of the teachers but rather their transfer, but Judge Rivers was charged with sifting the charges to determine if dismissals were in order. While the hearings were on, the one principal involved, Isadore Gordon of PS 137, and the five assistant principals elected to withdraw from the district, and McCoy agreed to withdraw specifics against them, despite the fact "that I had just given them unsatisfactory ratings. We just wanted to get rid of them. Odd isn't it? They transferred out as we originally wanted. But all the fuss first." In addition three of the teachers transferred out. Ten remained.

In an opinion, which the Ocean Hill–Brownsville board refused to accept, and which was not binding on Donovan, Judge Rivers recommended that the ten be returned to their schools. He said the evidence supplied failed to convince him the teachers should be dismissed. The local governing board had stated publicly that it would not abide by the Rivers findings, since it had not sought dismissal of the teachers.

Reverend Oliver, referring to the Rivers decision said, "A retired judge made a retired decision."

The nine teachers, whose dismissal was in effect denied by Judge Rivers, were Fred Nauman, Cliff Rosenthal, Barry Goodman, Abraham Olener, Burt Landsman, Paul Satlow, David Bergen, Theresa Galano, and Richard Douglass. Nauman was UFT chapter chairman at JHS 271 and a guidance counselor. Charges against him were dismissed by Judge Rivers because no witnesses were produced against him.

McCoy had one, he said, but she became a victim of the anger in Ocean Hill. The story is typical of the emotions triggered in the Ocean Hill–Brownsville district last spring, of angers quick to rise, perhaps never to subside. "One morning that May," Mc-Coy said, "Dorothy Hopkins, a teacher at 271, wasn't let through the barricades in front of the school. The cops stopped her and asked for her ID. Well, any fool knows that teachers don't carry IDs. But she was black and she had an African hair style and she was stopped. She got mad and mouthed off. I had to verify that she was a teacher. Miss Hopkins worked under Nauman in that school. Next morning she's back. She's dressed in Afros, with the beads, the whole thing, and she's grabbed again. This time she blows her top. She's arrested. We called Galamison who got her a lawyer, but she gets some other legal advice. What happens? She fails to show up in court for her hearing. A bench warrant is issued. By this time she's so teed off, she refuses to come to the Rivers hearings. There goes our witness. That's why there's no witness to what Nauman was doing as a so-called guidance counselor."

Shanker, in the UFT newspaper, *The United Teacher*, hailed the Rivers decision as upholding "the UFT's contention that these teachers were wrongly charged and not afforded even the most elemental due process in their forced removal."

However, in the letters sent to each of the nineteen that May, they had been notified that if they wished to question their transfers, they would be heard by the Ocean Hill–Brownsville board. It appears to be one part of the letter which was totally ignored, not only by the teachers involved, but by the union. Teachers, spoken to at random, appear unaware of that portion of the letter.

So, at the end of the 1967–68 school year, the professional fate of ten teachers was still at issue. With the schools closed there were of course no further confrontations, but there continued arbitration efforts throughout the summer. Among those involved at various times were long-time mediator Theodore Kheel; Dr. Kenneth Clark, an educator, director of the Metropolitan Applied Research Center, and a member of the state Board of Regents; Vincent McDonnell, chairman of the state mediation board; Victor Borella, labor adviser to Governor Rockefeller; and Harry Van Arsdale, Jr., president of the New York City Central Labor Council. None reported any measure of success.

During the summer McCoy recruited teachers to replace the 350 who had boycotted the district's school in May and June. With assistance from the Board of Education he attempted some recruitment among southern black teachers colleges. He tried recruiting teachers in Puerto Rico. He found few teachers who could meet not only the New York City requirements but those of Ocean Hill–Brownsville as well. As far as many of the black teachers were concerned, "it was just another case of them being down in those oppressed schools so long that they just couldn't do the job. We found some though." Most of those who eventually came to Ocean Hill were youngsters, recent graduates of teachers colleges, Peace Corps alumni, Vista people. One of them who decided to transfer into Ocean Hill was Marshena McCoy, McCoy's oldest daughter, who went immediately into the "Project Read" program. A sampling of the new teachers shows them to be young—average age twenty-four. They have majored not only in education in college, but in psychology, political science, and history. Some have masters degrees, some have graduate school credits, some have time in law school. Many come from universities within New York City—Columbia, NYU, City College. Many come from out of state, some from Ivy League schools. Quite a few previously taught in yeshivas. Some have teaching and guidance training and some do not. Many have done volunteer work with organizations which involved them with black and Spanish-speaking children in urban settings. Most were products of the Board of Education's Intensive Teacher Training program, with state certification and city licenses. Most are white and more than half are Jewish. Not many have extensive teaching experience, but this is not new for Ocean Hill–Brownsville. In the last school year, 75 per cent of the district's teachers had fewer than two years teaching. What they all had was "enthusiasm," says McCoy, and they brought with them "a new atmosphere." In the preschool days, with so many new programs undergoing summer shakedowns, "the kids did a beautiful job. They weren't hostile. They were not *telling* a community how their kids ought to be taught. They wanted to help. It was their choice to come here. That's what we liked about them the most. They wanted to come."

The UFT, however, dismissed this new young staff of teachers (described by *Newsweek* as a staff "With Love. . . ." and by *Time* as "Teachers Who Give a Damn") as "scabs" and "draft dodgers." With the question of the ten transferred teachers still undecided, it urged its members to strike to force them back into the Ocean Hill–Brownsville schools.

In addition to the ten, more teachers became an issue. In May and June, 350 teachers had left the district's schools in a sympathy boycott. Only 200 teachers were left in the district. McCoy hired 350 replacements "and we had more waiting on line." During the summer, 150 of the 350 requested and received transfers. Two hundred declared their intentions, through the UFT, of returning to school. McCoy and Oliver, contending that those teachers had "abandoned" the children, said they would not be allowed back. Subsequently 100 of the remaining 200 transferred out. A nucleus of 100 remained. This was later reduced to a hard core of 79, including the 10 in dispute. These teachers, because of the new ones hired by McCoy, became excess on the table of organization. Donovan said the teachers who had been transferred and who had struck would go back to school September 9. McCoy said no. Shanker said the UFT teachers were the regular teachers in the district and that "McCoy's teachers" would not be paid. Donovan agreed, saying his office had not "formally" assigned the new teachers to Ocean Hill.

The stage was set for September 9, and after summer ended on Labor Day, both sides' positions became, if possible, more rigid. The UFT newspaper headlined: "In Defense of Education, Officers and Executive Board Urge. . . . Don't Open Schools on Sep. 9th!" Reverend Oliver released a governing board statement which read "our governing board, our unit administrator, and his staff have made a heroic effort against overwhelming odds to bring the dawn of community control to our schools. . . . Some would seek to prevent the dawn, but the people are too enlightened now to return to the days of educational genocide."

Said Shanker, "I think it is quite obvious that there will be substantial powers delegated to local school boards and that we will move toward decentralization. This will bring problems and conflicts and increasing efforts—as we saw last year—to take away teachers' rights and due process."

Said Oliver, "True community control requires that the wishes of the community be respected. To seek to impose upon us now those who have been properly transferred out is to scoff at the will of the people, and this is always unwise."

McCoy, during the preschool period, made few public appearances or utterances. He stayed in his cluttered office on the first floor of a new cooperative apartment house at 249 Hopkinson Avenue, in the middle of the Ocean Hill–Brownsville district and talked curriculum, interviewed teachers, directed workmen to locations where school repairs and construction were under way. He was in his office, as usual, shortly after 7 o'clock each morning. It was, and is, the best time to see Rhody McCoy, if one desires more than five uninterrupted minutes.

Ten days before school was to open he said to me what he was to repeat so often, "We don't want those teachers back. I can only conclude that those who seek to impose them on us do not want to see black and Puerto Rican children learn.

"I appreciate Shanker's point of view. But I believe it's out of place. As for his tactics, I think they're dangerous. We sit and talk about community involvement and control. He talks about union power. They appear to me to be diametrically opposed." He paused, emptied his pipe, took another out of a brass and walnut rack and filled it. "Want to hear one? We had one principal, a lady, she walked out last spring. She said she couldn't stand the hatred. White versus black. She just couldn't stand it. After she's out she calls me up one day to make sure her evening job teaching in the community center won't be discontinued just because she's on strike during the day. How does that grab you? I guess the hatred isn't so bad at night. Or maybe it was the extra sixteen bucks a night she got for evening classes. She wasn't the only one. Guys were calling to ask, 'If we pull out, will our night

jobs stay?' It was all I could do to just hang up on them. This is
the kind of thing you had out here. Unionism at its worst.
Shanker's making it a racial thing. The teachers believe it's racial.
Here, he says it's a case of blacks pushing out white teachers, that
the UFT is fighting for a principle, and the principle would be
the same if it was a white community pushing out black teachers.
Who made it black and white? Shanker."

It was Shanker later on who vowed never to send teachers to
classes dominated by "Sonny Carson and the Panthers." Robert
(Sonny) Carson is chairman of Brooklyn CORE, and the Black
Panthers are a youthful para-military group whose members wear
black berets and string 50-caliber machine gun bullets around their
necks. Their aim, they contend, is to protect blacks from unwar-
ranted attacks by policemen. Police and others regard the Panthers
as dangerous and believe they are responsible for two recent shoot-
ing attacks on Brooklyn policemen. Both Carson and Panther
members were in front of JHS 271 during the spring confrontations.

In that week before the official school opening, Ocean Hill–
Brownsville made plans to open its schools on schedule, with firm
commitments from its newly hired teachers that they'd be there
for work. Most of them had not, and have not, been approached
by UFT recruiters, although most of those to which I spoke said
they intended to become union members "after this blew over."

That Thursday, September 5, the Board of Education adopted
a city-wide decentralization plan that would transfer some operating powers to local districts. These included the right to replace
their present superintendents; the right to recruit and hire teachers; the right to discipline and dismiss teachers according to law;
the right to modify and add to the curriculum; the right to select
textbooks and prepare budget requests; the right to manage school
expenditures. There was one nay vote, that of Reverend Milton
Galamison, who said he was against the plan because "powers
should not be delegated to local boards unless they are elected by
the people" and because the board "did not give all that it could
have under the law." The same day Shanker said he would recommend to his executive board and to his membership a strike against
the school system, and declared that McCoy "has ruined a school
system."

The strike vote, taken Sunday, September 8, was overwhelming.

On Monday and Tuesday the city's schools were effectively shut down by the UFT. Ocean Hill–Brownsville had classes as usual. All teachers in the district reported for work, making their entrances through networks of police barricades. The ten transferred teachers stayed on strike, as did their UFT supporters. School attendance was about 60 per cent, which McCoy considered "damned good" considering "all that flak going on." Tuesday evening, September 10, the UFT, the CSA, and the Board of Education reached a "Memorandum of Understanding" which provided that those teachers from Ocean Hill–Brownsville "wishing to return there shall resume their professional duties." The local governing board refused to recognize the agreement since it had not been party to any of the discussions which led to the agreement. Once again it was Milton Galamison who voted against approval of the agreement at a central Board of Education meeting. He was joined in a no vote by Hector Vasquez.

The most incredible feature of this agreement was the stipulation that those 350 teachers who had walked out of their classes in Ocean Hill last spring would be paid for the six weeks they were on strike. Strikes by public employees are forbidden under the state's Taylor law. They are illegal. Here was the Board of Education offering to pay its employees for remaining on strike while their students went uncared for. The board thus condoned, and rewarded, illegality. "How much," said McCoy, "do they think this community will take?"

The community wasn't taking. That Wednesday the transferred teachers were prevented bodily from entering the district schools. Shanker called a new strike for Friday. Again the city's schools were closed. The Ocean Hill–Brownsville district, with the unwanted teachers once more away, operated with efficiency.

On Sunday the Board of Education, under orders from State Education Commissioner Allen, suspended the local governing board and ordered the ten disputed teachers assigned to central Board of Education headquarters.

That Monday Mayor Lindsay happily announced that a "settlement" had been reached in the dispute. It involved, he said, Ocean Hill–Brownsville *agreeing* to take the teachers back. But as usual, the mayor did not look long and hard. He acted as he had throughout the dispute, as if he hoped it would all just go away. What he called an agreement was a statement by the gov-

erning board released after a meeting with him at City Hall.
It read:

> We deplore that we were forced to negotiate with threats over our
> heads: (a) threat of an injunction against the unit administrator;
> (b) threat of an injunction to close our eight schools; (c) threat of
> an injunction to have a new election for the governing board. Since
> the legal machinery of this sick society is forcing these teachers on
> us under threat of closing our schools and dissolving this district, the
> Board of Education should return to our district any of the teachers
> who wish to return.

There was no agreement. The board did not say it would accept the teachers back. It said simply that if the Board of Education wanted them back it would have to force them on the local
board and on McCoy. Donovan took the action.

So the strike kept on. Throughout the city, parents' demands
kept some schools open. District superintendents were ordered by
Donovan to keep schools open each day, unless, in their judg-
ments, conditions within them became dangerous to the children.
In most black areas of the city schools were open and well attended. The IS 201 and Ocean Hill–Brownsville complexes operated normally. There were scattered incidents at other schools
where parents, supporting the UFT, demanded that schools be
closed.

On Saturday, September 28, the mayor met with the Board of
Education and the UFT at Gracie Mansion. Shanker presented a
new demand for ending the strike. Not only were the ten transferred teachers to be returned, together with those of their supporters who had walked off their jobs in the spring; not only were
there to be Board of Education observers in the schools; but, to
use the mayor's words, the union "wants a five-man team of observers in the Ocean Hill–Brownsville schools. It wants to appoint
two of those five members, and to share in the choosing of the
third, and to have veto power over the other two. It wants the
city and the board to give those observers absolute power to shut
the schools down. That demand is simply unacceptable." When
the demand was outrageous, the mayor found it easy to be firm.
But he also said "The Ocean Hill–Brownsville board illegally transferred the teachers in question out of their schools."

Sunday afternoon, the mayor came out in front of Gracie Mansion to announce once again that there was agreement, despite the exclusion of the Ocean Hill–Brownsville board from the negotiations. In the agreement Shanker had not gotten the right to close the schools, but he had succeeded in getting two UFT members on each of the five-man observer teams assigned to the Ocean Hill schools. Later that evening, the UFT's executive board approved the agreement, and the rank and file, 6,422 out of 50,000 teachers eligible to vote, gave final approval. On Monday, September 30, the schools would be open.

Reverend Oliver said the mayor was standing by while the UFT "raped" the demonstration project and the Ocean Hill–Brownsville community. Asked what he meant, Oliver said flatly, "You know what rape means."

That Monday, 850 policemen stood poised in front of the district's eight schools. Barricades had been imported by the truckload. Checkpoints were set up by police in front of each school and for a block around each building. Students were allowed through. So were teachers. Parents who were members of the PTAs, the Brownsville Community Council, or the local governing board made it through. Everybody else was kept away. Fred Nauman, the nominal leader of the transferred teachers, walked into JHS 271 at 8:15. Others followed soon after. No move was made to stop him. Standing by were the Police Department's top echelon—Chief Inspector Sanford Garelik, Assistant Chief Inspector Lloyd Sealy, and First Deputy Police Commissioner John Walsh.

The next day, Tuesday, October 1, brought a renewal of hostilities. This time Vann led a teacher-student boycott of JHS 271. That school was later ordered closed as were three others in the district as angry parents, teachers, children, and police clashed in the streets around the schools. Nine people were arrested. Ten policemen reported injuries. Shanker threatened another strike. Mayor Lindsay declared that "no further disturbances will be tolerated" in the school district. But another day of truce came by itself—Wednesday and the school holiday of Yom Kippur.

The next day McCoy came up with what he considered a plan to keep schools open: to satisfy the sense of the City Hall order; and yet to keep the UFT teachers ineffective. He said with a trace of glee that he had decided to reroute the returning teachers through a program of "sensitivity training." He would remove them from their classrooms and assign them to orientation lectures inside the schools or at colleges around the city.

"After all," he said, "they've been gone from here for some time. They could *use* the reorientation." He was sitting in his office, behind a container of coffee, talking about his new "sensitivity" program when Dr. Nathan Brown, Donovan's executive deputy, came in with a letter from Donovan. He delivered it to McCoy with somewhat of a false smile, then left the office somewhat gingerly. McCoy read the letter.

What was it?

"A missive. It was Nate Brown delivering another missive. I said a missive not a missile."

And?"

"I read it."

Did you digest it? Was it important?

"Well, Dr. Donovan's missives are singularly difficult to digest. Let's say I read it. As for its importance . . ." McCoy shrugged.

Late that Thursday, Reverend Galamison, in his constant role of mediator, suggested that a solution to the problem lay perhaps in the affiliation of the Ocean Hill–Brownsville district with a university, perhaps Harvard. The district could then experiment under the aegis of the college, thus removing it from direct control of the Board of Education. The university in turn could use the district as a training ground, and would serve as a buffer between it and the union, City Hall and the central board.

"Next week we'll pray for rain," said McCoy.

On Monday, Oct. 7, Donovan once again formally suspended the local governing board—as he had done two weeks before—and announced that the eighty-three teachers would be back in the schools the next day. McCoy said he would formally relieve the teachers of their classroom assignments. Donovan said if McCoy did that he would himself be relieved, as would the principals of the schools.

Said McCoy that Monday. "I *will* relieve the teachers of their assignments. I do it with the realization of the consequences to me and to the principals."

Did he think Donovan would close the Ocean Hill–Brownsville schools?

"He can order the schools closed, but it won't work. We can take care of our own schools. It may involve keeping the Board of Education out. But I seriously doubt if he can shut them down."

McCoy did not say it boastfully, but rather with the knowledge that so much had already been begun out in his district that new administrators, including Bernard Donovan, would have little conception of how to run existing programs. He was proved right, when, after the principals *were* relieved, Donovan had to reinstate them three days later because the substitute principals were unable to "swing" the way Ocean Hill demanded.

McCoy said, "The Board of Education has never been able to enforce its rulings. Look how they suspended the governing board. It kept right on functioning, so it was reinstated. Now it's suspended again. It doesn't mean a damn."

He was asked if he had warned Donovan that the superintendent could possibly lose his job over his handling of the Ocean Hill–Brownsville dispute.

"I wouldn't tell him something like that so early in the morning," said McCoy with a smile. "Now over lunch, that would be something else, especially if he picked up the tab."

Late that night it was revealed that a UFT vice president, John O'Neill, had been fired by Albert Shanker for reportedly disagreeing with the UFT president over Ocean Hill–Brownsville. O'Neill was booed and hissed at a union meeting for speaking out against Shanker's call for yet another strike against the school system, and was deposed when he vowed to oppose any motion made for a new strike.

He did oppose it and in a statement he said why. "I do so because as a union officer I cannot stand by while a series of reckless and desperate actions destroys our union. In addition, as a citizen and parent, I cannot in conscience stand by while this series of actions tear our school system apart.

"Basically, the problem is that the strike weapon is irrelevant to the dispute in Ocean Hill–Brownsville. The conflict there is political and social—arising out of a very complex set of conditions—the thrust of the black and Puerto Rican peoples against the 'ins.' The struggle of the poor to get into the middle class; all the while President Shanker tries to sell the incredibly simplistic notion that this is a simple labor-management dispute in eight shops.

"To go along with the reality that the strike is not pertinent to the problem, the bald fact is that this strike cannot be won in any conventional sense. Three weeks of strike without any real solution should be clear evidence of this. Will six weeks bring any better results? Will nine weeks?

"President Shanker has two goals in this dispute. They are the removal of the governing board, Rhody McCoy, the eight principals, and/or the closing down of the district's schools. Precisely what would such an action solve? The children will have to go to school somewhere, the schools will have to be re-opened someday (in passing I doubt very much that President Shanker wants them re-opened under the control of the state Department of Education), the community leaders and parents will still be active —and if not in Brownsville, then someplace else. In answer to this line of argumentation, our president takes the position that 'we have to teach them a lesson and they won't bother us.' Is there anyone so naive as to think that a social movement with the power of the black and Puerto Rican community (a majority in our school system) can be held back or even turned aside by 'teaching them a lesson'? Is there a shred of evidence in all sociological theory to support this proposition? If anything, and, it is already clearly evident, our rash action in Brownsville has turned a brush fire into a conflagration sweeping across the city. In fact close observers of the scene say that 'Shanker has accomplished in five months what would have taken five years under normal conditions in furthering the demands of community militants!' "

On Tuesday morning, O'Neill came to McCoy's office and offered a four-point peace plan. It involved taking back the teachers; withdrawal of police and observers; and establishment of a human relations committee composed of UFT members, local governing board, and community members.

Shanker dismissed O'Neill's opposition. He said there was a "dubious morality," in a union official who runs for office on a platform and "betrays the trust of the members who voted for him."

That afternoon McCoy formally relieved the eighty-three teachers of their classroom duties. Later that afternoon Bernard Donovan sat under television lights in the library of the Board of Education at 110 Livingston Street, and announced: "I have today relieved Mr. Rhody McCoy of his duties as unit administrator of the Ocean Hill–Brownsville district and assigned him to central headquarters. Yesterday and again today I requested Mr. McCoy to remain in his position as unit administrator if he were willing to carry out the directives of the Board of Education and the instructions of the superintendent of schools. Mr. McCoy has indicated to me clearly that he intends to obey the directions of the suspended Ocean Hill–Brownsville school board and not those of the Board of Education or the superintendent of schools. It is necessary, therefore, for me to relieve Mr. McCoy of his duties. I regret having to take this action but I have done so in order that the orderly operation of the schools may proceed." At the same time the district's principals were relieved of *their* administrative duties.

Donovan said later that when the governing board's suspension is up on November 5, "it is contemplated that Mr. McCoy could resume his post if we come to a solution of this problem.

"Mr. McCoy told me that in conscience he owed his loyalty to the board which selected him. There is no personal animosity between us. Each of us is doing what in conscience he presumes is right."

The next day McCoy's principals were barred from their schools by police. But McCoy showed up at his office, on time, and opened the door with *his* key. He said if there was an attempt to bar him "They'll have to carry me out." He spent the day with his suspended governing board and with representatives of his teachers telling them to stay in the schools "for the kids' sakes." The rest of his time was spent on the phone with his superior, Bernard Donovan, as he explained the educational intricacies of the Ocean Hill–Brownsville experimental projects, something the central board apparently had not had time to concern itself with before.

"Donovan's crew doesn't know its way around here," McCoy said. "We have a good operation and I have to keep it running. After all I'm responsible to a lot of people."

Later that week Donovan ordered JHS 271 closed when the transferred teachers complained of being harassed and threatened by the newly hired teachers. Then, on Friday, McCoy, still officially not the boss of his school district, stormed down to the Board of Education to complain that temporary principals in the eight schools were subverting some of the experimental programs in the district. Following a three-hour meeting he announced with some satisfaction that all eight principals would be back in their schools the following Monday and that JHS 271 would be open. Sure enough, later that day Donovan made the formal announcement. Shanker promptly called another strike for Monday and for the third time this fall New York's teachers walked off their jobs.

Mayor Lindsay empanelled a fact-finding group to study ways of ending the strike, but it died before it could meet with any of the antagonists involved. Added to the UFT walkout was the support by the CSA and, later that week, action by the custodians of the schools. They locked school gates, changed locks, and failed to appear at the posts.

One locked school was PS 73 in Ocean Hill–Brownsville. An assistant principal rushed into McCoy's office one morning to announce that the school was shut tight.

"Get a crowbar and open the door. I don't care how you do it, just open the doors," said McCoy.

The administrator said that he didn't know where to get a crowbar.

"Buy one," said McCoy.

Except for that one incident, the Ocean Hill–Brownsville schools functioned normally through the strike. While there was confusion and tension elsewhere in the city, the experimental district was calm. McCoy came in as usual, a little after 7 o'clock each morning, although he officially didn't have a job; consulted with his governing board, which officially had no status; and continued to run his eight schools just as he had for a year. Superintendent Donovan continued making phone calls to McCoy and received progress reports. Publicly he repeated often that McCoy *was* relieved and that he really had no idea if and when the Ocean Hill–Brownsville administrator would be reinstated.

The impression was unmistakable. Bernard Donovan was doing most of the talking, but the signals that were making the district work were all McCoy's.

He's so busy keeping his schools running that he has just about forgotten the slip of paper he typed out last spring and slipped into the middle drawer of his desk. It is his resignation, "in the best interests of this project and the education of the children." Not that it makes much difference. Out in Ocean Hill–Brownsville they wouldn't even read it.

The Brooklyn Dodgers / JASON EPSTEIN

Whatever the outcome of the New York City school strike, the conflicting interests which caused it are irreconcilable. The city will have either to transform its public school system radically, which seems unlikely, or find that it has no school system at all, in which event it will be up to the parents themselves to contrive alternative ways to educate their children. Since the crisis in New York reflects a conflict within public education generally, it is of more than merely local interest to try to understand what the problem really is.

On the one hand, there has arisen over the past ten years or so an indeterminate but substantial and articulate minority of parents, mainly but not exclusively from the ghettos, who are convinced that the public schools are incompetent and cannot be reformed by their present personnel: that furthermore many teachers are indifferent to their pupils while some are even hostile or brutal toward them. These teachers are protected by their union, the United Federation of Teachers, so that a parent who feels that his child has been ignored or abused is unlikely to get much satisfaction if he pleads his case through conventional channels. Through years of negotiation with the Board of Education the UFT has established principles of collective bargaining and job security so that during a recent five-year period, according to the *New York Post*, fewer than fifty teachers out of a total of 60,000 have been fired from the system, even though by the third grade some 60 per cent of the children are doing so poorly that their chances for success in the higher grades, according to the Board of Education, are unlikely. The teachers are inclined to blame this on the children, saying that they are unteachable. The parents, understandably, see the case differently.

On the other hand, there are the teachers themselves, protected in the present crisis not only by their union but by the tenured supervisory staff of principals and other administrators who have

THIS ARTICLE appeared in *The New York Review of Books*, October 10, 1968. Reprinted with permission from *The New York Review of Books*. Copyright © 1968 The New York Review.

for their part built their own defenses over the years through civil service, political alignments, and elaborate, if informal, traditions of mutual support within their own bureaucracies. These teachers and supervisors argue that they are doing the best they can: that the number of children from broken homes, from backgrounds that are "culturally deprived" and who reflect the anger of their parents toward white teachers makes their work impossible.

This hostility between the embittered parents and the defensive teachers has been growing for years, sustained partly by a temporizing Board of Education whose conventional liberalism had kept it from seeing that the confrontation, when it finally came, would be revolutionary and would not respond to the expedient manipulations on which it had so far relied. The immediate cause of the present strike, for example, was the decision of a group of schools in the Brooklyn ghetto to fire nineteen teachers who, for whatever reasons, were unacceptable to the local governing board which had been chosen by the parents to supervise their schools. A confidential report, prepared for the Board of Education and released in the last few weeks, reveals that last spring the board had quietly agreed to transfer the unwanted teachers out of the neighborhood if the local governing board agreed not to make the firings a matter of principle: in other words, the central board would get the teachers out of the neighborhood if the local board did not also insist that it was within the right of any community to fire and hire teachers at its own discretion, a right which clearly conflicted with the principles of collective bargaining and job security on which not only the UFT but unionism itself depended.

The decision by the local board to elevate the conflict to the point where the UFT was left with no choice but to intervene on behalf of its general membership was anything but whimsical. The antagonists in the New York school crisis are as wise to each other's maneuvers as the members of opposing professional football teams. Though spectators may be baffled by the various strategies on the field, the participants make their moves with a practiced grace which imparts to the action a kind of predictable formality. The analogy with football breaks down in only one respect: the ball never changes hands. The parents are always on the offensive, while the teachers try to hold the line. When they fired the nineteen teachers, the Brooklyn parents and their militant leadership decided, at last, to make a rush for the goal, the goal, in this case, being the unequivocal right of the community to hire and fire its own teachers. They did not, however, go so far as to burn down the stadium, an event which is likely to occur if the local governing board is dissolved, as the UFT has urged—and as some members of the central bureaucracy would like.

There have been attempts by the press to discredit the governing board on the grounds that while it was legitimately elected by a significant majority, fewer than 25 per cent of the eligible parents bothered to vote. On the other hand this is a greater proportion of voters than participates in primary elections in the same neighborhood. It has also been argued that when the cases of the nineteen teachers had been submitted to a retired Negro judge, the judge found the charges against them to be insubstantial. The governing board has ignored these findings on the grounds that the judge refused to hear important evidence and that the right to decide who should teach in the district belongs to the governing board and not to a retired judge. As this is being written, State Commissioner of Education James Allen has agreed to suspend the governing board temporarily, and the UFT has agreed to the temporary transfer of the teachers, provided the governing board is not restored until the ten teachers are returned to their schools. The danger here is that the temporary vacuum in the district will be filled by genuine extremists whose actions are likely to be unpredictable.[1]

To understand the situation concretely one must try to identify with the individuals concerned; with the teachers who have invested perhaps ten or twenty years in their jobs and who are now totally dependent on them, underpaid, and for the most part un-

---

[1] While the original issue in the strike had been the decision of the local board to fire the ten teachers, the local board had also, over the summer, hired some 200 additional teachers, many black but the majority white, to replace members of the regular staff who, for various reasons, did not satisfy the governing board. The local board now insists on firing 100 of these regular teachers whose places have been taken by the new appointees, most of whom are not union members and many of whom are recent college graduates who presumably have not satisfied the city's licensing requirements for teachers. Thus, while the state commissioner has attempted to side-step the issue by agreeing to transfer the ten teachers temporarily out of the district, the governing board, which has also been temporarily dismissed by the state commissioner but which refuses to accept the commissioner's authority, has escalated the conflict by demanding that the 100 teachers be sent out of the district too. Meanwhile the central bureaucracy has stupidly made matters worse by demanding that the governing board dismiss the teachers it had hired over the summer.

employable in other capacities; and with the parents, particularly those from the ghetto, whose affection for their children and whose hopes for their futures may be assumed to be like those of parents generally but who are continually exposed to the humiliation and failure to which their children are subjected in the public schools. It is inconceivable that any but the most callous parent would agree with the teachers that his child is ineducable. The more likely, indeed the more rational, expectation is that the parents will find the school at fault and will, in the manner of oppressed groups generally, support leaders who will take matters into their own hands.

The justice of such an expedient is not, of course, lost on the members of New York's upper-middle class whose members, because they can afford it and have the right social connections, almost without exception send their children to private schools, partly out of clannishness but increasingly because they too recognize the incompetence of the public schools. There has thus arisen within the city an imperfect but significant alignment between, on the one hand, this class and the racial minorities and, on the other, a rather more deliberate coalition of unionists, civil servants, and their political representatives.

Mayor Lindsay, reflecting the interests of his class but probably at the expense of his interests as a politician, has taken the side of the former group and has, in the last few weeks, reconstructed the Board of Education accordingly. With the reluctant agreement of the state legislature, which is ultimately responsible for the city's schools and which, last spring, voted to expand the board from nine to thirteen members, Lindsay has shifted the balance on the board so that its majority can no longer be expected to support the interests of the entrenched teachers and supervisors as it had routinely done for years. The aim of Lindsay's new board is to decentralize the system; in other words, to shift the power within the system from its central administration to the various communities within the city such as the one in Brooklyn which summarily dismissed the nineteen teachers and precipitated the present strike.

Events, however, have considerably exceeded the mayor's expectations, for in firing the nineteen teachers the Brooklyn group had obviously decided not to await the orderly transfer of power which the new board promised, a decision which somewhat recalls the case in Russia when the soviets chose not to stay put for the deliberations of the provisional government. As this is being written it seems unlikely that the contested teachers, of whom only ten are still on the scene, the others having discreetly withdrawn, will be permitted to re-enter their schools; nor are the police in this case likely to figure as a counter-revolutionary force, for while some school supervisors have been heard to suggest that what New York needs in the present emergency is a more aggressive mayor than John Lindsay, it is hard to imagine that Lindsay will permit the police to drag the parents, who have so far prevented the teachers from entering their classrooms, away from the school-house door.[2]

When the strike was first announced, however, Mayor Lindsay did briefly seem to have persuaded or forced the local governing board to let the teachers return to their classes. He did this, presumably, by threatening to dissolve the local board and call for new elections, but the board's agreement under this pressure included the implied threat that it could not speak for other leaders in the neighborhood or for the more militant residents. Nevertheless Lindsay's assurances that the local board had given in were sufficient for the union to agree to call off its strike, provided also that the central board agree that the rights of teachers thoughout the city would be protected as the system decentralized.

To many advocates of decentralization, such an undertaking on the part of the central board seemed to ignore the fundamental condition of decentralization itself: that parents should be free to decide who should educate their children. Thus two of Lindsay's new appointees to the central board voted against the agreement. These were Hector Vasquez, a Puerto Rican businessman, and Milton Galamison, a militant and highly sophisticated black leader who had opposed the school system for years and who recognized that in accepting the union's terms, the board would effectively foreclose the possibility of genuine decentralization, the very purpose for which it had been reconstituted by Mayor Lindsay. Nevertheless a majority of board members, including two other Lindsay appointees, voted for the agreement, though John Lotz, a hold-over from the pre-Lindsay board but himself a strong advo-

[2] For further insight into the mentality of the New York City school supervisors, see the extensive interview between Walter Degnan, the president of the Supervisors Association, and the Ocean Hill administrator, Rhody McCoy in the opening issue of *The New York Advocate*, a journal of New York affairs.

cate of decentralization, cast his vote under protest. Presumably he, like the mayor, wanted to end the strike and hoped that the new board could manage, despite the self-defeating deal with the union, to turn control over to the neighborhoods by some sort of future compromise.

As it turned out, none of this made any difference. When the ten teachers attempted to return to their classes, their way was blocked by an angry demonstration. Only armed force could have got them safely into the school. Furthermore, their places had been taken by new teachers recruited by the local board. Amid accusations that Lindsay had gone back on his word, the union resumed its strike. The union's accusations, however, were gratuitous. There was nothing that Lindsay or anyone else could do. The Brooklyn board had rebelled and the conventional remedies —the police and the withdrawal of public funds from the ghetto schools—were obviously unthinkable.

Thus, the crisis in New York has been elevated to a conflict of opposing principles reflecting powerful and apparently irreconcilable class interests: the interest of the excluded class in improving its position through the education of its children; and the interest of an established, if largely ineffective, professional group in maintaining the prerogatives which it had won through bitter struggles of its own, even though this group now seems to stand in the way of the legitimate ambitions of the emerging class boiling up just beneath it. In such circumstances a satisfactory political compromise is hard to imagine. Nor, of course, can the conflict be arbitrated as if it were a conventional dispute between labor and management, for in this case labor and management are on the same side, confronting an angry and deeply disaffected clientele. It is also unlikely that Mayor Lindsay's new board can keep abreast of the crisis, for even if the present strike is settled the result will offer only temporary solution. The issue will inevitably erupt again and again as one neighborhood after another supports leaders who will claim the right to decide who shall educate its children.

Yet it is premature and in any case frivolous to conclude that the apocalypse is at hand, for out of such crises as this there often arise solutions which previously had remained invisible or seemed unspeakable. For instance, decentralization is already a fact in three New York neighborhoods: the Two Bridges district in Lower Manhattan, a district in central Harlem surrounding the by now famous IS 201, and, for better or worse, the currently disputed district in Brooklyn. While nearly all the schools in New York have been closed by the present strike, the schools in these districts have functioned normally under their locally appointed leadership and, according to reports in the press and from other observers, the teaching in them, largely by nonunion faculties, has been livelier than is generally the case in New York schools.

The outcome of the present conflict will probably, or so one hopes, encourage a variety of educational experiments, perhaps some of them along the lines suggested some years ago by Milton Friedman, the conservative economist at the University of Chicago. Friedman's idea was that parents of school-age children be given vouchers worth a year's schooling, to be redeemed in any legitimate institution they might choose. Thus all parents could enjoy a version of the privilege which the parents of private school children had long since claimed for themselves.

The advantage in Professor Friedman's proposal and the reason that it arises from his generally conservative outlook is that it promises to restore the principle of competition to a market place which is currently monopolized by a single, overpowering institution and which, since it has no competitors, except for the handful of private schools, can remain as complacent as it likes. The effect of the impasse in New York City is that the monopolistic system is now incapable of performing even the minimal functions which have routinely been expected of it. It cannot be trusted to keep the children off the streets and out of their parents' way nor can it continue to pretend that it is performing an educational service at all. In such circumstances, since the lives of their children are at stake, one would expect the parents to begin contriving educational alternatives of their own.

Professor Friedman's system of vouchers is, of course, unworldly and was evidently suggested for polemical purposes. Nevertheless, the proposed decentralization of the New York school system implies, at least in theory, a similar strategy. While blank checks would not be handed out to individual parents, they would, in a genuinely decentralized system, be given to individual school districts to spend as the parents, represented by their community boards, saw fit. To many of the paternalistic proprietors of the present system, such an expedient must seem not only a threat to their personal security but evidence of insanity, for the unspoken assumption of the liberal majority which has traditionally dominated public education in New York is that the poor, particularly

the blacks, are not only rather hard to educate but they are consti-
tutionally incapable of running their own institutions. Thus last
month when it was a matter of electing a new board president,
Lloyd Garrison, a distinguished lawyer, an impeccable liberal, and
a former board president, placed in nomination the name of Rose
Shapiro, a hold-over from the pre-Lindsay board, whose advocacy
of decentralization has been, to say the least, disingenuous, and
whose singlehearted project as a board member has been to preserve the existing institution from any change whatever.

Yet, in the past three years a group of Harlem street-workers,
many of whom are themselves school dropouts, have managed,
with the help of the Urban League of Greater New York, to establish a series of storefront schools whose success has been exem-
plary. These schools have recruited, largely from East Harlem's
Benjamin Franklin High School, several hundred incipient dropouts and have, in the last two years, sent more than a hundred of
them on to college. These street academies, as they are called, are
staffed mostly by teachers who are not licensed by the city of New
York. Though they are all college graduates and many of them
are experienced teachers, most of them have not passed the ritual
examinations which New York City teachers are required to pass
and few of them have been trained in teachers colleges. They are,
by the standards of the city schools, unprofessional. Yet these
amateurs, several of whom are former members of the Peace Corps,
have clearly succeeded where their professional counterparts have
failed.

They have, in effect, contrived out of the wreckage of the Harlem
public schools, a system of demonstrably successful private schools
which suggest not only that the idea of professionalism in education is of dubious validity but that the ghetto can perfectly well,
if left to its own devices, create and manage its own institutions
without the help of a centralized authority. These schools were
financed originally by the Ford Foundation and have been supported since by several private corporations. If the decentralization
of the public schools is to have any meaning at all, public funds
should now be made available for similar undertakings, and not in
the ghettos alone. For the retreat from the public schools is evident
throughout the city and one hears nearly every week of groups of
parents who have decided to set up schools of their own.

Professor Friedman's voucher system derives from his conservative bias against monopolistic public institutions, but there is

nothing in his scheme to contradict more recent notions of participatory democracy, which follow from traditions of community anarchism and radical populism. What we seem to be undergoing, not simply in the public schools but in the country generally, is a spontaneous and apparently irresistible surge of democratic fundamentalism, arising from a revulsion toward established social and political institutions. As Professor Friedman's conservatism comes full circle to emerge as a version of anarchism, so the advocates of law and order with their implication of frontier justice and their hatred of the Supreme Court are the ideological poor relations of the Yippies with their universal disdain for social institutions of every kind. While it should be obvious that these forces will remain bitterly opposed to each other, they nevertheless indicate a tendency against which the fortunes of the public school bureaucracies in New York and the other great American cities seem even less promising than those of Hubert Humphrey and his residual New Deal liberalism.

Who can say what political structures, if any, will emerge from such chaos? But in the isolated case of the New York City public schools there are provisional grounds for hope. It was Dewey's idea that the world itself is a sufficient school for most purposes. One learns by taking part in the world's work: to exclude experience from the process of learning is to exclude learning itself. It was Dewey's misfortune, and ours, that he submitted his proposals at the very moment when the schoolteachers were insisting that they had become a professional class, that education was a process which began on weekday mornings at eight and ended at three, and that unsupervised events outside the schoolroom were not only incapable of offering illumination but were actually distractions from the pedagogical process.

In the present collapse of the New York City schools there is some hope, if there are individuals to seize the opportunity, that the discredited professionalism, which public education has claimed for itself, may now begin to give way to an unpredictable variety of educational enterprises arising from the trials and errors of the various communities within the city. Obviously there are plenty of hazards to be encountered in these experiments, including the real danger, especially in the poorer neighborhoods, that the ambitions of the parents for their children's success will lead to an authoritarian and abstract academicism, contrary to Dewey's notions. But it is also reasonable to expect parents—especially those who have fought so bitterly against the present system—to learn from their errors, as the professional educators have seemed unable to do, what is likely to be in the best interest of their children. At any rate, there must, at this moment, be thousands of young students in New York who are learning more from their everyday experience about the nature of political systems and the complex meanings of democracy than they could ever learn if they were back in their classrooms reading the official myths of American history.

Epilogue

Urban School Reform in the 1970's

In the 1970's, the pressures for coping with the failure of urban education will shift from pleas for integration and compensatory education to demands for the complete restructuring of city school systems and increased community control. While in many city school systems the trend is barely observable, in some the first stage of battle has already been waged.

The ineffectiveness of even minimal efforts at school integration is readily observed in the major cities of the country. From small school pairings to attempts at staff rotation, organized opposition has forestalled the sometimes worthy intentions of community reform groups, boards of education, and school superintendents. Continued failure and more overt racist responses have raised serious questions regarding the energy expended for integration by civil rights groups throughout the country. Patterns of migration in the last five years have intensified segregation, making any meaningful integration a large-scale undertaking. The relative value of small-scale integration efforts has become increasingly less justified.

Investments in compensatory education, reinforced by federal and state funds, have also produced no successful models. Generally, these programs are a continuation of the regular school program in more concentrated form, for more hours. The Headstart evaluation demonstrated the short-range advantage of a special educational experience that was all but lost when Headstart students entered the regular school system. Foundation funding for

"Urban School Reform in the 1970's" by Marilyn Gittell is reprinted from *Education and Urban Society*, Vol. I, No. 1 (November, 1968), pp. 9–20, by permission of the publisher, Sage Publications, Inc.

compensatory education has also proven ineffective, largely because new techniques are not readily applied in an outworn structure. In New York City, a vast input in a single school administered by a local university proved eminently unsuccessful, largely because of the inability to cope with the system: the director of the project stated publicly that the failure of the project could be attributed to the red tape and routine of the school bureaucracy, which denied all efforts at innovation. The same experience is repeated in similar experiments in large cities throughout the country. None of the compensatory or special education programs have proven valuable. Compensatory education programs have become related more to the satisfaction of public demands than to actually serving the end of improving the educational experience.

Reform of the System

The failure of school integration and compensatory education efforts have led many school reformers to the conclusion that only reform of the total system can provide the necessary environment for the meaningful solution to urban educational problems. Presently, there appear to be two major groups of school reformers; one group espouses the more traditional approach of reform from the top—changing administrative personnel, introducing new systems, and recruiting from outside the school structure. This group of reformers is comprised largely of school professionals. The Philadelphia school system is currently undergoing this kind of reform under its new superintendent and board chairman. Program-planning-budgeting has been adopted, and top administrative personnel have been moved in from other cities and other disciplines.

The second group of reformers is largely made up of nonschool professionals and lay local community groups, based particularly in the ghetto. This group rejects pure administrative reform and demands a redistribution of power in the school system through decentralization and increased community control. Decentralization is defined as a delegation of decision-making power to local districts within the city. The community role is manifest in local election of local boards with discretion over personnel and budget. This latter type of reform movement is probably most developed in New York City. It has launched three demonstration school projects (in July, 1967) based on the concept of increased community participation.

Community groups connect their powerlessness to the growth

of a centralized professional bureaucracy that controls the policy process to their exclusion. Accordingly, they seek more fundamental reform, expanding the role of the community by concentrating greater decision-making in an independent local school district. They see the large city-wide school system as unable to respond to the diversified needs in areas throughout the city. The emphasis is on balancing power between professionals and parents and/or local residents. Those who seek reform of the total structure are concerned primarily with the need to redistribute power within the system, to include the very people who are most directly affected by school policy. The most extreme pronouncements for community-controlled local schools in the cities have come from a five-city black educators organization, which emerged from a Harvard conference in the winter of 1968. The group has met twice since that time and has developed a strong statement of purpose and intent as well as a rationale for community control and independent districts. Harlem CORE was one of the original groups actively to encourage this kind of total reform; it had a bill introduced in the last two state legislative sessions (both of which were defeated) to create an independent Harlem school district under state supervision. Legislative proposals for independent districts and community control were introduced in the last year in Massachusetts, Michigan, and Kentucky. Interest has been developing in several cities, particularly in Boston, Detroit, Chicago, and Washington, D.C.

Education Reform in New York City

New York has been a forerunner in education reform, and, judging by past experience, events in the city will likely serve to signal action in other cities. It is possible, therefore, to project some of the trends that are likely to materialize in all large urban school systems from the accumulated experience in the school reform movement in New York during the past year.

The politics of school decentralization in New York, as it developed in the city and in the state legislature during 1968, suggests the general alignment of forces and the current power structure in education in large cities at the present time. Those groups most resistant to change are the professionals, who have a vested interest in maintaining their status and power under the present structure. The professionals monopolize a good share of the policy process and are very reluctant to relinquish control. Teachers' organizations and unions vary in their relative strength in different cities as do boards of education; accordingly, the leadership varies. The coalition of established education groups, however, can be anticipated in every large city. The Board of Education in New York City resisted all compromises for increased community control and decentralization, supporting a plan for what can only be labeled a minor administrative decentralization. Special interest groups in education were generally supportive of the existing system (except for the Public Education Association) as were parent associations, but the major impetus against reform came from the United Federation of Teachers, the Council of Supervisory Associations, and the Board of Education itself.

An extensive public campaign was waged against decentralization in New York City. Much of it was based on emotional issues, particularly exploiting fears of black power and local corruption. In some instances, certain actions in the three experimental demonstration school projects were cited to indicate the "dangers" of community control. Although *The New York Times* supported the Regents Plan on its editorial page, news reporting on the demonstration districts tended to overdramatize what were labeled black racist goals. More often than not, these goals represented honest efforts to increase the number of black teachers and administrators in the system and to introduce more black culture into the curriculum. In some cases, the local district boards were acting to define their powers, since the Board of Education had failed to delegate authority during the first year of the experiment. In one of the districts, principals were appointed by the local board, with the approval of the state commissioner of education, and given the title "demonstration school principal." These appointments were not made in conformity with prescribed civil service procedures in the New York City School System, and the Council of Supervisory Associations challenged the appointments in court. The transfer of teachers and hiring of state certified teachers was actively challenged by the UFT. It is clear that both groups considered even these experimental districts a threat to their position and power.

The Controversy

Beyond the more emotional concerns, there are basic issues related to community control that must be seriously considered.

Local control does challenge some of the basic concepts associated
with the traditional city reform movement, which was originally
set up to root out corruption and party control of the school system. Ironically, some of the reforms instituted in the first half of
the century now plague American cities and their school systems.
The rigidity of the merit system and of civil service examination
and promotion procedures is a major element in the overcentralized
and insensitive bureaucratic structure that has failed to respond to
basic educational needs in the 1960's. The enormous emphasis on
professionalism has greatly undermined the role of the lay citizenry
in the policy process. A major element in the alienation of a large
segment of the new city population is the great reliance on professionals that is integral to the reform ethos. This is not to suggest
that reform in the 1970's will include an absolute rejection of professionalism but rather to hope its role will be tempered. Civil
service organizations have become a powerful force in state and
local decision-making, and their efforts and goals are often not so
much professional as self-serving. Their defense of the *status quo*,
particularly in the school situation, is couched in the rhetoric of
the preservation of professionalism. This is particularly appealing
to middle-class groups, but it merely reinforces the skepticism of the
ghetto population. There must be some adjustment of inflexible
regulations; state and city standards and general protections can
be set in flexible legislation to prevent any large-scale abuses.

Fears about community control of the schools have been expressed in two other general areas: first, there is concern that integration will be abandoned or that its achievement will be thwarted
under community control; second, there is concern that parochialism will be encouraged, exacerbating local ethnic conflicts. The
first concern is, for many who express it, specious; the fact is, little
or no integration has taken place under the present centralized
structure and, instead, segregation is increasing in most cities.
Moreover, there is, potentially, greater opportunity for meaningful
integration once ghetto schools have been improved. Certainly, the
Supreme Court decision in 1954 would prevent any overt denial
of integration under community control, and integration could still
be enforced by city and state agencies.

As regards the second area of concern, one can either view local-
ism from the narrow perspective of parochialism or see it as a
means for encouraging a sense of community identity. In ghetto
communities, in particular, local control may foster a more inti-

mate feeling of belonging; it may arouse a concern with educational policy and a feeling that the schools are really a part of the community. Local control can encourage greater community involvement and participation because of the stake the community feels it has in the school system. From the evidence already available in the three demonstration school projects in New York, this can be anticipated. In each of the three demonstration areas (all poverty areas), there has been greater voter turnout, larger attendance at school meetings, and more direct participation of lower-class groups in school affairs in the last year. Local ethnic clashes *are* more in evidence because decisions are localized; slight differences in class and social status also produce more conflict. These conflicts, however, may well be healthy and, in themselves, may activate new elements in the community. If the goal is greater participation and citizen interest, conflict may be a necessary component. Such clashes should not be viewed as necessarily negative in their import. They must be evaluated in terms of the goals set or the model of political relations considered most productive to developing responsive policies.

Some who disparage community control do so because they recognize that there is no educational component integral to such reform that will guarantee better reading or achievement-test scores. Those who support reorganization of the total system admit to that fact. Underlying the concept, however, is the assumption that only in an improved environment can solutions be tried and tested fairly. It is also suggested that any reform of the system that brings about greater community involvement will assure an expansion in the number and kinds of alternatives offered and a greater willingness to experiment; new participants will be a fertile source for new ideas, and the system itself should become more responsive to innovation.

Evaluating Reform

The most important consideration in the evaluation of any political system should be its ability to change. The very process of change is relevant; so, too, a school system, or any plan for school reform, must also be evaluated. If local control does not work or if it becomes obsolete in five to ten years, the test of the system will again be its ability to change with the demands of the time. Since community control embodies a design for the redistribution of power (or, at a minimum, a shift in the current balance of power), the test of effective school reorganization would be measured by whether a change in the power structure is actually achieved. Compromise will sometimes result in an abandonment of the basic elements of community control. It is for these reasons that even the term decentralization is inappropriate. Decentralization, more often, than not, will be construed as *administrative* decentralization, introducing no new participants but, instead, shuffling the roles of the professionals or, more than likely, merely changing titles.

A meaningful plan of community control must guarantee new power bases to local participants. That means local control over two major sources of power: jobs and funds. In so far as policy prerogatives are concerned, this means control over the budget and the selection of personnel. The extent to which these two powers are granted to local districts may vary according to such factors as state and city civil service regulations, tenure laws, state certification requirements, mandatory expenditures, the method for allocation of funds, and the presence of a union contract. The fewer the constraints, the greater the possibility for local power. Some constraints will undoubtedly be necessary; others will have to be abandoned. Complete independence of local school districts under state supervision would provide the greatest measure of local control. This would give every local district the same status as the city-wide district has under the present structure. Under a compromise plan, the more limited the role of the city board of education, the more power in the local district. Retention of a city board, a sizable headquarters staff, or both would be an indication of limited local control. The method of selecting the local board, the drawing of local boundaries, and the size of the local district are all significant elements in determining the commitment to local control. The local board must be locally elected if local loyalty and the recruitment of new participants are to be assured. Election procedures should guarantee that established organizations do not easily monopolize the local board. Boundaries should not be drawn to undermine ethnic solidarity and thus avoid the emergence of new and significant power groups. If the districts are too large, they will not be able to give a sense of identity to the community, and participation will be discouraged; with larger districts, the professionals will find it easier to retake complete control.

The failure of urban education in city school systems throughout the country and the ineffectiveness of those solutions that have been offered will persuade larger segments of the community of the need for more fundamental reform of school systems. More and more pressure will be brought to bear on school professionals to relinquish control, particularly as they have proved themselves unable to cope with the educational needs of a changing urban population. Ghetto communities will not much longer accept the argument that it is the home environment that causes educational failure. They will expect that the schools must educate their children. If New York City is an indicator for other cities, school professionals will be reluctant to accept the tide of change that is imminent. The greater the resistance to the movement for reform of the city schools, the more likely will be extremist responses from the community. The professionals will have their defenders in the middle-class who are convinced by the arguments based on efficiency and expertise. Immobility and unwillingness to compromise will likely produce more emphatic failures for both middle-class children and ghetto children. The crises in public education will lead to increased conflict until there is acceptance of the pressing need for reform. Administrative reforms can only offer temporary relief—even those now responding in this area will find that, unless they can again make the public feel a part of the educational process, their administrative reorganization will not resolve basic school problems.

The movement for greater community participation in the policy process in American cities extends beyond school reform. It represents the hope of a large segment of the population that has been alienated from the institutions of the society. Because education is so integrally a part of local government and because it represents such a vital link in the development of the community, it will be a major target of community activists in the next decade. The test of the vitality and responsiveness of the city school systems will come in the next decade. There will be those (as there were on the integration issue) who will claim that educational institutions should not be used to solve the ills of the society and that these institutions can only be a reflection of the larger system. Others will recognize the potential of school systems as a viable community force for change in the city. The future of city schools may well rest in the kind of response that is forthcoming.

Chronology of Events

September, 1966 East Harlem parents and community leaders boycott IS 201, demanding the school be either integrated or given to them to control. The Board of Education agrees to allow community participation; tacitly, it agrees to the demand for a black principal to be chosen by the community. The UFT sees these demands as extreme and counter-boycotts. The Board of Education and the mayor's office propose establishing a task force, headed by Ford Foundation president McGeorge Bundy, to recommend a solution. The proposal is rejected, but representatives of the board, the foundation, the UFT, and community groups meet informally throughout the winter to develop a realistic plan for community participation in school policy-making.

October, 1966 The Board of Education officially declares its support for the gradual administrative decentralization of its operations.

Winter, 1966–67 Parent unrest over school conditions grow. A group from the community of Ocean Hill in Brooklyn declares itself the rump school board in District 17. The UFT suggests to the Ford Foundation that the Ocean Hill group be included in a pilot program on decentralization.

April, 1967 The Board of Education adopts a mild decentralization plan, which includes the creation of demonstration districts. The three demonstration districts are to be IS 201 (Harlem), Two Bridges (Lower East Side), and Ocean Hill–Brownsville (Brooklyn). Mayor John Lindsay obtains the promise of $54 million in additional state aid from the state legislature should he submit a suitable plan for decentralizing city schools. The mayor appoints a panel of prominent citizens, headed by McGeorge Bundy, to prepare the plan.

July 29, 1967   The Ocean Hill Planning Council drops its original request for the More Effective Schools program after the superintendent of schools claims that not all schools in the district could be made MES schools. The teachers on the planning council oppose the change.

August 3, 1967   Of 4,000 eligible parents, 1,049 cast ballots for seven parent representatives to the local governing board. These elected representatives choose five community representatives. Two supervisors and four teachers, elected by colleagues in their schools, complete the membership of the local board.

August 21, 1967   State Education Commissioner James Allen, asked by Superintendent Donovan whether principals not on New York City civil service lists but having state certification can be hired, replies that the Board of Education can create a new category: demonstration school principal for elementary schools.

September, 1967   On the opening day of school, the UFT strikes all schools for a new contract. Key union demands include empowering teachers to expel disruptive pupils from classes and expanding the MES program. Many black parents, considering the disruptive pupil demand racially motivated, withhold support of the strike. As part of the settlement, the union gets a clause empowering it to spend $10 million of Board of Education money on an educational program; this marks the first time a union has won a contractual right to make policy. The new Ocean Hill board appoints Rhody McCoy as unit administrator. Eighteen assistant principals and five principals request transfers from the district.

October, 1967   The Council of Supervisory Associations files suit against the creation of the category of demonstration school principal; the UFT, as co-plaintiff, is ruled ineligible to act in that capacity.

November 12, 1967   The Bundy panel presents its plan to decentralize schools in New York City. The Bundy Plan recommends the creation of from thirty to sixty autonomous local school boards, each to have power over budget, curriculum, and personnel and to be composed of six elected parent representatives and five representatives appointed by the mayor from a list submitted by community groups. The plan also suggests that state licensing qualifications suffice for teachers and supervisors in the districts. The Bundy Plan draws heated reaction: Alfred A. Giardino, president of the Board of Education and a dissenting member of the Bundy panel, calls the plan too much too soon; the CSA condemns it; and the UFT attacks it as a "Balkanization" of the schools.

December, 1967 Mayor Lindsay revises the plan (notably, omitting high schools) and submits his revised plan to the state legislature.

March 4, 1968 Judge Rinaldi rules in the CSA suit that the Board of Education had the right to create the new category but that it had not sufficiently outlined that category to justify the appointments made under it.

March 26, 1968 In negotiations with the central board, the Ocean Hill governing board demands a clear grant of power instead of the vague mandate under which it is operating.

May 8, 1968 The Ocean Hill–Brownsville board orders the involuntary transfer of thirteen teachers, five assistant principals, and one principal to central headquarters for reassignment. Some of the teachers transferred were thought by the local board to be undermining the experiment. The UFT protests, claiming the transfers were in fact, firings and were done in violation of due process. The UFT strikes the district and 350 teachers walk out.

May 14, 1968 The superintendent of schools demands that McCoy and the local board supply written charges against the nineteen, and the Board of Education appoints its own examiner, retired judge Francis E. Rivers, to conduct an administrative hearing.

May 22, 1968 Although the Bundy Plan is backed by the governor and key Republican leaders, the state legislature discards it and substitutes the plan advocated by the state Board of Regents. The legislature passes the Marchi law, which postpones action for one year and authorizes the Board of Education to formulate an interim plan giving authority to local school districts and demonstration districts and expanding the membership of the nine-member mayor-appointed central board to thirteen.

June, 1968   Board president Alfred Giardino resigns leaving opponents of the Bundy Plan with a one-vote advantage over the Lindsay appointees.

August, 1968   Clarence Senior resigns from the central board and is shortly followed by Thomas Burke. The Lindsay pro-decentralization forces now command control of the "new" board. Ocean Hill receives permission from the central board to recruit new teachers, replacing striking teachers, to man the schools in the fall.

August 26, 1968   Judge Rivers rules that Ocean Hill has not proved its case against the ten teachers. He points out that, had the unit administrator simply requested transfers from the superintendent under board bylaws, no hearings would have been required.

September 4, 1968   The new board announces an interim decentralization plan (approved, in November, by the state Board of Regents) that gives some local control—except the election of school board members in regular school districts—to thirty local school boards and the three demonstration school districts.

September 9, 1968   The UFT strikes all city schools to reinstate the remaining ten teachers protesting the involuntary transfer at Ocean Hill and the 350 teachers out on strike since May 9. All three demonstration school districts are staffed and operate their schools; most of the city schools are shut down.

September 10, 1968   The UFT reaches an agreement with the Board of Education reinstating the ten teachers and the 350 supporting strikers and providing for hearings and arbitration on transfers. The Ocean Hill board, not a party to the settlement, states that it will not "prevent" the return of the teachers.

September 11, 1968   Ocean Hill residents bar returning teachers; the UFT threatens a new strike.

September 12, 1968   The Board of Education asks State Education Commissioner Allen to intercede.

September 13, 1968   The teachers strike again, claiming that the September 10 agreement was violated.

September 14, 1968   Commissioner Allen proposes a compromise: suspend the local board and temporarily transfer the ten teachers out of the district. The UFT refuses. A black caucus in the union, including two black officers and three black executive board members, opposes the second strike. Despite union refusal to accept the compromise, Allen orders the Board of Education to suspend the local board.

September 20, 1968   The suspension of the local board is lifted; the central board tells the local board that it may keep teachers hired to replace those in dispute. The disputed teachers are ordered back by the central board.

September 30, 1968   The second strike ends, and schools reopen. An agreement between the central board and the union (reached without the participation of the local board) returns disputed teachers to classroom duties.

October 1, 1968   Nine people protesting the return of the teachers are arrested, nonstriking teachers shut down JHS 271. The union threatens a new strike if their teachers are not protected from harassment.

October 6, 1968   The central board suspends the Ocean Hill board for thirty days for failing to assign disputed teachers to classroom duties.

October 7, 1968   UFT Vice President John O'Neill, removed from his staff position sometime earlier for disagreeing with the policies of the executive board, condemns the contemplated third strike by the UFT and proposes a plan to remove police and to assign disputed teachers to "pedagogical" duties.

October 8, 1968   Rhody McCoy and seven of his eight principals are relieved of duties and reassigned to central headquarters. McCoy refuses reassignment and remains in Ocean Hill.

October 9, 1968   Disorders cause the closing of JHS 271.

October 10, 1968   The NYCLU issues its report condemning the UFT for attempting to sabotage community control.

October 11, 1968   The seven principals are reinstated. JHS 271 reopens.

October 13, 1968   The UFT votes to strike. Their demands are: JHS 271 is to be kept closed; only principals who will abide by the

September 10 and September 30 agreements will be returned; the Ocean Hill project is to be termed a failure; the governing board and unit administrator, teachers and supervisors in the schools who are guilty of threats of violence and intimidation are to be permanently removed; the eight schools in the district are to be returned to the central school system.

October 14, 1968 Claiming that UFT members at JHS 271 were threatened with death, the UFT strikes for a third time.

October 16, 1968 Mayor Lindsay appoints a fact-finding panel headed by Theodore Kheel. (Four days later, the panel quits.)

November 15, 1968 The Appellate Division, in a 3–2 decision, upholds the Rinaldi ruling voiding the appointment of demonstration school district principals. The majority holds that the appointments are illegal; the minority feels that the central board had a "rational basis" for the appointments. The Board of Education appeals.

November 17, 1968 The third strike ends. The central board and the UFT, without the participation of the local board, agree to a plan placing the district under state trusteeship. The UFT receives a guarantee that, pending negotiation of a mutually satisfactory clause, involuntary transfers will be covered by the arbitration machinery of the contract. The Ocean Hill–Brownsville governing board and the unit administrator are to remain suspended until State Education Commissioner Allen lifts the suspensions. Charges against four teachers accused of harassing union teachers are to be heard by Commissioner Allen. A state trustee is to oversee the district, and a three member panel is to investigate complaints of harassment.

Aftermath Several weeks after the settlement, Rhody McCoy was reinstated as unit administrator; the governing board remained suspended until March. The district is still under a state trusteeship. Charges against the four teachers have been dropped for insufficient evidence. On January 15, the Court of Appeals overruled the lower courts, finding the central board's creation of the category of demonstration school principal correct on all counts. As a result, three principals have been reinstated to their positions in Ocean Hill.